MATH IN PRACTICE

TEACHING
Second-Grade Math

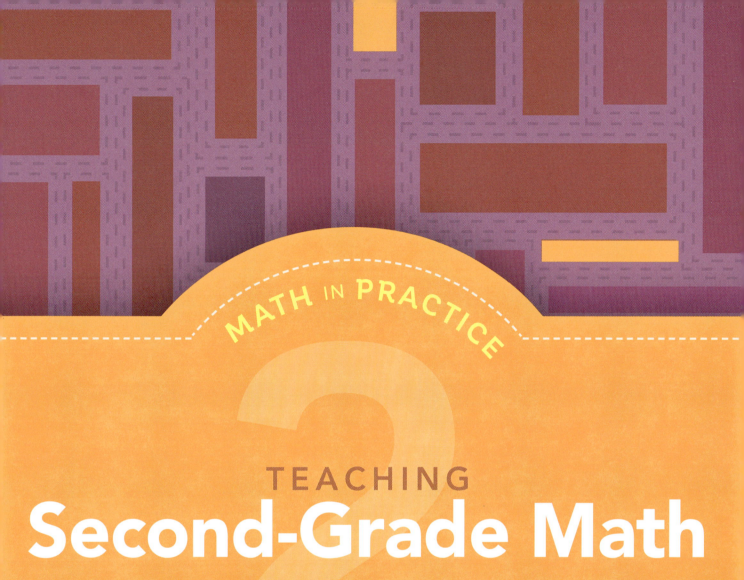

MATH IN PRACTICE

TEACHING
Second-Grade Math

Allison Peet • Susan O'Connell • John SanGiovanni

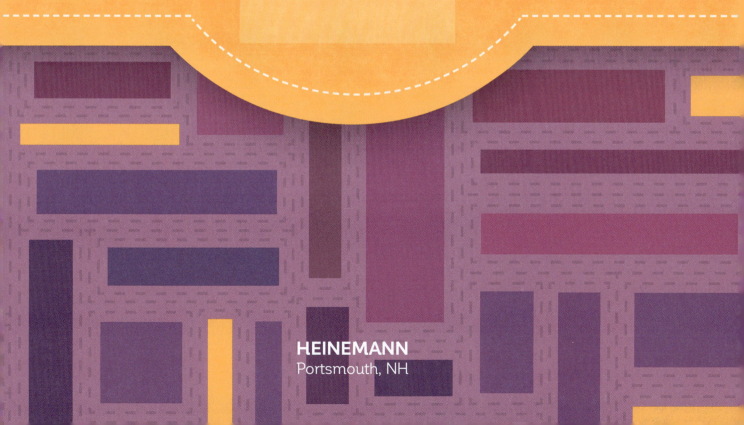

HEINEMANN
Portsmouth, NH

Heinemann
361 Hanover Street
Portsmouth, NH 03801–3912
www.heinemann.com

Offices and agents throughout the world

© 2016 by Allison Peet, Susan O'Connell, and John SanGiovanni

All rights reserved. No part of this book may be reproduced in any form or by any electronic or mechanical means, including information storage and retrieval systems, without permission in writing from the publisher, except by a reviewer, who may quote brief passages in a review, and with the exception of reproducibles (identified by the *Math in Practice: Teaching Second-Grade Math* copyright line), which may be photocopied for classroom use.

"Dedicated to Teachers" is a trademark of Greenwood Publishing Group, Inc.

Image credits: pages 79, 264, 266, 270, 290, 292, 293, and 298 © Houghton Mifflin Harcourt/HIP; page 322 (stop sign) © ArtLight/Shutterstock/HIP, (school crossing sign) © Shutterstock/HIP, (one way sign) © Alamy/HIP, (yield sign) © Houghton Mifflin Harcourt/HIP

Library of Congress Cataloging-in-Publication Data
Names: Peet, Allison. | O'Connell, Susan. | SanGiovanni, John.
Title: Teaching second-grade math / Allison Peet, Susan O'Connell, John
    SanGiovanni.
Other titles: Teaching 2nd grade math
Description: Portsmouth, NH : Heinemann, [2016] | Series: Math in practice |
    Includes bibliographical references.
Identifiers: LCCN 2016018173 | ISBN 9780325078267
Subjects: LCSH: Mathematics—Study and teaching (Elementary) | Second grade
    (Education)
Classification: LCC QA135.6 .P44 2016 | DDC 372.7/044—dc23
LC record available at https://lccn.loc.gov/2016018173

Editors: Katherine Bryant and Sue Paro
Production: Victoria Merecki
Typesetter: Publishers' Design & Production Services, Inc.
Cover and interior designs: Suzanne Heiser
Manufacturing: Steve Bernier

Printed in the United States of America on acid-free paper
20 19 18 17   VP   2 3 4 5

To Caden and Brian
AP

To Blake with love
SO

To Oscar and Deryn
JS

Contents

ix	*Acknowledgments*
1	**Introduction**
9	**Module 1** Exploring Problem Solving
40	**Module 2** Building Understanding and Fluency of Basic Math Facts
68	**Module 3** Building Foundations for Multiplication
85	**Module 4** Understanding Place Value
113	**Module 5** Comparing Two 3-Digit Numbers
133	**Module 6** Understanding Multidigit Addition
161	**Module 7** Understanding Multidigit Subtraction
184	**Module 8** Extending Understanding of Multidigit Addition
204	**Module 9** Extending Understanding of Multidigit Subtraction
219	**Module 10** Understanding Length Measurement
247	**Module 11** Exploring Time
264	**Module 12** Exploring Money
289	**Module 13** Representing and Interpreting Data
311	**Module 14** Describing Geometric Shapes
327	**Module 15** Partitioning Shapes
342	*Recommended Children's Literature*

Acknowledgments

We would like to thank many people who contributed to this book. Thank you to the teachers who shared work samples or allowed students to be photographed as they explored math tasks, including: Mark Baxendell, Marcia Beecken, Whitney Dennis, Erin Martindale, and Mary Jane Richmond. Thanks to the following educators who contributed lesson ideas: Melissa Bishop, Jeanine Brizendine, and Chris Oberdorf. Thanks to Stephanie Ross for taking wonderful photos of students at work. Thanks to Katherine Bryant and Sue Paro for their editorial help and suggestions. Thanks to the rest of our author team (Marcy, Laura, Cheryl, Kay, and Joan) for their collaboration and moral support through the many meetings and discussions surrounding the development of the grade-level books.

AP, SO, JS

I would first like to express my sincerest gratitude to Sue. I have admired your work and thinking around mathematics instruction for many years. It has been a true honor to be a part of this project. Thank you as well to John, for your collaborative work in creating mathematical images and representations for this series.

My own learning has grown, and continues to grow, as a result of the amazing professionals I have worked with over the years. Thank you to all of the educators who I've had the pleasure to collaborate with. A special thank you to Cheryl Covell, Barry Derfel, Beth Dryer, Jennifer Gondek, Mary McGrattan, Heather Sheridan-Thomas, Theresa Streeter, and Sarah Vakkas for supporting my growth around instructional reform in mathematics, and for continued collective expertise, wisdom, and humor in all things education.

Finally, my deepest gratitude to my family: to my mom, Ann, for her love and support of everything that I do; to my sister, Beth, for her interest in understanding what mathematics education can become; and to my children, Caden and Brian, for their patience, enthusiasm, and support of this project.

AP

Introduction

This book is about the teaching of mathematics to students in second grade. It does not focus solely on the content taught in second grade, because we recognize that math is about more than content. Our students are challenged to be able to use their math skills and knowledge, to be mathematical thinkers. It is not a book providing scripted lessons, because we recognize that the teaching of mathematics is not about reading scripts, but about listening to our students, making decisions, and having options for ways to support their math learning. It is not a book of activities, because we know that you can find activities everywhere, but rather a book filled with strong lesson ideas that are based on research-informed instructional strategies and can be modified to meet your students' needs. It is about providing you with options that allow you to choose effective teaching strategies and identify tasks that link to the standards expected of your second-grade students.

This book is more about the teaching of students than the teaching of content. It addresses ways to engage students, help them visualize math ideas, support them as they solve problems, help them make connections and develop insights, build their confidence in math, and learn to love mathematics. Students who think mathematically, reason and solve problems, understand the way numbers work, and have a positive disposition about math have truly met today's expectations. This book is about helping each of our students develop those skills.

A Focus on Teaching and Learning

We have known for a number of years that telling students how to do math procedures, asking them to memorize facts and formulas, and focusing on answers as right or wrong have not resulted in students who are skilled and confident in their math abilities. Today's standards have pointed us toward the adoption of teaching practices that value understanding and application, but it has been difficult to know just how to implement that within our classrooms.

Today's classrooms are standards-based classrooms. The lesson ideas and instructional practices throughout this book align with the National Council of Teachers of Mathematics (NCTM) Standards (2000), as well as the Common Core State Standards (CCSS). The content progressions in this book align closely with the progressions found in the Common Core standards. The instructional strategies are not an arbitrary list of strategies, but rather a compilation of consistently recommended approaches in line with the NCTM Process Standards, the Common Core Standards for Mathematical Practice, and the Mathematics Teaching Practices highlighted in *Principles to Actions* (NCTM 2014). They are informed by research and consistent with our current standards.

About the Math in Practice Series

This book is a part of the Math in Practice series, a comprehensive resource designed to identify critical math content, share essential instructional strategies, and provide resources to support teachers, administrators, and school communities as they rethink the teaching of K–5 mathematics. The series consists of eight books.

- *Math in Practice: A Guide for Teachers* outlines research-informed instructional practices that enhance math teaching and learning. It offers a rationale for changing the way we teach math to K–5 students and explores simple ways we can adjust our teaching to improve students' learning. A variety of highly effective instructional strategies are introduced, discussed, and illustrated throughout the book.

- Six grade-specific books, like this one, focus on the specific mathematics taught at each grade level, K–5. The instructional strategies introduced in the *Guide for Teachers* are shown throughout the lessons in the grade-specific books. These books include discussions about the math being taught, sample lessons that blend content and practice, a wealth of instructional tasks, practical teaching tips, and ready-to-use classroom resources.

- *Math in Practice: A Guide for Administrators* provides school and district administrators with an overview of math teaching and discusses what to look for in math classrooms. The book includes tips for guiding the math program and ideas for supporting teachers as they work to improve their teaching.

A variety of instructional strategies are introduced in *Math in Practice: A Guide for Teachers*. You will notice these instructional strategies illustrated throughout the lessons in this book. These strategies build deeper math understanding, promote mathematical reasoning and problem solving, strengthen math communication skills, and provide ongoing assessment information regardless of the math content being addressed. As you explore this grade-level guide, you will see how these instructional strategies enhance teaching and empower your students. The following instructional strategies are integrated into the lesson ideas you will explore in each module:

- problem solving integrated with content and skills
    - posing problems to provide a context for math skills and to challenge students to apply those skills

- use of representations (models) to build math understanding
  - encouraging the use of varied models, including manipulatives, drawings, and graphic representations, to explore and refine math understanding
- posing in-depth questions to prompt thinking
  - asking students to describe math concepts, explain how they performed math tasks, justify solutions, and predict outcomes
- ongoing opportunities for talk and writing about math ideas
  - challenging students to show and explain their thinking through both talk and writing
- connections to real-world situations
  - using real-world connections to help students make sense of mathematics and its abstract numbers and symbols
- formative assessment to drive instruction
  - posing ongoing tasks to determine students' level of understanding and then using the data to adjust instruction to support students' learning
- differentiation to meet the needs of varied learners
  - modifying our tasks and our delivery of instruction to ensure that all students have opportunities to learn mathematics
- focus on the development of mathematical practices
  - going beyond memorizing content to help our students think like mathematicians and do the work of mathematics.

About This Book

This book is organized into modules. Each module addresses an important math topic for second-grade students. It can be read from start to finish to provide an in-depth look at second-grade mathematics or it can be read by module to provide tips, insights, and strategies as you explore a certain math topic with your students. Some important points about the organization of this book:

- **The modules do not represent an order in which to teach the content.** They are simply a way to organize the math ideas so you are better able to access what you need at any point in time. Each module provides you with an overview of a math topic, as well as ideas for instruction and assessment related to the topic. This book is organized in modules to allow you to find the topic easily and see the development of that topic from simple to more complex ideas. Your state or school district likely has a pacing schedule or a sequence through which they suggest you teach the grade-level standards. This book is organized so you can access the information you need to enhance the teaching of any math topic.
- **This book does not recommend teaching by topic.** We do not suggest that you teach by modules. In fact, we highly discourage it! Math is not a set of isolated skills and should not be taught in that way. We strongly recommend revisiting

topics throughout the year at different levels of complexity and connecting each new concept to a previously learned concept. Teaching all measurement skills at one point during the year, for instance, and then moving on, does not give students the ongoing exposure they need to master and retain those skills. A measurement module gives you a wealth of ideas about teaching measurement, but your district pacing guide will help you identify when specific skills are introduced and revisited. It is likely you will be back in the measurement module at various points throughout the year as your students revisit skills or transition to more complex ones.

- **This book is about choice.** We encourage you to select lesson ideas and build your lessons from them. Teaching well is not about using every activity in the book. It is about finding those that address the needs of your students. For that reason, each module offers a wealth of additional ideas to get you thinking about options for teaching, reteaching, or enrichment.

- **This book does not specify lessons as being for your whole class or a small group of students.** Although in one classroom all students may benefit from an activity, in another classroom it may be the perfect choice for a small group of students who need additional exposure to a skill. Consider each lesson idea and how it might fit best with your students.

- **This book is a part of a series and the math you are teaching is part of a progression of math skills.** In each module, a variety of instructional ideas are presented—some that show the skill at a basic level and others that focus on more complex applications. Notes are frequently included to suggest ways to modify the task or your lesson delivery to meet the needs of varied learners in your classroom. But if your students lack foundational skills or understandings that make it difficult for them to grasp the module activities, connections are noted to the foundational skills in *Math in Practice: Teaching First-Grade Math*. This allows you to identify activities that address the gaps in your students' skills.

This book is a book for teachers, not students. It is organized to allow you to find topics, read about the critical math concepts, reflect on instructional activities, and use this information to plan and facilitate the best lessons for your students. It is filled with lesson seeds, rather than a set of scripted lessons. With your consideration, reflection, and modifications, these lesson seeds will grow into classroom lessons that engage and excite students and stimulate math learning.

Module Organization

Each module focuses on a key math concept at this grade level. It highlights the important math ideas and is filled with lesson ideas, practice tasks, assessment options, center tasks, discussion starters, and key vocabulary. Understanding the structure and key elements of each section of the module will help you better utilize the ideas and activities presented.

About the Math

The About the Math section describes the important math concepts being addressed through the module. Rather than simply listing math skills, this section provides a glimpse at the big ideas that underlie the skills and helps you identify key teaching points for the topics discussed within the module. It provides a glimpse into teaching the understanding of many skills that were previously taught in rote ways, offering you a better idea of how to build that understanding in your students.

This section includes a brief table to show the progressions for the skill, indicating the related skills and concepts at the grade level before and after. This table gives you a quick glimpse of what is introduced at this level and what is a continuation from the previous grade level. When appropriate, connections are made between the skills and concepts in this module and related skills and concepts in other modules. Math is not a series of isolated topics. The goal is to reflect on how each topic is connected to others in order to present math ideas in a connected way.

This section also includes:

- a brief overview of the mathematics related to the topic
- a discussion of the big ideas that underlie the math skills/concepts
- what is new this year and what is continued/expanded from previous years
- progressions for related skills in the grades before and after
- a connection to the content standards for this grade level (We use the Common Core standards for reference, although the mathematical content is relevant to whichever standards you use.)
- suggestions/recommendations for teaching strategies that build these skills
- a list of *I Can* statements to highlight student learning goals in student-friendly language.

Ideas for Instruction and Assessment

This section presents a variety of lesson ideas, practice tasks, and assessment options. You will not find scripted lessons in this book, since lesson planning should be specific to your students' needs and abilities. What you will find are lesson ideas that get you thinking about what to teach and ways to teach it.

This section presents lesson ideas and assessment options related to the key ideas highlighted in the About the Math section. You may choose to implement these very similarly to the way in which they are described, or to modify them depending on the needs of your students.

Our goal is twofold: (1) to provide you with a wealth of classroom ideas so you can select learning experiences that work for your students and (2) to provide elaboration on some tasks to allow you to experience a teacher's thought process as he or she works with students to build their understanding and math confidence. We want you to have lots of classroom ideas, as well as insights into ways you can enhance each activity for optimal student learning. To achieve both goals, you will notice three types of lesson structures:

1. **Lesson Ideas**—These appear early in the Ideas for Instruction and Assessment section and contain a description of the lesson, including ideas for teacher questioning that promotes student understanding. Rather than simply saying, "Probe for understanding about . . ." or "Ask students to discuss . . . ," a series of questions appears to allow you to hear the teacher's questioning process and imagine the student responses the questions might elicit.

2. **Thinking Through a Lesson**—In each module, one lesson idea has been elaborated on to become a reflective lesson. These lesson ideas contain the lesson description and teacher questioning, just like those above, but also include more detailed teacher notes that appear at various points throughout the lesson. These notes highlight teacher observations and suggestions as the lesson unfolds. They provide you with the behind-the-scenes thinking that guides us as we observe our students, make decisions, modify tasks, and provide needed support. These lessons also include references to the Standards for Mathematical Practice, highlighting opportunities to foster students' use and understanding of these key ways of thinking about and doing mathematics.

3. **Additional Ideas for Support and Practice**—These additional ideas offer ways to develop skills and understanding for students who may need more exposure, or ways to engage students in meaningful practice. They might become a whole-class lesson if additional instruction is needed, a small-group lesson for some students who would benefit from another exposure to the topic, an extension for those who need to be challenged, a center task for partner practice, or a way for students to independently practice the skill. They are meant to give you additional options to extend students' learning.

ICONS

You will notice specific icons as you are perusing lesson ideas. These icons connect us back to *Math in Practice: A Guide for Teachers* and the key instructional strategies that were highlighted. At any point, you can refer back to that book for more details on the strategies. These icons include:

Standards—When this appears in the About the Math section of a module, it indicates the specific content standards addressed within that module. When it appears in a Thinking Through a Lesson feature, it indicates the Standards for Mathematical Practice that appear within that lesson.

Show It—This indicates that skills and concepts are made visual through concrete objects or drawings.

Talk/Write—These discussion starters or writing prompts can be used to get students talking and writing about the key ideas related to the topic.

Literature—These lesson ideas incorporate the use of children's books to provide a context for the math skills and concepts being taught.

Differentiation—These ideas help you identify ways to modify tasks or modify your delivery of instruction for students who are struggling or those whose learning should be extended.

 Centers—These ideas offer a variety of ways for students to practice skills, alone or with partners, including ideas for math centers.

"I CAN" STATEMENTS

At the start of each module are "I can" statements that illustrate the instructional goals for the module from a student perspective. The activities and assessments in the module serve to guide students to these skills or understandings.

FORMATIVE ASSESSMENT

An essential component of effective math teaching is ongoing assessment to determine what our students know and what they may be struggling to understand. Throughout the book, you will notice formative assessment options that allow you to check for student understanding related to the math that is highlighted in each module. You may see samples of student work to help you visualize student responses, as well as suggestions for dealing with common errors. Ongoing assessment allows us to modify our instruction based on what our students know, or don't know, and keeps us focused on student growth.

VOCABULARY

A list of related math vocabulary words appears in each module. These words, although not an exhaustive list, represent some of the most critical terms related to the module's content. Discussing the meanings of these words, posting the words on a class Math Talk chart or word wall, and expecting students to use these words as they explore the math ideas deepens their understanding of the content and supports their ability to communicate with precision. Ideas for ways to develop these words are shared in Chapter 4 of *Math in Practice: A Guide for Teachers*.

Online Resources

Although you will find many resources throughout the pages of this book, additional resources are available on the accompanying website: http://hein.pub/MathinPractice. You will notice thumbnails throughout the modules that give you a quick glimpse of some of the accompanying materials. You will find:

- templates for lesson recording sheets or practice tasks
- resource materials like number lines, digit cards, hundred charts, or spinners
- ready-to-go center activities
- problem-solving cards related to the module topic for additional problem-solving practice.

These materials make your implementation of the lessons and activities easy and manageable. You will notice that many of the materials are in Microsoft Word rather than a PDF format to allow you to easily modify them to meet the needs of your students. Change the names to those of your students, modify the data to make them simpler or more complex, or delete parts to shorten the task.

> To access the online resources, visit http://hein.pub/MathinPractice. Enter your email address and password (or click "Create a New Account" to set up an account). Once you have logged in, enter keycode MIPG2 and click "Register."

How to Use This Book

As you read this book, consider the many ways you can use it to enhance your math teaching and support your students' learning. Read it to:

- better understand and gain insights about the math content at this grade level
- gain a deeper understanding of what comes before and after what you teach, and how our students' math understanding builds in a progression over several years
- explore the level of questioning that builds deep math understanding
- discover ways to make math concepts visible to all students through opportunities to investigate math in hands-on and visual ways
- reflect on ways to lead student investigations, rather than telling students how to do math
- find formative assessment ideas that allow you to identify what students know and reflect on sample student responses to find strategies to address what they struggle to understand
- gather a wealth of ready-to-use center/practice ideas that engage students in doing meaningful mathematics
- discover ideas to differentiate your teaching and tasks to meet the needs of different levels of learners
- gather problems and discussion starters related to the math content
- identify critical vocabulary to help students better understand the content and strengthen their math communication skills
- reflect on your current teaching practices to expand your repertoire of teaching skills.

This book provides you with insights into the math expectations for second-grade students; provides a wealth of standards-based activities; highlights research-informed instructional strategies; shares teacher notes that spur insights into classroom decision making; and provides a roadmap for teaching second-grade students to learn math, feel confident in their skills, and be excited to continue their math explorations in third grade. Read it, highlight it, and keep it close by as you and your students explore math together.

MODULE 1

Exploring Problem Solving

About the Math 2.OA.1

At all levels, students work to become effective problem solvers. Through ongoing problem-solving investigations, students expand their skills at comprehending problems and identifying the data needed to solve them. They develop a variety of strategies to find solutions, including choosing an appropriate operation, drawing a diagram, looking for patterns, or other problem-solving strategies (see *Math in Practice: A Guide for Teachers*, Chapter 1).

> The key ideas focused on in this module include:
> - extending understanding of using addition and subtraction to solve problems with unknowns in all positions, including problems with 3-digit numbers
> - exploring strategies for solving two-step problems.

Students were introduced to addition and subtraction in kindergarten, and in first grade they continued to explore the meanings of these operations. Through hands-on and visual activities, they developed an understanding of addition as *adding to* or *putting together* and subtraction as *taking from*, *taking apart*, or *comparing*. Based on these foundational understandings, they were able to identify the operation that made sense for solving each problem situation.

First graders explored problems in which the unknowns were in different positions. Through visualizing the situations or building equations with symbols for the missing data, students were able to make sense of problems like:

> Second-grade standards generally focus on problem solving within 100 (2-digit numbers); however, second-grade students explore addition and subtraction computation within 1,000 (3-digit numbers). Teaching computations in isolation is not advised. Linking computations to problem contexts helps our students develop a deeper understanding of subtraction. Throughout this book you will notice that problem-solving experiences extend to 3-digit numbers to match students' computational skills.

Bailey put some black shells into her bucket. She put 6 white shells into her bucket, too. She had 14 shells in her bucket. How many were black?

Students might have shown the situation with __ + 6 = 14 or might have explained that you could subtract to find out how many are black because you know how many there are altogether.

$$\_\_ + 6 = 14$$

Second-grade students continue to work with addition and subtraction problems with unknowns in all positions, but now the data increases in quantity to match students' computation skills, which include addition and subtraction with 2-digit numbers.

Blake put some yellow beads in a cup. She put 26 red beads into the cup. She had 44 beads in her cup. How many of the beads were yellow?

Visual representations of problem data help students better understand the operations. There are a variety of ways students might visualize the operations, including manipulatives, number lines, bar models, and a variety of graphic organizers. As the problem data gets larger, transitioning students to using place value models like base-ten blocks or drawings of sticks and dots, or exploring the use of bar models in which the bars are labeled with numbers to represent the quantities, allows them to move beyond drawing every item separately and helps to extend their skill at understanding and modeling problems. See Teacher Tips for Solving Math Problems on page 11.

In second grade, students are introduced to two-step problems. These tasks require attention to the question being asked, as many students perform one step and then stop, assuming they have found the answer. Through precise teacher questioning, clarifying the steps in the task, students begin to understand this two-step problem-solving approach.

Joe had 67 superhero cards. He gave 18 to Kevin and 21 to Brendan. How many did he keep for himself?

> *What do we want to find out?* (We want to find out how many cards Joe has after he gives some away to Kevin and Brendan.)

Learning Goals

I can make sense of problems and persevere in solving them.

I can build equations to show and solve problems.

I can solve problems with unknowns in different places.

I can solve two-step problems.

What do we know? (We know what he had before he gave them away. We know how much he gave away.)

Is anything confusing about this problem? (We should subtract, but there are 2 things to subtract.)

What could we do? (We could subtract one of them first.)

So, are we done? Why or why not? (No, because he gave some to Brendan, too.)

So what do we need to do? (We need to subtract 21 more.)

Now, are we done? Why or why not? (Yes, because we subtracted for both people.)

Does our answer make sense? Why or why not? (Yes, because it is a lot less than 67 and he gave away a lot of cards.)

Does anyone have a different way? (We could add both of the amounts he gave away, 18 + 21, and then subtract from what he had.)

Through class discussions, probing teacher questions, think-alouds to share reasonable thinking, and visualizing the process, students explore these more complex tasks. Encouraging students to stick with the task (persevere) and praising them for their effort is important when two-step tasks are introduced.

Second-grade students apply their problem-solving skills to other math content. They solve addition and subtraction problems related to length, time, and money, applying their problem comprehension and computation skills to a wider range of problems, discovering that problem solving connects to all math content.

Through instructional strategies like Focus on the Question, pinch cards, and writing story problems, students continue to explore, discuss, visualize, and justify problems and their solutions.

> **Lessons in This Module**
>
> **Solve Addition and Subtraction Problems**
> Revisiting Bar Models to Show Addition Situations
> Revisiting Bar Models to Show Subtraction Situations
> Using Number Lines to Solve Problems
> Choosing Models
>
> **Solving Two-Step Problems**
> Representing Two-Step Problems
> Exploring Different Methods

See Math in Practice: A Guide for Teachers, Chapters 1 and 2, for more on these strategies.

Exploring the Progression

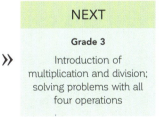

PREVIOUS	NOW	NEXT
Grade 1	**Grade 2**	**Grade 3**
Solving addition and subtraction problems using basic math facts with unknowns in all positions	Solving addition and subtraction problems using 2- and 3-digit numbers with unknowns in all positions	Introduction of multiplication and division; solving problems with all four operations

Teacher Tips for Solving Math Problems

As a teacher of second-grade students, you are probably quite skilled at teaching students to use comprehension strategies while they are reading fiction and nonfiction text. As we work with word problems, we also use instructional strategies that help children comprehend word problems before they begin to solve them. When students comprehend word problems, they understand the situation, as well as the known and unknown information. With this understanding in mind, students can skillfully choose operations to solve for the unknown, rather than randomly adding or subtracting the numbers they see in the problem. The following are some instructional strategies that help students comprehend and solve word problems effectively.

MULTIPLE READS FOR A VARIETY OF PURPOSES

Skillful problem solvers usually read word problems more than once. They may read the first time, ignoring the numbers, to get a general sense of what is happening in the problem, such as whether something is being added to, separated, or compared. They may read it again to see how the numbers fit in and then make a model to represent it. After solving, they may go back and read it again to make sure their answer makes sense.

> *First read: What is happening? Can I retell it?*
> *Another read: How do the numbers fit in? How can I show it?*
> *Read it again: Does my answer make sense?*

For two-step problems, the multiple reads might be:

> *First read: What is happening? Can I retell it?*
> *Another read: How can I get started? What should I do first?*
> *Read it again: What was I trying to find out? What should I do next?*
> *Read it again: Does my answer make sense?*

STUDENTS ACTING OUT PROBLEMS

Although second-grade students are able to draw diagrams and build equations to solve problems, there are still benefits to having them act out situations, particularly when they appear confused about the problem. Students demonstrate their understanding of the problem situation as they act it out.

USING TECHNOLOGY TO ACT OUT A PROBLEM

Interactive whiteboard technology allows us to import photos of students, or use fun clip art, in our problems and has the added benefit of letting us move the graphics to show addition and subtraction situations. This technology engages students, allows them to visualize the story problem, and provides a tool for them to actively show what is happening in the problem.

MODELING A PROBLEM WITH MANIPULATIVES

Using manipulatives (e.g., counters, base-ten blocks) allows students to actively explore the problem situation. Using these materials to represent the problem data and arranging or moving them to show what is happening in the problem allows students to see the problem more clearly.

RETELLING & GRAPHIC ORGANIZERS: BORROWING STRATEGIES FROM READING INSTRUCTION

Beginning/Middle/End

Students are often asked to retell the stories they read, frequently chunking information as the beginning, middle, and end of a story. This strategy can also be used with word problems, especially when there are events and actions involved in the word problem (adding to, putting together, taking from, separating).

What is happening in the problem?

Can you retell it in your own words?

How does the problem begin?

What happens?

How does it end?

Graphic organizers for retelling used during reading instruction can be helpful when retelling math problems. Students record information in the sections and record a question mark when the beginning, middle, or end is not known. This allows them to see the events in order and help them build an appropriate equation. Example:

There were some people at the soccer field. 19 more people arrived at the soccer field. Then there were 56 people at the soccer field. How many were there at the start?

Beginning	Middle	End
some people were at the field ?	19 more people came	there were 56 people there

The diagram helps students move through the task without the start data, charting what they know, and helps them see the story and construct the equation __ + 19 = 56.

Four Ways

A Four Ways graphic organizer helps students make connections between word problems and related models and equations. In this graphic organizer (see below), one of the four ways is supplied, and students must complete the other sections to match it (e.g., If the equation is supplied, the student is expected to write a word problem, represent the problem with a model or drawing, and write a sentence to explain his thinking, like why he chose the operation).

word problem	equation
model	my thinking

Part-Part-Whole

Students used Part-Part-Whole graphic organizers as work mats in kindergarten and first grade as a way to model and organize information from the word problem. By second grade, the 2-digit data begins to make this model more cumbersome, although students who struggle with part-part-whole understanding may still benefit from using the mats.

Two Steps

Second-grade students begin to explore two-step problems. Using a two-step organizer allows them to show both parts of the problem. Students show the steps they took using words, models, and equations.

Tell what the problem is asking you to find out.	
First, I . . .	Then, I . . .

DRAWINGS & DIAGRAMS

Helping students relate models to drawings and diagrams is an important step in the development of a problem solver.

Representational Drawing

By second grade, students should be creating drawings with representations (e.g., circles, Xs) rather than actual detailed drawings. 2-digit numbers might be represented with sticks and dots to represent tens and ones rather than with individual units. Representing in this way allows students to continue to visualize the problem data without showing the 56 red pencils and 25 blue pencils.

Number Bonds

Number bonds are similar to part-part-whole mats, with numbers in each section rather than drawings. Labeling these diagrams helps keep students focused on the problem data.

Toby picked 23 apples. Barbara picked 36 apples. How many apples did they pick together?

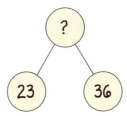

Bar Models

Students transition from part-part-whole mats to bar models to show problem situations. Bars represent parts and wholes, but a number is placed in each bar rather than counters. By modeling problems in this way, students are able to visualize the connections among the data and can then build the equation to match the situation (see Figure 1.1). Bar models show the comparison relationship between two quantities, which is often difficult for students to visualize (see Figure 1.2). And these models are particularly helpful when the start or change is unknown in a problem, allowing students to still visualize the problem situation with a blank box for the unknown (see Figure 1.3). There is not one way to create bar models, as shown in Figures 1.1–1.3.

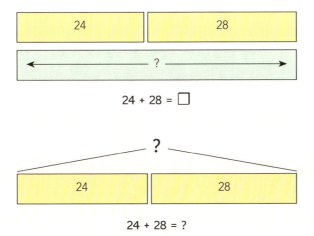

Figure 1.1 Students visualize the problem with a bar for the total and two bars for the parts or one bar with brackets to show the whole.

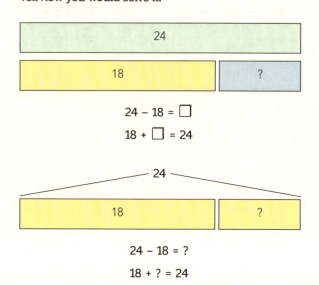

Figure 1.2 Students create two bars to show the two amounts being compared and are able to see the relationship between them (e.g., how many more or less).

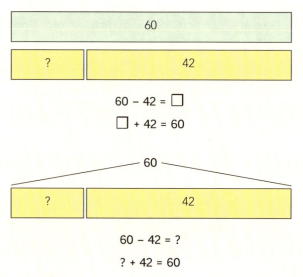

Figure 1.3 Students visualize the problem, placing a question mark for the unknown data. Rather than being confused or stopping because there is unknown data, they are able to visualize the entire problem.

Number Lines

Number lines are another way for students to visualize addition and subtraction. Drawing open number lines, and showing addition or subtraction as hops on the number line, allows them to keep track of the data as they visualize the problem and reinforces their understanding of decomposing numbers.

John rode his bike 17 miles on Saturday. He rode his bike 21 miles on Sunday. How many miles did John ride in all?

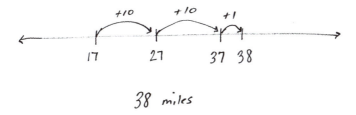

Ideas for Instruction and Assessment

SOLVE ADDITION AND SUBTRACTION PROBLEMS

Students have previous experience working with addition and subtraction problems with unknowns in different places. In second grade, the data increases in complexity, incorporating their skills of adding and subtracting 2-digit numbers.

Revisiting Bar Models to Show Addition Situations SHOW IT!

Students explore bar models to represent problem situations. Some students may have been exposed to bar models in first grade and be ready to jump into this lesson. Students who have had no previous exposure would benefit from an introductory activity (see page 28).

> Pose the following problem:
>
>> Gavin blew up 31 balloons for his party. His sister Jen blew up 7 balloons. How many balloons did Gavin and his sister blow up?
>
> *What do you picture in your head as you read this problem?*
> *Turn to your partner and tell them what is happening in the story.*
> *What are we trying to find out?*
> *How could we draw a model of the balloons that Gavin and Jen have?*
>
> Students may suggest drawing each individual balloon.
>
> *We could draw 31 balloons, but that's a lot of balloons to draw. Do we need to draw them all?*
> *Is there a way we can represent the balloons without drawing each one individually?*

Problem data should be adjusted depending on students' computational skills. Early in the year, students might explore 45 + 34, while later in the year they might explore 47 + 36 or 272 + 345.

Differentiation

Some students may need to continue to use counters or draw individual objects to visualize the problem data. Keep working with them on making the transition to less concrete models through discussions, hearing others' strategies, and connecting their work to other models.

With your partner, come up with a way to show this situation without drawing each balloon.

Listen and observe students as they work with partners.

Ask students to share their ideas.

A student might suggest a number bond. Have him share his idea with the class.

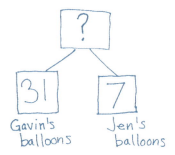

What does your number bond show?
Would a number bond be quicker than drawing all of those balloons?
Who thought of another way to model the problem?

If a student suggests a bar model, have her share her thinking with the class. If a student suggests a rectangle or box or something similar, use that idea to begin your discussion.

How could a rectangle show Gavin's balloons? How could I label it?

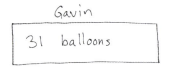

How would I show Jen's balloons?
How might her rectangle be different? (It would be shorter.)
Why do you think it would be shorter? (She only has 7 and he has 31, so he has a lot more.)

You're right; he does have a lot more. That bar could be shorter, but we don't have to worry about the size of it. As long as we show both parts, I think we will be able to see the problem.

How should we label the second rectangle?

Some teachers make bar models somewhat proportional, while others simply use it as a way to visualize the parts of the problem. At times, it may be difficult for your students to know how big they should make a bar and that can frustrate or block them. Having two equal bars can be thought of as two boxes to hold the data, as in a part-part-whole mat. It still enables them to visualize the parts and whole and determine the operation that makes sense.

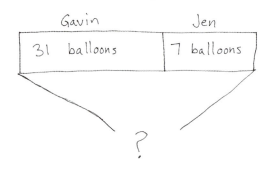

What part of our picture shows how many balloons in all? Turn and tell your partner.

Listen for students who recognize that the two rectangles together create a long bar that shows the sum.

Turn and talk: What does this diagram remind you of? Have you done anything similar to this before?

How is it like a part-part-whole mat? How is it different?

How is our model like a number bond? How is it different?

How can your bar diagram help you to construct a number sentence?

Work with your partner to write a number sentence that supports your bar diagram.

After pairs have had time to create a number sentence, ask for students to share.

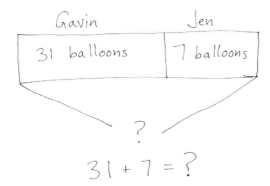

How many balloons did Gavin and Jen blow up?

How does your bar model show this?

Pose the problem:

> The Riva animal shelter has 42 cats and 26 dogs that need a forever home. How many animals are looking for a home?

Turn to your partner and retell this problem in your own words.

Work with your partner to make a bar diagram that could represent this problem.

Use your bar diagram to write a number sentence and solve it.

Listen and watch as students work, looking for students who may still struggle to create the bar model or connect it to a number sentence. Then, ask:

Compare your diagram and number sentence with another pair of students. Do you agree?

Continue with this problem, using similar questions:

> The Severna Park animal shelter has 51 cats and some dogs that need a forever home. 75 animals are looking for a home. How many are dogs?

Listen and watch as students work, looking for students who may still struggle to create the bar model or connect it to a number sentence. As groups finish, ask:

What was different about this problem?

How were you able to use the bar model to visualize the problem?

How did you show the unknown information (the number of dogs)?

Would it help to label the bars? Explain.

What equation matched your model?

Did anyone have a different equation? Explain.

To end the lesson, have students discuss with partners and then the class:

How do bar models help you organize your thinking when solving math problems?

> Provide additional opportunities for students to solve addition problems with bar models, including those that require regrouping once students have been exposed to that skill.

FORMATIVE ASSESSMENT

Give students the following directions:

Use a bar model to solve the following:

> Hillcrest Farms planted 48 apple trees. They also planted 24 cherry trees. How many trees were planted?

Write a number sentence that goes with your bar diagram and solve.

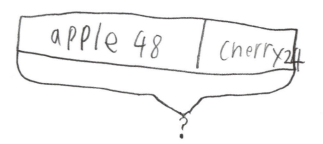

This student's work shows a bar model with 48 and 24 as the parts, and identifies the unknown with a question mark. The student writes the number sentence 48 + 24 = 72. The student does not show how he solved for 72. If there is a question as to the student's solution, the teacher might choose to conference with the student.

If the student has difficulty drawing the bar model, provide her with a Bar Model template.

If the student struggles to solve the problem, ask:

Do we know the parts?

Do we know the whole?

Which part of the diagram shows each part?

Which part of the diagram shows the whole?

If the student does not label the diagram, ask:

What does 48 stand for?

What does 24 stand for?

If the student does not write a number sentence, ask:

What equation matches this bar model?

Revisiting Bar Models to Show Subtraction Situations

Students construct bar models to show various subtraction situations.

Pose the following problem:

Two second-grade classes were collecting canned food for the food pantry. Altogether they collected 95 cans of food. If Mrs. Thurston's class collected 41 cans of food, how many cans did Mrs. Cotter's class collect?

Retell the story to your partner.

What are we trying to find out?

What do we know?

What type of math situation is happening here?

Provide each pair of students with two strips of different-color paper (about 1 inch wide and 8 inches long). Cut one of the strips into two parts.

How could you use these strips of paper to help you model the situation? Talk to your partner to come up with a plan. How might you represent the problem?

Circulate, looking for pairs to share their thinking with the class.

Encourage students to write on (or label) the paper strips.

How did you model the problem?

How did you show the parts and whole?

So what part shows what you are looking for?

Did anyone model it a different way? Explain your model.

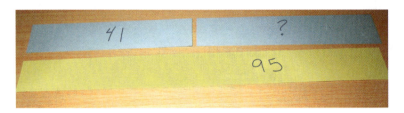

Write a number sentence (equation) that goes with your bar model and then solve.

What number sentence could you use?

Did anyone do it differently? Explain.

How many cans did Mrs. Cotter's class collect?

Have students draw their bar models and write the equation in their math journals.

> Bar models can have double bars like part-part-whole mats, or single bars showing the two parts. The important thing is that students' models accurately represent the problem and that they can explain what the parts of their models represent.

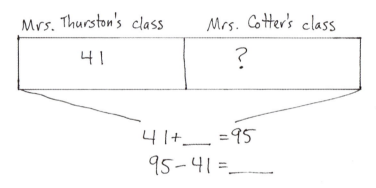

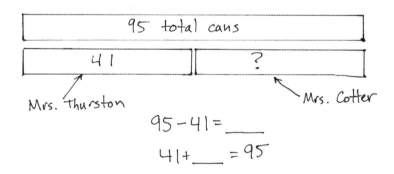

Have students turn to partners to discuss:

Does the model you chose make sense? How do you know?

Pose the following problem:

Michael was 52 inches tall. Missy was 48 inches tall. How much taller was Michael?

Turn to your partner and tell what you know about Michael and Missy.

> Notice that this problem connects to students' work with length measurement. For more problems with length measurement, see Module 10.

What are we trying to figure out?

How is this problem different than the problem before?

Would a part-part-whole model be the best model for this problem? Why or why not?

Discuss the comparison situation in this problem.

Provide each pair with a second set of 1-inch-wide paper strips of different lengths.

Talk to your partner about how we could use bar models to represent Michael's and Missy's height. Use the paper strips to guide your thinking.

Circulate around the room listening for pairs who consider using two different bars to represent the heights, one for Michael and one for Missy. Allow students to share their thinking with the whole class.

How did you use your paper strips to model the problem? Explain.

What does the longer strip represent? Why?

What are you looking for?

How did you show comparison?

Write an equation (number sentence) that goes with your bar model and solve the problem.

What equation did you write? (52 − 48 = ___. Or, 48 + ___ = 52.)

How much taller is Michael?

Have partners draw their bar model and write the equation in their journals.

Pose the following:

> Brian is 56 inches tall. He is 7 inches taller than Caden. How tall is Caden?

Have students work with partners to draw bars to model the problem.

Discuss how they showed the data when they knew one boy's height and the difference but did not know the other boy's height.

Have them share their models and explain their thinking.

Students benefit from ongoing opportunities to discuss, model, and solve a variety of problems. Make problem-solving experiences a regular part of your math routine, increasing the complexity of problem data as students are ready for the challenge.

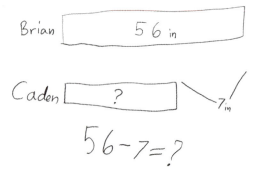

To end the lesson, have students talk with partners and then the class about the following:

What are the differences between a part-part-whole problem and a comparison problem?

How are the bar models different?

Adjust the problem data (2-digit or 3-digit numbers) to match your students' computational skills.

FORMATIVE ASSESSMENT

Give students the following directions:

Draw a bar model and write a number sentence to solve the following:

Tupper Falls is 215 feet tall. Hills Falls is 48 feet shorter. What is the height of Hills Falls?

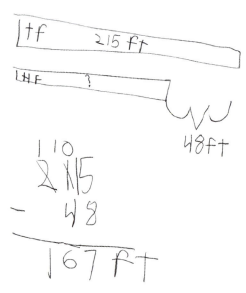

This student shows a comparison bar model and solves the problem. He labels Tupper Falls as 215 ft. and shows the difference as 48 ft. The student uses subtraction to find the height of Hills Falls.

If the student uses a part-part-whole model, ask:

Are we putting together or taking apart?

Are we comparing?

How do we show comparison?

If the student has difficulty drawing bar diagrams, provide her with a Comparison Bar Model template.

Using Number Lines to Solve Problems

Students explore using number lines to solve math problems.

Pose the following problem:

> Mrs. Ross brought snacks for the soccer game. She had a bag of 15 oranges and another bag with 8 oranges. How many oranges did she bring?

Turn and tell your partner what the problem is about.

What are we trying to find out?

Tell your partner a way you could model the problem.

Have students share their ideas with the class. They are likely to mention putting counters on part-part-whole mats, making number bonds, making bar models, or making drawings (e.g., circles to show each orange).

Could we use a number line to show this problem? Talk to your partners about how you could solve it with a number line.

Give students a number line and have them solve the problem.

What did you do to solve it?

Did anyone do it differently?

Probe students' strategies with questions such as:

Why did you split the 8 into 5 and 3?

Did we have to all show it in the same way on the number line? Explain.

Pose the following problem:

> There were two second-grade classes at Central Elementary School. Mr. Willson's class had 25 students, and Mrs. Cage's class had 23 students. How many second-grade students were at the school?

Have students retell the problem and identify what they need to find out.

Could we model this problem with a number line? Why might this one be harder than the last one?

Does our number line have to start at 0?

Turn and tell your partner where it could start for this problem.

> Have students share their ideas with the class. Then have them make an open number line and solve the problem.
>
> Have them share their number lines and how they chose the jumps (decompositions of the number) on the number lines.

> Students explore open number lines when modeling the addition and subtraction process (see Modules 6–9) and use open number lines as strategies when exploring length in Module 10 and time in Module 12. See the lessons in Modules 6–7 for more specific ideas on helping students understand number lines as models for 2-digit addition and subtraction.

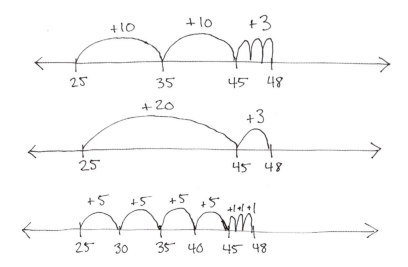

> *Turn and tell your partner something you have to remember when you use number lines.*

Pose the following problem for students to solve with number lines. Have them share and explain their strategies.

> Jacqui had 30 pieces of candy corn. She ate 15. How many does she have now?

> *Was there just one way to show this problem on the number line? Explain.*

To close, have students respond to these questions.

> *Why do we create models to show math problems?*
> *Turn and tell your partner different ways you can model math problems.*

Choosing Models

Students read problems and decide on the bar model that works best to solve each one.

> Pose varying problems from the list below, asking the following for each problem:
>
> *Draw a bar model to show the problem, then explain your model to your partner.*
>
> For part-part-whole models, say:
>
> *Show your partner which part of your bar model is the whole. Show your partner where the parts are.*

Exploring Problem Solving

MODULE 1

For comparison models, say:

Show your partner which part is the larger part and which part is the smaller part. Show where the comparison is.

Circulate to observe as partners create their bar models, then have them share and explain their choices with the class.

Ask students:

Record the information from the problem and label what you know.

What do you not know?

What are you trying to find out?

How will you show what is unknown?

Will you solve the problem using addition or subtraction? How do you know?

What equation shows the problem? Solve it.

Below are some possible problems. Others are available in the online resources.

Part-Part-Whole Models:

At the beginning of the month Clara had 24 pencils. At the end of the month, Clara had 13 pencils. How many fewer pencils did Clara have at the end of the month?

Tariq had 37 toy cars. His brother gave him 13 more. How many cars does he have now?

Comparison Models:

Penny ate 19 raisins at breakfast. Her brother, Jack, ate 7 more raisins than Penny ate. How many raisins did Jack eat?

There are 75 boys in second grade. There are 8 more boys than girls. How many girls are there in second grade?

Differentiation

These first problems intentionally use simpler data to allow students to focus on whether the situation calls for part-part-whole or comparison. As students gain confidence, the complexity of the data is increased. The online problems are in a customizable format to allow you to modify the data as needed.

FORMATIVE ASSESSMENT

Have students solve the following problem using a model to show how they solved it. Have them write an equation to match the problem.

Mr. Lange has a basket with 73 pens and pencils. If there are 27 pens, how many pencils are in the basket?

The equation could be represented as 73 − 27 = <u>46</u> or 27 + <u>46</u> = 73.

The model used should be appropriate to show the problem situation.

For additional formative assessment ideas, see Math in Practice: A Guide for Teachers, Chapter 5.

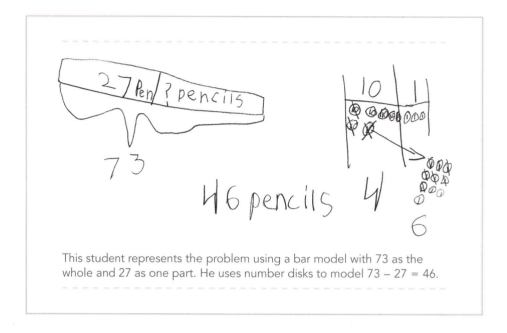

This student represents the problem using a bar model with 73 as the whole and 27 as one part. He uses number disks to model 73 − 27 = 46.

Additional Ideas for Support and Practice

The following ideas extend students' understanding of problem solving and provide meaningful practice.

INTRODUCTION TO BAR MODELS

Using this modified activity to introduce "single bar" models may be appropriate for students who have not been previously exposed to them. This type of bar model may feel a bit different for them because it does not have separate bars to show the parts and whole like they are used to with part-part-whole mats and number bonds.

> *We know that numbers can be broken apart into smaller parts. How have you shown those parts before?*

Let students share their ideas. If no one suggests part-part-whole mats and number bonds, remind them of these ways to model parts and whole.

> *Here is another way to show the parts and the whole. How do you think this diagram shows the parts? Talk to your partner.*

Show students the bar model for part-part-whole problems.

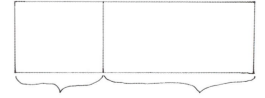

> *Are the short bars the same size? What might that tell you about the parts of the number?*

> [!NOTE]
> Note that using double bar models, with a bar showing the whole and a bar showing the parts, is always an option. Choose the model that works best for your students. It is good to have an alternate model for students who may have difficulty visualizing problems with one or the other.

How do you think this diagram shows the whole? Talk to your partner.
So the whole is when the parts are combined. It is the whole bar together.

> You might use brackets and/or color to show the parts and whole as students explain their thinking.

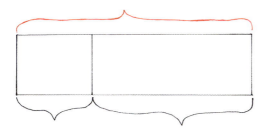

Choose 2 numbers to put into your bar diagram to show 2 parts.
Check your partner's numbers. Is the larger number in the larger part?
Create a number story to go with your bar diagram.
Label the parts of your bar model to go with your story.
Write the number sentence you would use to solve your story.
Share your number story and number sentence with your partner.
Where should we show the total since there isn't a bar for the total?

As students share their stories, models, and equations, show them on the board or have them place them under a document camera for others to see. Talk about the labeling and connect the parts of the equation to the model.

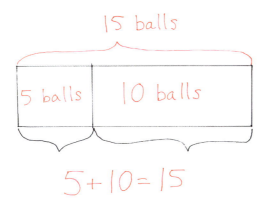

What different addition and subtraction equations are represented with this bar model? Think about part-part-whole mats and the different addition and subtraction equations they can represent.

After students have had experience with the part-part-whole version of the bar diagram, introduce the comparison version. This may happen during a different class period.

How is this bar diagram different from the first?
Sometimes we have situations when we compare numbers.

Show this bar model:

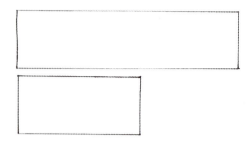

If we were thinking about comparing the lengths of 2 snakes, how would the parts of this bar model show the comparison?

Fill in the 2 parts, using 2 different numbers that are less than 20.

Which bar would represent your larger number? Explain.

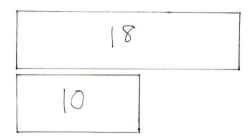

Create a comparison story and number sentence that would go with your bar model.

How will we know what the numbers in your model represent?

black snake — 18 inches
green snake — 10 inches

Share your story and number sentence with your partner.

Where is the answer on your model?

Use brackets or draw an extension to the bar to show the difference.

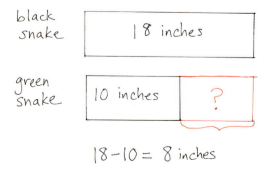

black snake — 18 inches
green snake — 10 inches ?

18 − 10 = 8 inches

Have some students share their number stories, models, and equations with the class. Talk about the labeling and how their equations match their stories.

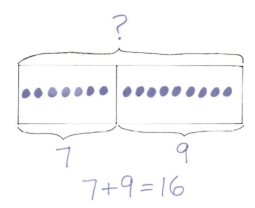

In the initial stages of using bar diagrams, students may need more semi-concrete support. They can draw dots in the diagram as shown.

Provide additional experiences as needed.

Compare It

Students distinguish comparison problems from other types of problems, then create models and solve the problems.

Give students an envelope with 3–4 problems that include comparison problems.

Have them read the problems and decide which ones show comparisons.

Have them work with a partner to model the comparison problems and build equations to match them.

Students often struggle to recognize problems that show comparisons. Frequent opportunities to visualize and discuss these types of problems are helpful.

Have students share with the class which problems were comparison situations and how they knew. Have them share and explain their models.

Following are some possible problems:

I had ____ grapes. I ate ____. How many are left? (*taking from* situation)

I had ____ baseball cards. My friend gave me ____ more. How many do I have? (*adding to* situation)

Blake had ____ blue balloons and ____ red balloons. How many balloons did she have? (*put together* situation)

There were ____ students on the playground. Some were boys and ____ were girls. How many were boys? (*take apart* situation)

Kellen was ____ inches tall. Liam was ____ inches taller than Kellen. How tall was Liam? (*comparison* situation)

Monday I rode my bike ____ miles. Tuesday I rode my bike ____ miles more than I did on Monday. How many miles did I ride on Tuesday? (*comparison* situation)

Differentiation
Fill in the blanks with the level of data that makes sense for students. For this task, putting students in like-ability groups allows them to work with others that are at the same level. Even if students work with different data, the situations are the same so the class can discuss which situations are comparisons.

My brother had ____ stickers. My sister had ____ more stickers than my brother. How many stickers did my sister have? (*comparison* situation)

Talk About It/Write About It

How are number bonds and bar diagrams alike? How are they different?

How are take away problems and comparison problems alike? How are they different?

Focus on the Question

Post the data below and ask students a different question about it each day. Students work with partners to retell the problem, identify the data needed to solve it, and talk about how they would solve it. Partners then share their methods with the class.

The school store keeps a tally of the sales each week. The items that were sold last week are recorded below:

School Store Sales

Pencils	11
Pens	15
Erasers	26
Notebooks	24
Folders	19
Three-Ring Binders	?
Sketchbooks	?

1. How many pens and pencils were sold at the school store last week? Tell how you would solve it.
2. How many more notebooks than folders were sold? Tell how you would solve it.
3. How many fewer pens than notebooks were sold? Tell how you would solve it.
4. There were 4 more notebooks sold than sketchbooks. How many sketchbooks were sold last week? Tell how you would solve it.
5. There were 32 three-ring binders and erasers sold in all. How many three-ring binders were sold? Tell how you would solve it.

SOLVING TWO-STEP PROBLEMS

Students are first exposed to two-step problems, using addition and subtraction, in second grade. They begin to develop their skills in drawing two visual representations and writing two equations. Using a two-step problem organizer can help students identify each step.

Thinking Through a Lesson

`SMP1, SMP2, SMP3, SMP4, SMP5`

Representing Two-Step Problems

Students use models and an organizer to show how they solve two-step problems.

Pose the following problem:

> Taylor rode his bike 46 miles on Saturday. On Sunday, he rode his bike 17 miles farther than he did on Saturday. How many miles did Taylor ride over the weekend?

Turn to your partner and retell the problem in your own words.

What are we trying to find out? (How many miles Taylor rode his bike on Saturday and Sunday.)

Record on the board: *Taylor rode _____ miles on Saturday and Sunday.*

Have students discuss the following with partners and then with the whole class.

What information do we know? (He rode his bike 46 miles on Saturday.)

Do we have all of the information that we need to solve this? (No; we need to know how many miles he rode on Sunday.)

What do we know about Sunday? (He rode 17 miles farther on Sunday.)

So, do we know how far he rode his bike on Sunday?

Think about how you might be able to figure that out.

Provide each student with the two-step problem-solving organizer.

What do we need to figure out first so we can solve this problem? (We need to figure out how many miles Taylor rode on Sunday.)

What information will help us find out? (He rode 46 miles on Saturday. He rode 17 more miles on Sunday.)

What operation would you use? What kind of problem is this? (We're thinking about 46 miles and then 17 more so we add.)

Look at your two-step organizer. Where should we show our work? (We should show it in the top Show It box.)

Go ahead and draw a model that shows your first step. Be sure to put labels so that we know what your model is showing.

Observe students as they create their models.

Compare your model with your partner's.

Tell them how you decided what to draw.

Circulate around the room listening to discussions.

Invite some students with different types of models to share them with the whole class. Make connections between the different models used to show the situation.

> In two-step problems, students often stop after solving the first part of the problem. Having them begin by writing a phrase identifying what they are solving for (e.g., Taylor rode _____ miles on Saturday and Sunday) keeps them focused on the final answer.

> Some students might mistakenly believe that Taylor rode only 17 miles on Sunday. Have students reread that sentence and explain to a partner what it means to go 17 miles farther.

> Students may slide this template into a page protector and use a wipe-off marker so that the template can be used for several problems.

> *Use your model to help you write a number sentence that could be used to find out how many miles Taylor rode his bike on Sunday. (46 + 17 = ____.)*
>
> *Compare your number sentence with your partner's.*

Invite students to share their thinking with the whole class, making connections between the model and the number sentence and discussing any other number sentences that may be suggested.

> *How many miles did Taylor ride on Sunday? (63 miles.)*

Refer back to the board: Taylor rode ____ miles on Saturday and Sunday.

> *Tell your partner if we have answered the question. Are we done? (No; we want to know how many miles Taylor rode on Saturday and Sunday.)*
>
> *What kind of mathematical situation is this? What operation should we use? (It's addition; we are putting the miles for Saturday and Sunday together.)*
>
> *Look at your template. Where would this information go? (It should go in the bottom Show It box.)*
>
> *Create a new model that could show how many miles Taylor rode on Saturday and Sunday.*
>
> *Use your model to help you write a number sentence that could be used to solve this problem.*
>
> *Share your model and number sentence with your partner.*

Have students refer back to the problem to tell you if they have solved it.

> *What equation did you use to solve it? (46 + 63 = 109 miles. Or, 63 + 46 = 109 miles)*

Refer back to the board: Taylor rode ____ miles on Saturday and Sunday.

> *Have we answered the question? Can you tell me your answer in the sentence we wrote on the board? (Taylor rode 109 miles on Saturday and Sunday.)*
>
> *Does that answer sound right? Explain. Turn and tell your partner. (Yes, because he almost rode 50 miles the first day and rode a little more the next day.)*
>
> *How was this problem different than other problems that we've done? (We had to make two models and two equations.)*

> **Students should justify their reasons for modeling the problem in the way they did. Asking others if they agree or disagree with a model is a great way to start class discussions.**

> **Asking students to reread the problem after solving it and to think about the reasonableness of their answer helps them develop an important habit of successful problem solvers.**

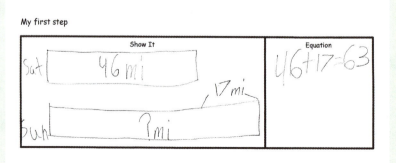

Then I

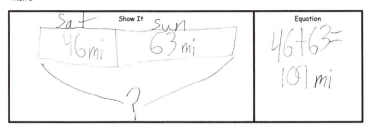

If time allows, pose the following problem for students to solve with their partners:

> There are 53 second-grade students at Sheridan Elementary School. Thomas Elementary School has 15 fewer second-grade students. How many second graders are there in both schools?

As students finish, invite them to share their solution and their thinking.

To end the lesson, have students talk with partners and then the class about:

> *What are some challenges when solving a two-step problem?*
> *How does the Two-Step organizer help to show your thinking?*

Differentiation
If you notice students who are having difficulty representing the two steps with models or equations, work with them in a small group while other students are working with partners, asking questions to guide their thinking.

Students might mention that they need to remember what the problem is asking them to solve, or that they need to create two models and two equations. As students get more experience with two-step problems, they can create their own two-step organizers. Part of the skill is identifying when two steps are required. For initial experiences, the organizer reminds them that two models and two equations are a part of the solution process.

Exploring Different Methods

Students solve two-step problems and share and compare the different methods they use.

Pose the following problem:

> Jill had 45 baseball cards. She gave 14 to Mike and 20 to Sara. How many did she have left?

Turn to your partner and retell the problem in your own words.
What do you need to find out?
Write that as a sentence with a blank for the answer.
What do you already know that will help you figure that out?
How would you solve it?

Ask students to solve the problem with a partner and be ready to share how they did it.

Two-step problems can have any combination of addition and subtraction; both steps may use the same operation, or each step may need a different one.

Common Error or Misconception
When trying to write equations for two-step subtraction problems, we may see students writing $45 - 14 - 20 =$ ____. Have students write two equations that show the two steps taken to solve the problem, so for this problem students might write $45 - 14 = 31$ and $31 - 20 = 11$.

Walk through the room to observe students' strategies. Identify students who may have solved it in different ways (e.g., either adding the 14 and 20 and then subtracting that from 45 or subtracting the 14, then subtracting the 20). Select those students to share their strategies.

> *John, can you explain how you and your partner solved it? Be sure to tell me the numbers you used and explain why you did it that way.*
>
> *What equations did you use to show that?*

Record the equations on the board as students talk.

> *Does anyone have any questions about how a classmate solved it?*
>
> *Did anyone solve it a different way? What did you do? What equations did you use to show the problem?*

Record the equations on the board as students talk. Have students compare the strategies and see that they resulted in the same answer.

> *Can you tell me the answer with our problem statement?*

Pose the following problem:

> Baby carrots come in a bag of 50. At snack time, Robin ate 23 carrots. Gail ate 18 carrots. How many carrots were left in the bag?

Have students talk about the context and important information in the problem.

Provide students time to solve the problem using their chosen method.

As students finish, have them circulate around the room to find someone who solved it the same way and someone who solved it differently.

Have some students share their strategies.

> *Is there more than one way to solve this problem? Explain.*
>
> *Who chose to add first and then subtract? Why did you choose that method?*
>
> *What was a different way to solve? Why did you choose that method?*

Pose additional problems for students to explore with partners. See the online resources for more two-step problems.

> *There are often different ways to solve two-step problems. The students' strategies just need to make sense with the problem situation.*

Differentiation
Use this time to observe for students who need support. Provide manipulatives and additional questioning as needed.

FORMATIVE ASSESSMENT

Have students solve the following problem using a model and writing the equations:

> Corbin had 48 marbles in his collection. He gave 8 to his friend Izzy and 8 to his friend Tyler. How many marbles did Corbin have left?

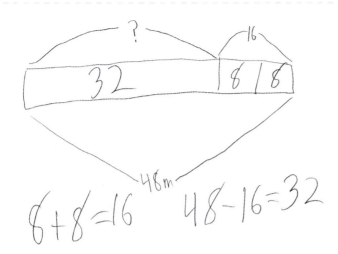

This student shows a bar model with three parts. When asked to explain his work, he said that he did 8 + 8 = 16 to see how many marbles Corbin gave to his friends. Then he subtracted 16 from 48 to find how many marbles were left. His method works and his equation reflects the problem situation. Remind him to label his model so it is clear what the numbers represent.

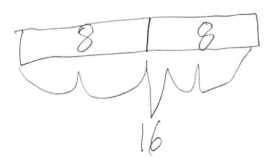

This student shows a model to figure out how many marbles Corbin gave away. She then subtracts 16 from 48 to find the answer. Suggest including an addition sentence for 8 + 8 and labels to indicate what the numbers represent.

If the student just does one part:

- Have him write a phrase for the answer before he starts solving: "Corbin gave some marbles to his friends and had ___ marbles left."

> - Have him record his equation next to each part of the model.
> - Ask: *Who did Corbin give marbles to? Did he give marbles to anyone else?*

Additional Ideas for Support and Practice

The following ideas extend students' understanding of two-step problems and provide meaningful practice.

TALK ABOUT IT/WRITE ABOUT IT

Teri said the answer to the following problem is 35 children. Mark said the answer is 17 children. Who do you agree with? Why?

There were 32 children on the playground. 15 children went inside. Then 18 children came out to the playground. How many children are on the playground now?

How are one-step problems and two-step problems similar? How are they different?

How many number sentences would you need if you were solving a two-step problem? Explain your thinking.

PASS A PROBLEM

Write a problem on the outside of a manila envelope.

Students work in teams to solve the problem and put their work (answer and model to show how they did it) into the envelope.

Then the envelope is passed to another team, who solves and puts their solution in the envelope.

After several teams have solved the problems, teams open the envelope they currently have and compare the answers and strategies.

PROBLEM-SOLVING CENTER

Post a problem of the week.

At some point during the week, students go to the center and solve it, showing models and equations.

Have students put their finished work in a basket.

On Friday, pull all of the work out of basket.

Give each student one (not his own) to look at and review.

Have a discussion about the problem and solutions.

ONE-STEP/TWO-STEP SORT

Write various one- and two-step problems on cards.

Students sort the problems into one- and two-step categories.

Students then pick a one-step and a two-step problem to solve.

Vocabulary

addition	number sentence
bar model	problem-solving strategies
equation	
model	
number bond	subtraction
	two-step
number line	unknown

General Resources

Additional Problems

Resources for Specific Activities

Bar Model Template

Comparison Bar Model Template

Four Ways

Two-Step Template

These resources are available at http://hein.pub/MathinPractice, keycode MIPG2.

ONLINE RESOURCES

MODULE 2

Building Understanding and Fluency of Basic Math Facts

About the Math 2.OA.2

Our goal is that our students are fluent with basic addition and subtraction math facts by the end of second grade. Math fact fluency allows them to do the mental math they encounter each day and helps them perform multidigit computations more smoothly. But fluency is not the only goal when studying math facts. If it were our only goal, we would simply ask students to memorize the facts. An equally important goal is to develop greater understanding of numbers through the exploration of math facts—to increase our students' number sense through investigations, discussions, and observations of these fact sets. The exploration of addition and subtraction facts in kindergarten through second grade is a perfect opportunity to:

- introduce and revisit properties
- explore the inverse relationship between addition and subtraction
- explore the meaning of equality and gain confidence with varied equations, including those with missing numbers in different positions
- build mental math skills by composing and decomposing numbers
- strengthen math connections and number sense by relating one fact set to another
- revisit problem solving.

The study of addition and subtraction facts spans kindergarten through second grade. Kindergarten students were introduced to the concepts of addition and subtraction and gained fluency with some +/−1 and +/−0 facts. In first grade, students continued to explore math facts, including +/−2, +/−10, doubles, and making ten, through stories, problem-based tasks, drawing diagrams, acting out situations with manipulatives, and building equations. They worked to gain fluency with these facts to build a foundation for the facts they explore in second grade.

In second grade, our students apply their understanding of doubles and making tens as they explore facts that are close to the doubles and making-ten facts. Through opportunities to visualize the new facts with the known facts in mind, our students make sense of the remaining math facts. For example:

- 5 + 6 is 5 + 5 + 1 (using their knowledge of doubles)
- 9 + 4 is 9 + 1 + 3 (using their knowledge of making ten).

These facts present a perfect opportunity to work with numbers flexibly. Students learn to adjust numbers and use their understanding of tens and doubles to find sums and differences for these facts.

The key ideas focused on in this module include:

- discovering how to apply an understanding of making tens to solve more complex facts (called the *using-ten* strategy), and gaining fluency with these facts
- discovering how to apply an understanding of doubles to solve more complex facts (called the *using-doubles* strategy), and gaining fluency with these facts
- promoting fluency with all addition and subtraction math facts.

Since kindergarten, the goal of math facts lessons has been both fluency and understanding. Instructional activities focus on an exploration of addition and subtraction fact sets as well as building automaticity with the facts. To do that, our lessons for each fact set follow this sequence:

1. Build understanding of the addition fact set (visualize the fact set through problems, manipulatives, and math talk; explore properties related to the fact set; make connections to other fact sets).
2. Work on fluency with the addition fact set (interactive activities to promote automaticity).
3. Build understanding of the related subtraction fact set (visualize the subtraction fact set through problems, manipulatives, and math talk); make a connection to the related addition fact set (visualize the facts as unknown addend facts).
4. Work on fluency with the related subtraction fact set (activities to promote automaticity).

Moving too quickly through the fact sets does not allow students time to develop understanding and fluency. This is particularly evident when it comes to subtraction fluency. Students often solve subtraction facts by thinking about addition. If you pose 10 − 6 = ___, they change the fact to "6 plus what is 10?" Giving students the time to gain fluency with a set of addition facts allows them to use those skills as they explore the related subtraction facts.

And when exploring using doubles and using ten, fluency with prior fact sets is critical. Fluency with making-ten and doubles facts allows our students to use that knowledge when faced with these new facts. Beginning the year with a fluency review of the foundation facts (+/−0, +/−1, +/−2, +/−10, doubles, making ten) ensures our students have a strong foundation for the facts to come.

USING TEN

In first grade, students identified addend pairs that make ten (e.g., 8 + 2, 7 + 3, 6 + 4). The understanding of, and fluency with, these facts now helps them determine answers to facts like 7 + 4.

"If I know that 7 + 3 is 10, then 7 + 4 is one more than 10, or 11."

This strategy hinges on our students' knowledge of the addend pairs that make ten, as well as their ability to decompose one of the addends in the expression. Double ten frames (see Figure 2.1) and double bead counters (see Figure 2.2) are ways to visualize these decompositions.

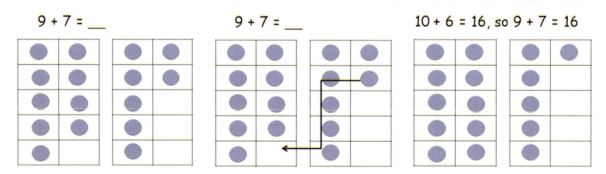

Figure 2.1 Students show 9 + 7 on a double ten frame. Then, students move one counter to fill a frame so they are able to see 10 and some more. They see the sum quickly, using the simpler 10 + 6 expression.

Using manipulatives helps our students to get a mental image of the way the numbers are broken apart and then put back together.

Once students understand the process, it's time to practice for fluency. Activities that are game-like, and offer opportunities for students to say and write the facts as they play, engage our students and give them the concentrated practice they need to commit these facts to memory. Math fact centers, partner games, and independent fluency activities help our students develop automaticity with math facts and should be a routine part of math class during second grade.

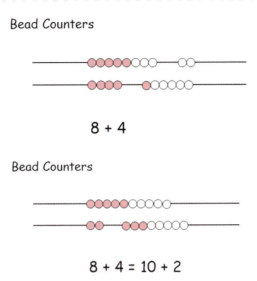

Figure 2.2 Students represent 8 + 4 with the beads (on the left) and then slide the beads, adding 2 in the top row and removing 2 in the bottom row, to show the simpler 10 + 2.

USING TEN WITH SUBTRACTION

First, students explore the meaning of *using ten* and work on their fluency with the addition facts. Then, once they have attained some fluency with these facts, we introduce the related subtraction facts.

$$11 - 7 = ?$$

Students know that 10 − 7 = 3, so if they break 11 into 10 + 1, they can just do 10 − 7 and then add the 1 to find that the difference is 4.

Our students' prior work decomposing numbers reminds them that numbers can be broken apart in various ways. The ability to break numbers apart in ways that make their computations easier strengthens our students' mental math abilities and builds their number sense. Eventually, students will simply know the differences for these facts, but these explorations help them better understand how numbers work.

When exploring subtraction facts, we also emphasize the connection between addition and subtraction, showing subtraction as the inverse of addition. Opportunities for students to combine and separate counters and cubes allow them to revisit this idea. When they put 7 counters and 4 counters together they get 11 counters, so how many will be left of the 11 if they take away 4? Through acting out problems and using manipulatives to show problem situations, students better understand how 7 + 4 = 11 relates to 11 − 4 = 7 (see Figure 2.3).

Students then use their understanding of inverse operations to help them with math fact fluency. To solve 11 − 7, students might change the subtraction fact to the related unknown addend fact, thinking, "7 plus what equals 11?" Having spent time developing fluency with using-ten addition facts prior to moving to the subtraction facts allows our students to more easily determine the missing addend. Also, experiences observing the three numbers that form the related equations (7 + 4 = 11, 4 + 7 = 11, 11 − 7 = 4, 11 − 4 = 7) strengthen students' understanding of the link between addition and subtraction and contribute to fluency.

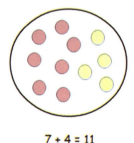
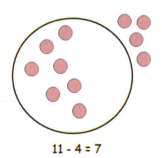

Figure 2.3 Explorations in which students visualize inverse operations (adding to/taking from or putting together/taking apart) help them build a stronger understanding of the relationship between addition and subtraction. On the left, additional counters were added, while on the right, counters were taken away.

USING DOUBLES

In second grade, our students use their understanding of doubles, as well as their fluency with doubles facts, to find the sums of facts that are close to doubles. Knowing that 6 + 6 = 12, our students might see 6 + 7 as just one more than the doubles fact, or 6 + 6 + 1. Through opportunities to visualize these facts with objects, counters, or connecting cubes as in Figure 2.4, our students see one quantity as just a bit more than the other and use the known fact to find the unknown fact.

> There is no one way to use these strategies to find sums and differences. One student might see 6 + 7 as near doubles, thinking 6 + 6 + 1, while another might think about making tens, changing 6 + 7 to 6 + 4 + 3 or 10 + 3. Either way makes sense.

Understanding the Concept

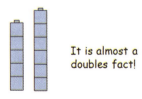

5 + 6 = 11 because 5 + 5 + 1 = 11

Figure 2.4 Students build towers to show the facts and see that 5 + 6 is the same as 5 + 5 and 1 more. Using the doubles fact allows them to quickly find the sum. The ability to use doubles facts to find near-doubles facts reinforces our students' understanding of the flexibility of numbers. Numbers can be decomposed to allow us to more easily do computations.

USING DOUBLES WITH SUBTRACTION

First, students explore the meaning of *using doubles* related to addition. Then, they practice their fluency with the addition facts to prepare them for the related subtraction facts. When students see 13 − 6 = __, they use their understanding of inverse operations to change the equation to 6 + __ = 13. Students might think about double 6 is 12, so the other addend must be 1 more than that to get 13.

Keep in mind that these strategies improve our students' mental math skills and strengthen their understanding of numbers and operations. Although ultimately we want our students to just know 13 − 6, we first focus on understanding the expressions, building number sense, and better understanding the way numbers work. Do we want our students to rely solely on a set of memorized facts, or would they also benefit from a deep understanding of numbers and operations? Won't our students gain confidence and become more capable mathematicians if they understand the structure of our number system, are able to use numbers flexibly, and know how numbers work? Our students can commit facts to memory and also develop the skills that make them mathematical thinkers.

> The study of math facts in second grade is about understanding operations, equations, and properties. It is about using known facts, like doubles and making tens, to make sense of and determine the sums and differences for related, but more complex, facts. And second grade is about gaining the strong number understandings and fluency with math facts that allow our students to tackle the more complex computations they will perform in third grade and beyond.

UNDERSTANDING THE EQUAL SIGN

Understanding the meaning of the equal sign is an important part of our math fact lessons. Posing facts with the sum or difference on either side of the equal sign (4 + 8 = 12 or 12 = 4 + 8) shows that the equal sign is not an indicator to write the answer, but a symbol to show that both sides of the equation have an equal value. Sometimes saying *same as* when talking about *equal* is helpful. And having students name the missing number in equations helps us determine if they really understand the operations and equations.

> Seeing the sum on the left side of an equation can be particularly confusing for students who do not understand the meaning of the equal sign. Having students think about making the sum on one side of the equal sign the same as the sum on the other side helps clarify the confusion.

4 + 8 = ____

12 = ____ + 8

4 + ____ = 12

5 + ____ = 4 + 6

8 + 7 = ____ + 5

Exploring the Progression

PREVIOUS	NOW	NEXT
Grade 1	**Grade 2**	**Grade 3**
Fluency with math fact sets +/−1, +/−0, +/−2, +/−10, doubles, and making tens	Applying the using-ten strategy and the using-doubles strategy to solve more complex facts; fluency with all basic addition and subtraction facts	Applying math fact fluency to multidigit addition and subtraction

Learning Goals

I can break numbers apart to find solutions to math facts.

I can use doubles facts to find the solutions to other facts.

I can name the number pairs that make ten and can use them to find the solutions to other facts.

I can solve subtraction facts by thinking about addition.

I know all my addition and subtraction math facts.

Lessons in This Module

Reviewing Fluency with Making Ten
Spin and Make Ten (addition)
Roll for Tens (addition)
Grab a Ten (addition)
Behind the Back Subtraction (subtraction)
Capture (subtraction)
Cover and Uncover (addition and subtraction)
Number Bond Cards (addition and subtraction)

Reviewing Fluency with Doubles
Roll for Doubles (addition)
Spin and Subtract (subtraction)
Spin and Double It (addition)
Number Bond Cards (addition and subtraction)

Understanding the Using-Ten Strategy for Addition
Double Ten Frame Addition
Another Way to Think About It
Ten Frame Recording

Developing Fluency with Using Ten for Addition
Match 'Em Up
Make a Fact
Plus Nine
BINGO

Understanding the Using-Ten Strategy for Subtraction
Talking About Numbers
Double Ten Frames
Finding Differences with Double Ten Frames
Here's My Problem, Pass It On

Ideas for Instruction and Assessment

REVIEWING FLUENCY

In first grade, students worked on fluency with pairs that make ten and with doubles facts. Their fluency with these facts impacts their ability to understand and apply the using-ten and using-doubles strategies. The following interactive games provide students with repeated exposure to these fact sets helping them gain fluency.

REVIEWING FLUENCY WITH MAKING TEN

Spin and Make Ten (addition)

Players take turn spinning a 0–9 spinner, or picking a 0–9 digit card, and saying what number is added to it to make ten.

Students then say and write the math fact.

Roll for Tens (addition)

Partners roll two 1–6 number cubes and two 4–9 number cubes.

They look for pairs that make ten, say the fact and record the equation, then roll again.

Grab a Ten (addition)

Partners remove all jokers and face cards from a deck of playing cards.

They lay 16 cards face up in a 4 × 4 grid.

Students take turns removing two cards that make ten (e.g., a 4 and 6 or a 2 and 8) and say and record the fact.

When cards are removed, they are replaced with cards from the deck.

Students keep playing until no tens can be made.

Whoever has the most cards wins.

Reshuffle and start again.

Behind the Back Subtraction (subtraction)

Each pair has ten connecting cubes. One partner makes a chain and puts it behind his or her back, then breaks it and shows one part to his or her partner. The partner has to say what is still behind the first student's back. Together, the students write the matching subtraction equations.

Building Understanding and Fluency of Basic Math Facts — MODULE 2

Capture (subtraction)

Pairs of students need a cup and ten counters. One student captures some counters with a cup. The partner has to say how many are under the cup and write the equation. Then, partners switch roles.

Cover and Uncover (addition and subtraction)

Use a set of 0–10 number cards for each pair of students.

One student makes pairs with sums of 10 and stacks the two cards one on top of the other so one card is hidden.

The other student predicts what number is hidden by subtracting the top number from 10.

Number Bond Cards (addition and subtraction)

One student pulls a card with a sum of 10 and covers one circle.

The student's partner writes the related addition and subtraction equations.

Then, students switch roles and pick another card.

REVIEWING FLUENCY WITH DOUBLES

Roll for Doubles (addition)

Partners roll two 1–6 number cubes and two 4–9 number cubes.

They look for two of the same number (doubles), say the corresponding doubles fact, and write the equation.

If no doubles are rolled, they roll again.

Students continue to roll and record any doubles facts they see.

Spin and Subtract (subtraction)

Partners take turns spinning the doubles subtraction spinner and saying and recording the fact.

Partners compare to see who spun the greater difference.

The greater difference wins the round.

Partners continue to spin and compare.

Spin and Double It (addition)

A student spins a 0–9 spinner, doubles the number, and says and writes the equation for the fact.

Developing Fluency with Using Ten for Subtraction
Minus 8 or 9

Understanding the Using-Doubles Strategy for Addition
Breaking Chains
Talk About It/Write About It

Developing Fluency with Using Doubles for Addition
Towers of Facts
Domino Sort
BINGO
Spin, Two, Three

Understanding the Using-Doubles Strategy for Subtraction
Exploring Difference with Breaking Chains

Developing Fluency with Using Doubles for Subtraction
Making Connections
Filling Digits
Spin and Inverse
Cover Them

For additional fluency tasks for previous math facts, see Math in Practice: Teaching First-Grade Math, Modules 3–7.

Check students' fluency with previously learned math fact sets at the start of the second-grade year. Throughout the year, practice for fluency should be a daily classroom routine.

Number Bond Cards (addition and subtraction)

One student pulls a card with a doubles fact and covers one circle.

The student's partner writes the related addition and subtraction equations.

Then, students switch roles and pick another card.

UNDERSTANDING THE USING-TEN STRATEGY FOR ADDITION

Students convert their addends to make an easier problem. They decompose an addend and compose a part with the other addend to make a ten.

`SMP3, SMP4, SMP5, SMP7`

Thinking Through a Lesson

Double Ten Frame Addition

Students use double ten frames to visualize the strategy of using ten by moving counters to fill one frame.

Give each pair of students a double ten frame template and 20 two-color counters.

Pose the problem:

> At the beach, Bailey found 9 shells and Molly found 6 shells. How many shells did they find?

Work with your partner to show this problem using your ten frames.

Observe as students model the problem, looking for the different ways they show it.

> *How many shells did they find?* (15.)
> *What equation shows this problem?* ($9 + 6 = 15$.)
> *How did you know the sum was 15?* (I counted all of them. Or, I started at 9 and counted on with the counters on the other frame.)
> *Did anyone do it a different way?*

If any students moved a counter from the frame with 6 to fill the other ten frame, have them share their thinking. If not, try a think-aloud as you write $9 + 6 = 15$ on the board.

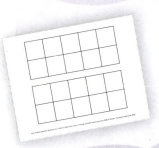

> Students visualize a mental math process by using ten frames and counters. This allows them to better understand how to simplify computations by decomposing and recomposing numbers.

> Using red counters to represent the first addend and yellow counters for the second addend can help students better visualize the ways they are decomposed.

> The first answer is a beginning-level counting strategy of counting all. The second is a more-developed strategy of counting on.

Show 2 ten frames with 9 red counters on one and 6 yellow counters on the other. This might be done on an interactive whiteboard that allows you to slide counters, with a document camera, or with magnetic counters.

I was thinking it would have been easier if one of the ten frames was filled. Would that make it easier? How? (You wouldn't have to count them all because it's easy to add to 10.)

Could we fill a ten frame? How could we do that with the counters we have? Talk to your partner about what you could do.

Have students share their ideas, asking questions to make their thinking visible to others in the class.

What could you do? (We could move a counter to fill a ten frame.)

Slide a yellow counter from the frame with 6 to the frame with 9, filling that frame.

But if you moved the counter would you have the same answer? (Yes, because you just moved it. You didn't take it away.)

How does that help you find the total number of counters? (You can see the 10 and 5 more.)

Do you need to count to find the total? (No.)

Write 9 + 6 = 10 + 5 on the board.

> Asking students to explain and justify their suggestions pushes them to think deeply about their actions and allows others to hear their thinking.

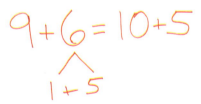

> Students have been working with double ten frames since kindergarten. They should be able to immediately recognize these numbers without counting. They can tell the number that results from 10 and 1 more, 2 more, 3 more, and so on.

Pose the problem:

> Blake found 8 shells and Liam found 5 shells. How many shells did they find?

How could you show this problem using your ten frames? (We could put 8 on one and 5 on the other.)

Talk to your partner about how you can solve it. How many shells did they find?

Observe as students model and solve the problem. Look for students who are counting the 8 and 5, and those who are making a 10.

How many shells did they find? (13.)

What equation shows this problem? (8 + 5 = 13.)

How did you know it was 13? (I counted all of them. *Or,* I started at 8 and counted on with the counters on the other frame. *Or,* I moved some to make a 10, and then just saw that it was 10 and 3 more.)

This student models 8 + 5 with 2-color counters.

The student moves two counters to make a ten. Now she can add 10 + 3.

Show 8 red and 5 yellow counters on the whiteboard ten frames, and slide two yellow counters from the frame with 5 to the frame with 8, filling that frame.

What number do my frames show? (13.)
How do you know? (It's 10 and 3 more.)

$$8 + 5 = 10 + 3$$
$$\wedge$$
$$2+3$$

5 can be decomposed into 2 and 3. When 2 is recomposed with 8, the equation becomes 10 + 3.

Emphasize how easy it is to see the total when one frame is filled.

Have students use their counters and ten frames to solve these equations by making tens. Talk about each one using similar questioning.

8 + 6
9 + 5
9 + 8

Does it matter which frame you fill? Could you make a 10 with either frame? Try it both ways for 9 + 8.

Have students share their ideas. Show both ways on the board.

Could you use this strategy without the counters and ten frames? (Yes; we could make the tens in our head just thinking about what two numbers make a 10, such as 8 and 2 or 9 and 1.)

Write *8 + 9* on the board.

Turn and tell your partner what you would do. (I would take 1 from the 8 and make the 9 a 10.)

What new addition problem did you make? (7 + 10.)

Where did the 7 come from? (I took one from the 8.)

What is the sum? (17.)

> Some students may make connections to the commutative property, knowing that 9 + 8 is the same as 8 + 9.

$$9 + 8 = 10 + 7$$
$$\wedge$$
$$1+7$$

$$9 + 8 = 7 + 10$$
$$\wedge$$
$$7+2$$

We can decompose either addend.

To end the lesson, have students write in their math journals about how they would solve 8 + 4 by making a ten.

Another Way to Think About It

This activity gives students the opportunity to connect using what they have done with counters to a more symbolic way of showing using ten.

Students are given an equation and asked to think about using ten to solve it.

Equation	Another Way to Think About It	Another Way to Think About It
9 + 7 = 16	9 + 1 + 6 = 16	10 + 6 = 16
8 + 7 =		

In the middle column of the recording sheet, students decompose an addend to allow them to make a ten.

In the last column, students rename the fact by making the ten and adding what's left.

FORMATIVE ASSESSMENT

Pose the following:

> Jason said that knowing his tens facts helps him add 7 + 4. How could that help? Explain.

I know 7 + 3 = 10 + 1 = 11

This student tries to communicate that he broke 4 into 3 and 1. He adds 7 + 3 to make his 10. He then adds 1 more to make 11. There is some faulty communication in the recording of thinking, in that 7 + 3 does not equal 10 + 1. Conference with the student to check his reasoning. Ask, "Does 7 + 3 equal 10 + 1? How can we record our thinking with more precision?"

If students have difficulty explaining their thinking, provide them with a double ten frame mat and 2-color counters to model.

If students struggle with their explanation, have them list all pairs of numbers that have a sum of 4.

Ask:

> Can any of those partners make a 10 with 7?
> Which one?
> How many are left?
> What does 10 and 1 make?

Ten Frame Recording

In this activity, students observe facts displayed on ten frames and then show how they would think about the fact using ten.

Students first record the fact illustrated on the ten frame.

Then, students show the fact by using the same data but filling an entire ten frame (10) and showing the remaining ones on the second frame. Students record the new equation.

  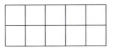 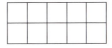

Fact: _____   As ten and some more: _____

> **Students begin by thinking about making tens, but ultimately should know the sums for the facts. The more exposure they have to the facts, the more likely they are to simply know 7 + 9 = 16 without thinking about making tens.**

DEVELOPING FLUENCY WITH USING TEN FOR ADDITION

Match 'Em Up

In this game, students match equations that illustrate how decomposing numbers can help with making ten. (See the online resources for Match 'Em Up cards.)

Students might match a 9 + 7 fact card with a 9 + 1 + 6 card.

This match shows that we can make ten (9 + 1) by taking 1 from 7.

The fact can now be thought of 10 + 6.

Make a Fact

Students select two ten frame cards (representing the numbers 6–9) and create an addition fact.

Students should say and write each fact.

The ten frames provide a visual aid as they think about the fact.

Plus Nine

Students take turns spinning a 6–9 spinner and adding 9 to their spin.

Although they may think about making a ten, they should say and write the +9 fact (e.g., 7 + 9 = 16 or 8 + 9 = 17).

If they do not know the sum, partners can talk about using ten and find the sum for the fact.

BINGO

Have students write the following numbers in the boxes on a 5 × 5 grid: 11, 12, 13, 14, 15, 16, 17, and 18.

> **Differentiation**
>
> The goal is fluency with addition and subtraction facts by the end of second grade. Set up centers that allow students to work on a designated fact set (e.g., using-ten addition or using-ten subtraction) based on their needs. Centers might contain varied folders of games, and students select the ones that match their designated fact set.

Students can write a number as many times as they want and anywhere they want.

Students play in partners or groups.

Two sets of using-ten fact cards are shuffled and placed facedown in the center.

A player picks a fact card, and everyone decides what the answer is.

Each player covers that number on his board with a cube or counter.

Only one number is covered each turn.

Then, the next player picks the card, and everyone decides on the sum and covers it on their grid.

A player wins when she has covered five in a row, vertically, horizontally, or diagonally.

Then, the cards are shuffled and play begins again.

UNDERSTANDING THE USING-TEN STRATEGY FOR SUBTRACTION

Students explore using ten to subtract, making connections to addition.

Talking About Numbers

Students talk about ways to subtract, sharing various strategies, including those that involve thinking about a ten.

> Pose 16 – 6.
>
> *How would you subtract 6 from 16? Explain.*

Have students share their thinking.

> Pose 16 – 9.
>
> *Turn and talk: How would you subtract 9 from 16? Be ready to explain your idea to the class.*

Let students share some ideas and have a brief discussion about each one. As students talk about their thinking, record their ideas on the board or chart paper. Ask the other students to agree or disagree that the strategy works.

> *Someone said we could draw 16 circles and cross out 9 of them. Do you agree? Does that show subtraction?*
>
> *Someone said we could make a chain of 16 cubes and a chain of 9 cubes and see how much longer the 16 chain is. Will that work? Explain.*
>
> *Someone said they thought about addition and said 9 + ____ = 16 and knew 9 + 7 = 16. Does that make sense? Why?*
>
> *Someone said we could take 6 away and then take 3 more away. Why would we do that?*
>
> *How does it help you to take 6 first?*

Number talks are a great way to begin discussions about students' thinking. As students share their ideas, model them on the board, ask questions about their thinking, and allow students to think about each other's methods.

Building Understanding and Fluency of Basic Math Facts

MODULE 2

Someone said we could think about taking 10 away and then put one back. Does that make sense?

Have students look back at all of the methods and observe the differences. What do they notice?

Is there just one way to do this?

Pose 17 − 8.

Turn and tell your partner two ways you could solve it.

Listen as students share their strategies with partners.

Double Ten Frames

Through teacher demonstration and student exploration with double ten frames, students visualize a possible strategy for thinking about tens when they subtract.

Show a double ten frame with 17 counters (10 on one and 7 on the other).

Turn and tell your partner how many counters are on my frames.
How did you know that so quickly?

Listen to my problem:

> Patrick had 17 baseballs when he went to the park. He lost 9 at the park. How many did he have when he got home?

What operation are we doing in this problem? Explain.
How many did he lose?
So, I can show it like this, right?

On your ten frame, remove 4 from the filled frame, leaving 6, and 5 from the other frame, leaving 2.

So, how can we find how many he had left?
Is there another way to do this? Talk to your partner.

Have students share some ideas. Pick a couple that relate to tens to discuss.

Someone said we could take one whole ten frame away and then put 1 back on the other frame. Would that work? Why?

Show it on your frame. Take all 10 counters off one, but slide one of them to the other frame.

Why did we move that one counter?
How many baseballs did he have left? How do you know?
So first we took 10 away.

Write *17 − 10 = 7* on the board.

Then we added 1 back.

Write *7 + 1 = 8* on the board.

Give each pair a double ten frame and twenty counters.

Have students work with partners to solve the following:

    15 − 9
    17 − 8
    14 − 6

> **Differentiation**
> Although some students may already be thinking flexibly about numbers and breaking them apart to find differences, others may benefit from additional examples and more time. Listening to their partner discussions allows you to determine which students need additional support.

> For more ideas on using models to build math understanding see Math in Practice: A Guide for Teachers, Chapter 3.

> Students may also suggest that to subtract 9 from 17 we could take all 7 from the 7 frame, and then take 2 more from the 10. (17 − 7 = 10 and 10 − 2 = 8). Doing it in this way also has them thinking about tens as they subtract to have a difference of ten, then use their understanding of number pairs that make ten to immediately know the answer. Have students discuss and model this method, too.

This is not the only strategy students can use to solve these expressions, but having some experience adjusting the expression to think about tens strengthens their number sense and shows them how numbers can be broken apart or put together to help us do mental math.

As students remove counters from their double ten frame mats, look to see if they remove randomly or if they take from the partially filled frame first before removing the others. Doing this reinforces the idea of using ten, a benchmark.

Practice tasks that integrate problem solving allow students to gain continued problem-solving practice as they work on understanding math facts.

Common Error or Misconception

Fluency with subtraction is more difficult for students than fluency with addition. To promote fluency with subtraction, (1) allow students time to gain addition fluency and (2) help them use the idea of inverse to find the difference (e.g., for 13 − 9, have students think 9 + ____ = 13).

Talk about each one, emphasizing the way students could use what they know about tens to help them find the solutions.

Finding Differences with Double Ten Frames SHOW IT!

Students pick fact cards and then use double ten frames to show and solve the subtraction facts.

Students select a using-ten subtraction fact card.

Students create a model of the fact on a double ten frame mat by filling one frame completely (10) and placing the remaining counters on the other frame.

Then, they show this amount on the recording sheet by drawing dots.

Students then remove the counters from their double ten frame to show the subtraction and model this on the recording sheet by crossing out dots to represent what was removed.

Students then record the equation with the difference.

Using-Ten Fact	Double Ten Frame Model	Equation

Here's My Problem, Pass It On

Students select a using-ten subtraction fact card.

They write a word problem for the fact.

Students then pass their problems to a partner.

Partners solve the problems and pass the problems and solutions on to another student to confirm their solutions. Problems are returned to their owners at the end of the activity.

DEVELOPING FLUENCY WITH USING TEN FOR SUBTRACTION

Minus 8 or 9

Students take turns with partners picking a number card (11–17) and stating the number.

Then, the player spins a −8/−9 spinner and subtracts either 8 or 9 from the total on the card.

That player says and writes the fact.

After three rounds, students add their three differences.

The partner with the greatest sum after three rounds wins.

Then, players play again.

UNDERSTANDING THE USING-DOUBLES STRATEGY FOR ADDITION

Breaking Chains SHOW IT!

Students build chains and split them as close to half as possible. They record equations to show them. Students then observe to see connection to doubles facts.

Give each pair of students 19 connecting cubes.

Show the following on the board:

19 = __ + __
17 = __ + __
15 = __ + __
11 = __ + __
9 = __ + __
7 = __ + __
5 = __ + __
3 = __ + __

For each of these, make a chain to show the total, and then show how you break it as close to in half as you can. Then, fill in each equation.

Watch and listen as students work on completing the equations. Then, have students share their solutions as you fill in the blanks.

What did you find for 19? (9 + 10. Or, 10 + 9.)

Does it make sense that there was more than one way?

Record the equation with addends reversed next to the first one (e.g., 19 = 9 + 10 and 19 = 10 + 9).

Continue to build a class chart as students share their findings.

What do you notice when you look at the chart? (The numbers are almost doubles. Or, The numbers are just one different, like 5 and 6 or 3 and 4. Or, If 6 + 6 = 12, then 6 + 7 = 13, because it's just one more.)

Have students show a chain of 15 cubes.

Break the chain to show me the two parts. Hold them side by side.

How are they different?

Write *7 + 7 + 1 = 15*.

Turn and talk to your partner: What does this show?

Can you write an equation to show doubles and one more for 19? 17? 13?

Have students write doubles +1 equations for all of their chains.

> In this investigation, students begin by knowing the total number of cubes. Having them record the equations with the sum first is a natural way to show what they are doing in the activity. And showing equations with the sum at the start helps students get comfortable with equations that start with the sum and are followed by the addends. They need to see that both ways to write equations work with the meaning of the equal sign.

> Students revisit the commutative property.

> Although not all students may come up with this insight, listen for these types of responses and then ask students to think about the idea and agree or disagree with it.

Turn and share: How does knowing doubles help you find the sum of other math facts?

Explain.

Talk About It/Write About It 😊✏️

What do you notice about the sums of these using-doubles facts?

1 + 2 = 3

3 + 4 = 7

5 + 6 = 11

7 + 8 = 15

8 + 9 = 17

Why are the sums all odd numbers?

Differentiation

Although some students are moving to fluency practice, you may need to continue work on understanding the strategy with a small group of students. This can be done while the other students are practicing facts at centers.

FORMATIVE ASSESSMENT

Pose the following:

> How could thinking about doubles help you know the math fact 6 + 7? Explain.

You minus one from 7+7

7+7=14

14−1=13

This student chooses to subtract 1 after adding 7 + 7. He shows his thinking by writing 7 + 7 = 14 and 14 − 1 = 13.

If students have difficulty identifying a possible doubles fact, use connecting cubes for a model. Ask:

> What doubles fact can you make if you add one more cube?
>
> What doubles fact can you make if you take away one cube?

DEVELOPING FLUENCY WITH USING DOUBLES FOR ADDITION

Towers of Facts

Students pick a using-doubles fact card.

They build a tower to show the fact using two colors of connecting cubes (e.g., for 6 + 5 they might build a tower with 6 blue cubes and 5 red cubes).

Then they say and write the fact.

Domino Sort

In this activity, students sort through dominoes to find all of the ones that represent using-doubles facts (e.g., the domino for 7 with 3 dots on one side and 4 on the other, or the domino for 9 with 5 dots on one side and 4 on the other).

After completing the sort, students draw the domino and write both addition equations for all of the dominoes in their using-doubles pile.

BINGO

Have students write the following numbers in the boxes on a 5 × 5 grid: 3, 5, 7, 9, 11, 13, 15, 17, and 19.

Students can write a number as many times as they want and anywhere they want.

Students play in pairs or groups.

Two sets of using doubles fact cards are shuffled and placed face down in the center.

A player picks a fact card and everyone decides what the answer is.

Each player covers that number on her board with a cube or counter.

Only one number is covered each turn.

Then the next player picks the card, and everyone decides on the sum and covers it on their grid.

A player wins when he has covered five in a row, vertically, horizontally, or diagonally.

Then, the cards are shuffled and play begins again.

Spin, Two, Three

Students take turns spinning the using-doubles spinner (see the online resources) and saying and writing the math fact.

After three turns for each player, players add the sums for their three facts.

The player with the largest sum wins.

Differentiation
Modify the game to finding sums after two spins each.

UNDERSTANDING THE USING-DOUBLES STRATEGY FOR SUBTRACTION

Exploring Difference with Breaking Chains

Students build towers and split them as close to half as possible. They record subtraction equations to show them. Students then connect their equations to the related addition equations.

> Give each pair of students 19 connecting cubes.
>
> Show the following on the board:
>
> 19 – ____ = ____
> 17 – ____ = ____
> 15 – ____ = ____
> 13 – ____ = ____
> 11 – ____ = ____
> 9 – ____ = ____
> 7 – ____ = ____
> 5 – ____ = ____
> 3 – ____ = ____

Work with your partner to build chains with the connecting cubes and then break them as close to in half as possible.

Can you make two subtraction equations to show what you see?

> Listen and watch as students work.
>
> Ask them to share their data and create a class chart.

Does this remind you of another chart we made?

> Place the chart made while exploring using-doubles addition next to the one that was just created.

What do you notice? (The same three numbers are in the equations. *Or,* They are almost doubles.)

Does that make sense?

How would knowing this help you find the difference for these subtraction facts?

FORMATIVE ASSESSMENT

Pose the following:

> How could knowing an addition fact help you find the answer to 17 – 9? Explain.

Students might identify that 17 is 1 more than 16, and that 8 + 8 = 16, so 8 + 9 = 17. Some students might show that 9 + 9 = 18, and 17

Although you are exploring understanding of the using-doubles strategy for subtraction, continue to reserve some time during the math lesson for continued fluency practice with the addition facts.

is one less, so 8 + 9 = 17. Others might use their knowledge that 8 + 9 = 17, so 17 − 9 = 8.

> 17−9=8
>
> I used 9+8

This student shows that 17 − 9 = 8 because he uses his understanding of 9 + 8.

If students have difficulty subtracting, give them linking cubes to support their thinking.

DEVELOPING FLUENCY WITH USING DOUBLES FOR SUBTRACTION

Making Connections

Making Connections is an activity for students to connect using-doubles addition facts with using-doubles subtraction facts. Students make sets of matching addition and subtraction fact cards in a memory-style matching game.

To do this, students spread out the addition and subtraction facts face-down. A match is made when corresponding fact cards are flipped over. For example, the 17 − 9 or 17 − 8 cards would match the 8 + 9 or 9 + 8 fact cards.

Filling Digits

Students take turns spinning digits to complete the equations.

Students use the digit to complete one of their equations.

If the digit doesn't fit, the player loses her turn.

The first player to complete all of the equations wins the game.

Afterward, students write about observations of the using-doubles sums (all are odd) and how the equations are connected (subtraction is related to addition).

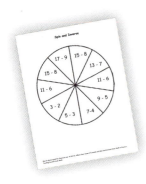

Spin and Inverse

Players spin and solve the math facts (e.g., 17 − 9).

Players say and write the fact in their journals or on notebook paper and then write the related addition fact next to it.

For example, a student spins 17 − 9, and writes 17 − 9 = 8 and 8 + 9 = 17.

Cover Them

Partners each have a set of digit cards, but remove the 0 card from the set leaving only the 1–9 cards.

Each player selects any six digit cards he wants and places them in a row faceup.

Partners take turns picking a fact card with a using-doubles subtraction fact, saying the fact, and placing a counter on the difference if they have it.

If a player has already covered the difference card, she cannot move on that turn.

The first player to put counters on all six of his cards is the winner.

Cards are shuffled and play begins again.

Monitoring Progress

Our goals in math fact instruction are both understanding and fluency. A variety of tasks appear throughout this module to assess for understanding of specific strategies, including tasks that ask students to write the math fact that corresponds to a designated addition or subtraction problem, identify connections between different fact sets, or demonstrate their understanding of addition and subtraction as being inverse operations. Assessment of fluency looks quite different. Fluency is our students' ability to recall facts without relying on counting strategies. Rather than measuring it in a specific number of seconds, it is more about identifying those students who simply recall the fact rather than having to model, count, or do a mental manipulation to come up with the answer. There are a variety of ways we can check for fluency, and using varied ways is recommended.

TEACHER OBSERVATION

One of the most effective ways to determine fluency is through observing students as they work. As students work on fluency tasks, circulate through the room observing them as they say and write the math facts. Record notes as you identify students in one of three categories:

1. fluent with the set of facts (simply know them)
2. strategic (able to use a strategy like counting on to find the answer, but not fluent)
3. unable to use strategies to find answers.

As you watch students play math fact games, consider:

- Which students are automatic in their math fact recall? (They are ready to move to a new set of facts.)
- Which students are relying on strategies to determine the sums and differences, rather than moving toward automatic recall? (They need more time for fluency practice.)
- Which students are giving incorrect responses or require tools to find sums or differences? (They may benefit from small-group support to develop strategies for finding sums and differences, like exploring patterns or talking about related fact sets; these students need more activities at the building understanding level.)

Listening to their verbalizations as they explore math facts activities provides great insight into their understanding and fluency, and allows us to determine appropriate interventions for strengthening either understanding or automaticity.

TEACHER INTERVIEWS/CONFERENCES

It is important to identify students who are struggling with either understanding of the concept or fluency with the facts. Brief conferences or interviews can provide this information. Meeting one-on-one with a student, while others are working on fluency tasks, allows you to ask questions and listen carefully to their responses. For ideas on recording anecdotal notes, see Recording Progress on page 66.

FACT CHECKS

Fact checks look similar to the math fact tests students have done for years, but they are not intended to be speed drills. Fact checks:

- can be used as practice or assessment
- are brief; rather than 100 facts, they might contain 20–25 facts
- are focused; rather than including every math fact, they contain math facts related to the fact set being assessed (e.g., doubles or making tens)
- are used to identify specific facts that are unknown, in order to help students with those facts
- are not used to compare students to each other, but are a way for students to see how many facts they can correctly answer and then set goals to improve on that on the following attempt.

This teacher conferences with a student to determine his understanding and fluency with a set of facts.

It is impossible to completely eliminate the element of time, because the goal is fluency and allowing students to have unlimited time to complete the task would not allow us to distinguish between whether they are fluent or using strategies to find the answers. But we recognize that timed tests add undue stress to students, and that it is not necessary for them to know their facts at a lightning pace. Rather than setting a time goal that all students must achieve, consider using time as a personal motivator by providing a specific amount of time (e.g., two minutes) and challenging students to see how many facts they can correctly answer in that amount of time, then further challenge them to "beat their own record" by getting more facts correct on the following attempt. Students do not even have to be aware that you are collecting the papers at a certain time. It should never be about trying to speed through a set of facts.

Another option is to administer fact checks in small groups and watch students as they complete the facts. By doing this, you are able to determine if they are fluent or if they need to stop and "figure out" facts by tapping their pencil in a counting rhythm or drawing lines on their paper.

Two sets of fact checks are available in the online resources. In one set, the sums or differences are unknown. In the other set, there are unknowns in different positions in the equations. Focusing on the set with unknown sums allows you to check for basic fluency, but the other set of fact checks allows you to assess students' flexibility with the facts. They may know 9 + 7 = ____, but when they see 7 + ____ = 16 they are unable to use what they know to identify the unknown. Speed is not the goal—understanding the way numbers work is the goal.

The key to fact checks is what we do with the information we gain from them. Consider the following:

Progress Graphs

Each time students complete a fact check for a specific set of facts, have them graph their results. Coloring in a simple bar graph to show the number of correct facts for each fact check they take allows students to set their own goals and see their own progress.

Individual Conferences/Interviews Following Fact Checks

As your students are engaged in practice tasks or visiting math centers, invite individual students to meet with you to review their most recent fact check:

- Examine blank or incorrect math facts.
- Ask students which facts are difficult for them to remember.
- Provide tips and reminders to help them master those specific facts.
- Record a few unknown facts on index cards and give the cards to the student to bring home for practice.

TEACHER-ADMINISTERED INDIVIDUAL FACT CHECKS

For some students, it may be more effective to do periodic teacher-administered checks (see photo on page 66). Using a set of fact cards, assess the student's fluency beginning with simpler facts and moving toward those that may be causing difficulty:

- As a child misses a fact, set the card aside.
- When a child misses several facts, stop and set a goal for those facts.
- Give the missed fact cards to the student, discuss any strategies that might help him better remember those facts, and determine a time frame for when you will recheck the facts.

Math fact fluency builds over time. Using varied assessment options, allowing students to be a part of setting goals and celebrating progress, and choosing options that minimize stress help our students stay motivated and develop a positive and confident attitude.

Vocabulary

commutative property

inverse

near double

using doubles

using ten

ONLINE RESOURCES

General Resources
0–9 Digit Cards
0–9 Spinner
0–20 Number Cards
Additional Problems

Resources for Specific Activities
–8/–9 Spinner
Addition Fact Checks
Another Way to Think About It
BINGO Board
Domino Cards
Double Ten Frame Mat
Doubles Subtraction Spinner
Filling Digits
Finding Differences with Double Ten Frames
Match 'Em Up Cards
Math Fact Progress Graph
Plus Nine Game Spinner
Spin and Inverse
Subtraction Fact Checks
Ten Frame Cards
Ten Frame Recording Sheet
Using-Doubles Fact Cards
Using-Doubles Math Facts Teacher Recording Sheet
Using-Doubles Spinner
Using-Ten Fact Cards
Using-Ten Math Facts Teacher Recording Sheet

These resources are available at http://hein.pub/MathinPractice, keycode MIPG2.

This teacher checks for fluency, then briefly discusses missed facts and shares strategies to help the student gain fluency with them.

RECORDING PROGRESS

Throughout this module, you will find a variety of questions and tasks that allow you to assess whether your students understand the big ideas of that fact set (e.g., *How would knowing doubles facts help you find the sum of 6 + 7?*). Keeping track of your observations and insights as you watch and listen to your students thinking during lessons, interviews, and activities helps you determine the best ways to support their growth. Gathering and recording anecdotal data from interviews or observations helps you choose individual teaching points, group students appropriately by needs, and more effectively communicate with parents about each child's progress. A template for recording observation notes is shared in the online resources (see sample on page 67). Note that columns two and five focus on student understanding of the fact set and provide a place for the teacher to take notes on student misunderstandings. Columns three and six focus on supporting fluency and provide a place for teachers to make notes about missed or problematic facts. Columns four and seven indicate a place for the teacher to record when fluency has been achieved.

Student Names	Applies Knowledge of Doubles Facts to Solve Using-Doubles Facts	Working on Fluency with Using-Doubles Addition Facts	Knows Using-Doubles Addition Facts	Applies Knowledge of Using-Doubles Addition Facts to Find Using-Doubles Subtraction Facts	Working on Fluency with Using-Doubles Subtraction Facts	Knows Using-Doubles Subtraction Facts

The teacher keeps track of student progress related to math fact understanding and fluency and is able to make grouping or other instructional decisions based on the data.

For additional lesson ideas, fluency games, and teaching resources, see *Mastering the Basic Math Facts in Addition* and *Mastering the Basic Math Facts in Subtraction*, by Susan O'Connell and John SanGiovanni (Heinemann, 2011).

MODULE 3

Building Foundations for Multiplication

About the Math   2.OA.3, 2.OA.4

Students have been exploring addition and subtraction since kindergarten. In third grade, they will begin a study of multiplication and division. In order to prepare them for multiplicative thinking, second-grade students benefit from opportunities to explore and observe equal groups of objects. They explore groups with even and odd numbers of objects, recognizing even numbers as numbers that can be represented with paired objects. In addition, they explore rectangular arrays and use addition to find the total of the equal rows of objects.

Students are used to thinking in an additive way (e.g., three more than what I have). In order to get students ready for multiplication, which requires a very different kind of thinking, students benefit from experience with the following:

- skip counting to find the total of like sets
- thinking about *groups of*, *rows of*, or *pairs of*
- visuals that show equal groups or equal rows.

Although second-grade students do not study multiplication, they begin to develop a mindset that will help them better understand it.

The key ideas focused on in this module include:

- exploring the concept of odd and even numbers
- examining equal groups related to repeated-addition equations (e.g., 5 + 5 + 5 = 15)
- visualizing equal groups with arrays and area models.

EVEN AND ODD NUMBERS

When asked what an even number is, many students reply, "A number that ends in 0, 2, 4, 6, or 8." Those are examples of even numbers, but they do not tell what an even number is. The concept of an even number is linked to multiplication and division. An even number is a number that is divisible by two, which means that you can divide it into groups of two (pairs) with none left over, or you can split it into two equal parts. Although second-grade students have not studied multiplication yet, they are able to visualize these concepts as they divide a set of counters into pairs to see if they are all partnered (see Figure 3.1) or as they shade the sections in 2-column grids starting at the bottom to see if they are shaded in pairs (see Figure 3.2).

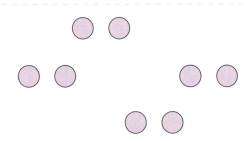

Figure 3.1 Students know that 8 is an even number, because 8 counters can be placed in sets of 2 with no leftover counters.

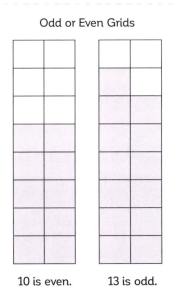

Figure 3.2 Students shade grids to show even and odd numbers.

Students can visualize even numbers as they split a chain of connecting cubes to see if they can make 2 equal parts (see Figure 3.3). They notice they can build an equation for even numbers that is a doubles equation (the sum of two equal addends). Through hands-on and visual investigations, students develop an understanding of the concept.

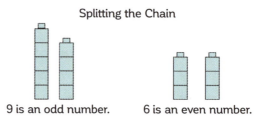

Figure 3.3 Can the chain of connecting cubes be split into 2 equal parts? If so, it is an even number of cubes.

EQUAL GROUPS, ARRAYS, AND AREA MODELS

As third graders explore multiplication and division, they use two important models: a rectangular array (see Figure 3.4) and a rectangular area model (see Figure 3.5). These two models are used in second grade as examples of repeated addition (still focusing on additive thinking), but will become important models to represent multiplicative thinking starting in third grade. 5 rows of 3 counters is seen as $3 + 3 + 3 + 3 + 3 = 15$ total counters. By exploring repeated addition and building addition equations, second graders are becoming familiar with models that will transition to multiplication models next year (5 rows of 3 counters are $5 \times 3 = 15$ total counters).

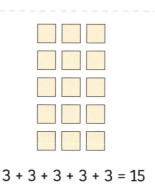

$3 + 3 + 3 + 3 + 3 = 15$

Figure 3.4 Students find sums based on rectangular arrays.

$3 + 3 + 3 + 3 + 3 = 15$

Figure 3.5 Although students find sums using the area model in second grade, they use this same model to transition to multiplication in third grade.

Building Foundations for Multiplication 71

MODULE 3

Experiences with skip counting, pairs and equal groups, and models that capture key ideas about multiplication provide the foundation for the introduction to multiplication and division in third grade.

Exploring the Progression

PREVIOUS	NOW	NEXT
Grade 1	Grade 2	Grade 3
Skip counting; exploring counting patterns	Exploring odd and even numbers and equal groups	Introduction to multiplication and division

Learning Goals

I can use models to decide if a number is odd or even.

I can explain what makes a number odd or even using words and pictures.

I can build repeated-addition equations to go with arrays and area models.

Ideas for Instruction and Assessment

EXPLORING THE CONCEPT OF ODD AND EVEN NUMBERS

Through a variety of hands-on investigations, students explore the concept of odd and even numbers.

Odd or Even Grid Models [SHOW IT]

Students attempt to create rectangles that are 2 tiles wide to explore odd and even numbers.

> Each pair of students needs a 1–20 chart and a set of 20 square tiles.

1	2	3	4	5	6	7	8	9	10
11	12	13	14	15	16	17	18	19	20

Work with your partner to use your square tiles to create rectangles that are 2 tiles wide.

The rectangles may be any length.

After you have created a rectangle, count to see how many total tiles you used.

Shade that number on your 1–20 chart.

Lessons in This Module

Exploring the Concept of Odd and Even Numbers
Odd or Even Grid Models
Splitting the Chain
Even Steven and Odd Todd

Visualizing Equal Groups with Arrays
Sticky Note Arrays
Making Arrays

Students record information from their investigation on the 1–20 chart. The organization of the chart makes patterns easily visible.

With your partner, figure out which of the numbers (from 1–20 tiles) form rectangles that are 2 tiles wide.

Observe as students try to create rectangles with 1–20 square tiles.

Have students share the numbers with the class.

Have students talk with partners about what they notice as they observe the shaded numbers—the numbers that created rectangles.

What do you notice?

Does that make sense? Why?

What happened when you had 5 tiles? Could you create a rectangle that was 2 tiles wide? Why or why not?

What did you notice about all of your rectangles? (They had groups of 2 tiles, or pairs.)

> Students usually first notice a simple pattern of every other number. Probe further to see if they can explain the pattern of groups of two.

Explain to students that the numbers that could be formed by those groups of two are called *even* numbers.

Write the word *even* on the word wall or Math Talk chart, and include an illustration of a rectangle. Include the word *pairs*.

Explain that the numbers that did not form a rectangle with pairs of tiles are called *odd* numbers.

Write the word *odd* on the word wall or Math Talk chart, and show a picture of five square tiles not forming a rectangle.

Have students record the words *odd* and *even* in their math journals.

List three even numbers and three odd numbers.

Draw a rectangle model for three even numbers. Remember our rectangles are 2 tiles wide to show pairs of tiles.

Show why odd numbers can't be shown as these kinds of rectangles.

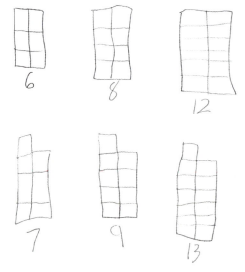

> **Common Error or Misconception**
>
> As students explore multiplication with area models (rectangular grids) in third grade, they sometimes mistakenly think a number is even because it can be modeled with a rectangle, not truly understanding that what made these numbers even was that two tiles were in each row of the rectangle. Although 25 tiles can form a 5 × 5 rectangle, 25 is not an even number. Emphasize the two tiles in each row of these rectangles, rather than just the fact that a rectangle is formed.

Review students' journal entries to see if they are able to show odd and even numbers using rectangles.

Building Foundations for Multiplication

MODULE 3

Thinking Through a Lesson

SMP3, SMP7, SMP8

Splitting the Chain SHOW IT!

Students create chains with 1–20 connecting cubes and split them to determine if the number of cubes is odd or even.

Draw two circles on the board. Label one *Even* and the other *Odd*.

Turn to your partner and tell them what you know about even and odd numbers.

Have a student count out 16 connecting cubes and put them in a chain.

We are going to continue exploring odd and even numbers.

Turn to your partner and predict if you think 16 will be even or odd. Why? (I think it will be even, because I think we can make a rectangle with 2 rows.)

Ask another student to see if he can break the chain right in half so both parts are equal (have the same number of cubes).

Once the chain is split, hold the two chains up next to each other.

Turn and share: What do you notice when you can split the chain in half? (They are the same length. *Or*, Each cube matches with one on the other chain.)

Would that make 16 an odd or even number? Explain. (It's even, because each cube is matched with the one on the chain next to it; it is like the rectangles we made.)

Record *16* in the *Even* circle.

Have a student count out 17 connecting cubes and put them in a chain.

Do you think 17 will be even or odd? Why? (It will be odd; it is one more than 16, so it won't have a partner.)

Ask another student to see if she can break the chain right in half so both parts are equal.

Hold the two unequal chains up next to each other.

Can you split this exactly in half? Why or why not? (There is one more on one side, so they aren't in pairs.)

What if there is a leftover cube? Would that make it an odd or even number? Turn to your partner and explain your thinking. (It would be odd, because they wouldn't all have a match.)

Record *17* in the *Odd* circle.

Give each pair a set of 1–20 cards, 20 connecting cubes, and a piece of chart paper with two circles drawn on it.

> Students will likely mention that even numbers can make rectangles that are two tiles wide, or that every other counting number is an even number, because that has been their only exposure to even numbers.

> Listen to students' predictions. Many students will connect their thinking to the previous lesson. Make note of students who do not, and focus additional questioning on them.

> Using a different manipulative and a different way of modeling even numbers than in the previous lesson deepens students' understanding of the concept.

> Rather than asking one student to answer, frequently ask students to turn and share answers with partners to keep everyone involved in the lesson and thinking about the math.

Have students label one of the circles *even* and label the other one *odd*.

> Work with your partners to investigate whether the numbers are odd or even, using your connecting cubes.
>
> One partner picks a number card and creates a chain with that number of cubes.
>
> The other partner tries to split the chain in half.
>
> Place the number in the *odd* or *even* circle once you decide where it belongs.
>
> Then switch jobs and try it for a different number.

Observe as students work.

Differentiation
Students who are quickly grasping the concept of odd and even with numbers twenty or less can be challenged to investigate numbers greater than twenty.

Students sort numbers into even and odd groups after exploring with connecting cubes.

Have students share their numbers and record them in the circles on the board.

> *What do you notice about the odd and even numbers?* (The even numbers are all doubles and the odd numbers aren't.)
>
> *Does that make sense? Explain.* (Yes, because doubles means that they would all have a partner; the two chains would be equal, so they have to be even numbers.)
>
> *What patterns did you notice when working with the 2-digit numbers?* (Numbers that have 0, 2, 4, 6, or 8 ones are even; numbers that have 1, 3, 5, 7, or 9 ones are odd numbers.)
>
> *Do you think that is always true? Can you find an example of a number that doesn't follow that pattern?*

Give students a few minutes to look at their data or try some other numbers to test that idea.

Differentiation
Students can be challenged to give an example of an even number that is more than 20 and an odd number that is more than 20 and then prove it.

What do you know about tens? Are tens even or odd? (Even.) *Why?* (Ten would be 5 and 5, and 20 would be 10 and 10.)

Have students work with their partners to make a list based on the following questions:

What is always true about even numbers? (They are doubles. Or, We say them when we count by twos. Or, If you used counters and lined them in twos, they would always have a partner. Or, They end in 0, 2, 4, 6, or 8.)

What is always true about odd numbers? (They are not doubles. Or, They are 1, 3, 5, 7, and 9. Or, You can't split them in half. Or, If you lined them up, one wouldn't have a partner.)

Have pairs share their answers and add the ideas as phrases on your Math Talk chart that was started in the previous lesson.

> Students are working together to build a definition of odd and even numbers. When asked what an even number is, we do not want the answer to be "a number that ends in 0, 2, 4, 6, or 8." Those are examples of even numbers, not a definition of the concept. Although we want students to see the patterns in the ones digits of odd and even numbers, we expect them to understand that even numbers can be broken into two equal parts or can be broken into groups of twos.

Even Steven and Odd Todd

Students listen to a story about odd and even numbers, *Even Steven and Odd Todd* by Kathryn Cristaldi, and classify numbers related to events in the story as to whether they are odd or even.

> For more ideas on integrating children's literature into math lessons, see Math in Practice: A Guide for Teachers, Chapter 2.

Before Reading:

Briefly introduce the book.

We are going to read a story about two boys named Even Steven and Odd Todd. Listen to figure out why those are their names.

During Reading:

Read *Even Steven and Odd Todd*.

Every so often, stop to ask students if they notice some reasons behind the boys' names.

After Reading:

Turn and share: Why are their names Even Steven and Odd Todd?

Give students a list of the following items/events from the story:

- 10 goldfish
- 3 knocks at the door
- 6 cats
- 5 streamers
- 8 gerbils
- 5 needles on the cactus
- 12 pancakes
- 4 slices of pizza
- 12 sprinklers in the flower garden

3 odd-shaped suitcases

4-leaf clovers

9 squishy worms

Have students fold a paper in half and label one side *Even Steven* and the other side *Odd Todd*.

Work with a partner to decide whether each of these items or events apply to Even Steven or Odd Todd.

Write it on the correct side of your paper.

Be ready to explain why.

Have partners share their ideas with the class, explaining why each one is either even or odd.

With your partner, write one more event for the story. Be sure to show something even and something odd.

Have partners share their new story events.

Ask the class to agree (thumbs up) or disagree (thumbs down) with their odd and even examples.

FORMATIVE ASSESSMENT

Pose the following:

Decide if the following numbers are odd or even: 6, 9, 12, and 17. Justify your answers.

This student correctly identifies that 6 is even, 9 is odd, 12 is even, and 17 is odd. The student shows pairs of circles with 9 and 17 having 1 extra.

Building Foundations for Multiplication 77

MODULE 3

> If a student does not consistently identify even and odd numbers, ask if he can explain what even and odd mean. Provide the student with manipulatives and have him model the numbers and explain why they are even or odd.

Additional Ideas for Support and Practice

The following ideas extend students' understanding of even and odd numbers and provide meaningful practice.

ODD AND EVEN TOWERS

Have students pick a 1–20 number card.

Students then shade the tower by beginning at the bottom and shading each row until they have shaded the number of sections for their number (e.g., this tower is shaded to show the number 8).

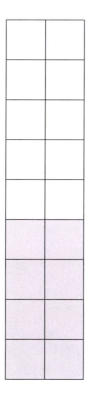

Odd numbers will have only one of the two sections shaded in the last row.

Have students complete the recording sheet and decide if each number is odd or even.

This student builds towers with connecting cubes and discovers that 17 is an odd number.

Scoops of Cubes

Have a basket of connecting cubes at the center.

Students scoop connecting cubes with both hands, then put the cubes into pairs.

Students record the number of cubes they scooped.

How many did you scoop?
Can you count by twos to get the total?
Are there any leftovers?

Have students make a chart:

Odd: Numbers with 1 Left
Even: Numbers without Leftovers

Talk About It/Write About It

What is an even number?

Kavitha said 13 was an even number. Is she right? Justify your answer.

Liam said that the sums of all doubles facts are even numbers (e.g., 4 + 4 = 8). Is he right? Explain your answer.

Reach the Beach

Each pair will need a copy of the Reach the Beach game mat.

Players see who can reach the beach first.

Players decide who will move when an odd number is rolled and who will move when an even number is rolled.

Players take turns rolling a number cube (a 1–6 cube or 0–9 die will work).

Players decide together if the number rolled is even or odd.

The player who is designated to move on *odd* moves one space if an odd number is rolled and the player who is designated to move on *even* moves one space if an even number is rolled.

Play continues until someone lands on the beach ball.

Then, players put counters back at the start and play again.

If you would like a record of students' work, have them record the number rolled in each sun on the game mat.

Differentiation
Allow students to use counters to determine odd or even if needed.

Odd/Even Folded Book

Have students fold a paper in half.

Students label one side *odd* and the other *even*.

Students show what they know about each concept using words, pictures, numbers, and/or examples.

Additional Literature Links

The following children's books address the concept of odd and even:

The Missing Mittens by Stuart J. Murphy

One Odd Day by Doris Fisher

My Even Day by Doris Fisher

The Odds Get Even by Pamela Hall

Books might be placed in centers for students to read.

Students might write another page for the story, or classify story events as odd or even.

ODD/EVEN CHALLENGE

Have students add odd and even numbers to see what happens.

Can they discover these rules?

> odd + odd = even
> even + even = even
> odd + even = odd
> even + odd = odd

Can they explain why they work?

> **Differentiation**
> This investigation about odd and even sums provides an enrichment task for students who understand odd and even numbers.

VISUALIZING EQUAL GROUPS WITH ARRAYS

Students build a foundation for multiplication with investigations in which they see repeated addition through arrays.

Sticky Note Arrays

Students create arrays with square sticky notes and then write repeated-addition equations for the arrays.

On the board, make an array to show 3 rows of 4 square sticky notes.

Turn and share: How would you describe how I placed the squares on the board?

What do you notice about the rows?

When things are arranged in equal rows like this, we call that an array. An array always has the same number of objects in each row.

Write the word *array* on the word wall or Math Talk Chart. Include a drawing to show an array.

How many squares are there altogether?

How did you figure out how many squares there were?

Did anyone add to find the total?

If a student did add, invite that student to share what she did. If not, model how you could think about adding to solve the problem.

How many squares are in the first row? How many squares are in the next row? How many squares are in the last row?

How would we write that as an addition equation?

Record *4 + 4 + 4 = 12* by the array.

What we just did is called repeated addition.

Why do you think it might be called that? (We added 4 and then 4 again and then 4 again.)

> **Common Error or Misconception**
> Students often confuse rows and columns. Review the meanings of the words and add them to the word wall or Math Talk chart.

Add *repeated addition* to the word wall or Math Talk chart, with an example of a repeated-addition equation.

On the board, make an array to show 5 rows of 3 square sticky notes.

Work with your partner to write a repeated-addition equation for this array.

Have students share the equation (3 + 3 + 3 + 3 + 3 = 15) and explain what the 3s represent in the equation.

Give partners some sticky notes and a piece of chart paper.

Have them make an array with their sticky notes and write the repeated-addition equation.

Post the charts around the room and have each pair explain their model and equation.

Making Arrays SHOW IT!

Students make arrays with square tiles and record the repeated-addition equations.

Give each pair of students 12 square tiles.

Work with your partner to make an array with your tiles and write the repeated-addition equation.

Watch as students create arrays, looking for pairs who make different arrays (e.g., 3 + 3 + 3 + 3 = 12 or 6 + 6 = 12).

Have some students share their arrays and equations, calling on students who have done it in different ways.

Record the equations on the board:

    3 + 3 + 3 + 3 = 12 (for 4 rows of 3 squares)
    4 + 4 + 4 = 12 (for 3 rows of 4 squares)
    6 + 6 = 12 (for 2 rows of 6 squares)
    2 + 2 + 2 + 2 + 2 + 2 = 12 (for 6 rows of 2 squares)

How are your arrays and equations alike?
How are your arrays and equations different?

Assign one of the following sums to each pair: 16, 18, or 24.

How many different arrays can you make for your number?
Use your square tiles to make the arrays, then draw each array and write the repeated-addition equation that goes with it.

After students have worked on arrays and equations for their sum, have pairs that worked on the same sum (16, 18, or 24) meet together to compare their models and equations.

82 MATH IN PRACTICE
Teaching Second-Grade Math

MODULE 3

This student builds arrays with square tiles to explore repeated addition.

FORMATIVE ASSESSMENT

Pose the following:

Write a repeated-addition equation for the following array:

Explain your equation.

Write a repeated addition equation for the following array:

Explain your equation.

$3 + 3 + 3 + 3 + 3 = 15$

I am adding three, five times

Student A shows 3 + 3 + 3 + 3 + 3 = 15. The student identifies that she has added 5 groups of 3.

Write a repeated addition equation for the following array:

$3+3+3+3+3+3=18$

Explain your equation.

I did $3+3+3+3+3+3=18$

Student B shows 3 + 3 + 3 + 3 + 3 + 3 = 18. Ask the student to count how many rows there are, and how many groups of 3 he added.

If a student shows 5 + 5 + 5 = 15, have the student circle the rows. Remind the student that rows go across rather than up and down.

Vocabulary

array
equal rows/columns
even
leftover
odd
pairs
repeated addition

ONLINE RESOURCES

General Resources
1–20 Number Cards
Additional Problems

Resources for Specific Activities
1–20 Charts
Even or Odd Number
Reach the Beach

These resources are available at http://hein.pub/MathinPractice, keycode MIPG2.

Additional Ideas for Support and Practice

The following ideas extend students' understanding of arrays to show repeated addition and provide meaningful practice.

TALK ABOUT IT/WRITE ABOUT IT

What is an array?

What is repeated addition?

Colin said that this array shows 3 + 3 + 3. Is he right? Explain.

ROLL AN ARRAY

Version 1

Partner A rolls to see how many rows.

Player B rolls to see how many in each row.

Players draw the array, write the repeated-addition equation, and solve the problem.

Repeat.

Version 2

Each player rolls two dice.

The rolls represent the number of rows and number in each row.

Each player draws her array, writes the repeated-addition equation, and solves the problem.

Players compare their sums.

The greater sum wins the round.

Repeat.

MODULE 4

Understanding Place Value

About the Math   2.NBT.A.1; 2.NBT.A.2; 2.NBT.A.3; 2.NBT.B.8

Throughout the elementary years, our students are developing an understanding of our number system as a base-ten system. It takes 10 ones to make a ten, 10 tens to make a hundred, and 10 hundreds to make a thousand. The ways in which we write numbers, add and subtract numbers, and compare numbers are all based on place value concepts. Understanding place value is foundational to understanding how numbers work.

The key ideas focused on in this module include:

- understanding how to read and write 3-digit numbers
- decomposing numbers in different ways based on place value
- mentally adding and subtracting 10 and 100 to and from 3-digit numbers.

In first grade, students explored place value with 2-digit numbers. Second-grade students extend their understanding of place value to 3-digit numbers. Place value understandings in second grade include the following:

- The digits in a 3-digit number represent hundreds, tens, and ones.
- 10 tens is a hundred.
- We represent 1 hundred, 2 hundreds, 3 hundreds as 100, 200, 300 . . .
- Because of our base-ten system, patterns appear when we count by hundreds, tens, and ones.

- Numbers can be decomposed based on place value (expanded form).
- Numbers can be decomposed in different ways (235 = 2 hundreds, 3 tens, 5 ones or 2 hundreds, 2 tens and 15 ones).
- We can mentally add and subtract 10 and 100 from a 3-digit number.

Explorations at this level focus on building a deeper understanding of place value. Having students build numbers with base-ten materials and talk about the value of each digit focuses them on the meaning of place value. Although a student may identify a 3 in the tens place of 134, she may not know that the 3 stands for 3 tens or 30 ones. Having students build numbers with base-ten materials and count the number of flats (hundreds), rods (tens), and units (ones) allows them to make connections to both the standard and expanded forms for written numbers (see Figure 4.1). When writing a 3-digit number in expanded form, students decompose the number into its place value components. 235 becomes 200 + 30 + 5. Rather than simply saying there is a 3 in the tens place, they show that 3 as 30, reinforcing place value understanding.

200 + 30 + 5 = 235

Hundreds	Tens	Ones

Figure 4.1 As students build 3-digit numbers, they notice the connection to the way numbers are written in both standard and expanded forms.

In first grade, students realized that 2-digit numbers could be decomposed in different ways. 25 is 20 + 5 or 2 tens and 5 ones, but it might also be thought of as 1 ten and 15 ones. In second grade, we explore different ways to decompose 3-digit numbers. Explorations with manipulatives allow students to find other ways to decompose 235, extending their understanding of place value (see Figure 4.2). Students will later apply this understanding in third grade; when subtracting 3-digit numbers like 235 − 127, the task is immediately simpler if students rename 235 as 2 hundreds, 2 tens, and 15 ones.

2 hundreds + 2 tens + 15 ones = 235

Hundreds	Tens	Ones

Figure 4.2 Exploring different ways to decompose numbers deepens students' understanding of place value. Could 235 also be renamed as 1 hundred, 13 tens, and 5 ones?

Skip counting by fives, tens, and hundreds focuses students on patterns. As they skip count by tens beginning at any number, they notice how the tens digit changes with each number said. Consider the patterns in each skip-counting sequence below:

156, 166, 176, 186, 196, 206, 216, 226, 236 . . . (tens digit increases by 1 ten)

245, 345, 445, 545, 645, 745, 845 . . . (hundreds digit increases by 1 hundred)

130, 135, 140, 145, 150, 155, 160, 165 . . . (tens and ones digits show counting by fives; 2 fives make a ten)

Exploring patterns related to place value opens up discussions about the concept and shows students the structure of our number system. It is predictable and filled with patterns!

In second grade, students investigate adding and subtracting 10 and 100 from a 3-digit number by building numbers with concrete materials, like base-ten blocks, adding to or taking 10 and 100 from the model that was built, and then recording the new number. As our students observe the numbers they have recorded, they gain insights that allow them to predict 10 and 100 more than and less than a number, until they no longer rely on the manipulatives. Their skip-counting work also supports students to mentally add or subtract 10 or 100 to or from any number. The patterns they encounter allow them to understand that adding or subtracting 10 changes the tens digit by one, while adding or subtracting 100 does the same for the hundreds digit. Our goal is for them to apply this place value understanding to mentally perform the task.

Learning Goals

I understand that a 3-digit number is composed of hundreds, tens, and ones.

I can read and write 3-digit numbers.

I can break numbers apart in different ways.

I can mentally add and subtract 10 and 100 from a 3-digit number.

MATH IN PRACTICE
Teaching Second-Grade Math

MODULE 4

Lessons in This Module

Understand Place Value to Hundreds
- Bundling Tens and Hundreds
- The Flower Shop Problem
- Counting to 1,000 Using Tens and Hundreds
- Pencils in Boxes
- Adding and Subtracting 10 and 100
- Counting up by Hundreds, Tens, and Ones

Decompose 3-Digit Numbers
- Comparing Place Value Models
- Representing Numbers in Different Ways
- Decomposing in Different Ways
- Introducing Expanded Form

SMP1, SMP4, SMP7, SMP8

> Students can create large place value mats by folding an 11 × 17-inch sheet of paper into thirds and then labeling the sections hundreds, tens, and ones.

> Be sure students in each group are working together. Each student should be actively bundling straws, both for understanding the concept and to reduce the time spent making the bundles.

A strong understanding of place value supports our students as they read and write numbers, add and subtract numbers, and compare and order numbers. Place value is an ongoing and critical topic in K–5 mathematics.

Exploring the Progression

PREVIOUS	NOW	NEXT
Grade 1	Grade 2	Grade 3
Exploring 2-digit place value	Exploring place value concepts up to 3 digits	Extending place value skills to multidigit numbers; rounding numbers to the nearer 10 or 100

Ideas for Instruction and Assessment

UNDERSTAND PLACE VALUE TO HUNDREDS

Students will use various models to make connections between counting strategies and place value. Students will record numbers using their understanding of place value.

Thinking Through a Lesson

Bundling Tens and Hundreds

Students develop an understanding that 100 can be thought of as a bundle of 10 tens.

Provide small groups of students with a large quantity of straws, craft sticks, or coffee stirrers (between 300–500), rubber bands, and a place value mat.

   Estimate how many straws you think you have.
   Work together to bundle the straws, using any strategies you choose.

Look for and make note of groups who bundle tens and hundreds.

If some groups struggle with organization, ask: ● ▲

   How can we count the straws in a way that is fast and accurate? (We can put them into groups.)
   Why would that help? (It's faster.)
   How can we organize these straws into tens? (We can bundle them.)

As groups complete the bundling:

How did you bundle your straws? (We bundled by tens. *Or,* We put tens together to make hundreds.)

Why might it help you to put 10 bundles together to make 100? (We won't have as much to count.)

Tell students you are going to count both ways—with tens and with hundreds.

Pick a group that bundled by tens and ask students to help you count by tens to find their total (e.g., 10, 20, 30, 40, 50, 60, 70, 80, 90, 100, 110, 120 . . .).

Pick another group that bundled by tens and model bundling their straws by 100.

Let's put these in groups of 100.

How will we know when we have a group of 100? (We can count by tens until we get to 100 and that's a group.)

Model counting bundles of 10 to 100, forming groups of 100.

Now, how can we count the straws? (We can count the hundreds and then the others.)

Count with students (e.g., 100, 200, 300, 310, 320, 321, 322).

Turn and talk to your group: What did you notice about counting it that time? (It was faster. *Or,* We didn't have to say as many numbers.)

Work with your group to count your straws by making groups of 100.

Watch as students count and find the total.

Pose the number 274.

Ask for a volunteer to read the number out loud, then have group members respond to the following:

How many hundreds are in this number? (2 hundreds.)

Show me 2 hundreds using your straws.

How many tens are in 274? (7 tens.)

Show 7 tens using your straws.

How many ones should we show? (4 ones.)

Add your 4 ones to complete your model of 274.

Let's count our straws together, starting with the hundreds.

Count the straws as a whole group (100, 200, 210, 220, 230, 240, 250, 260, 270, 271, 272, 273, 274).

Provide groups with different 3-digit numbers to model, using straws or pictorial representations. Choose numbers with varying digits, such as 317, 150, 206, and 192.

> Although students will likely group by tens based on their bundling experiences in first grade, some may decide to group by hundreds. Their first-grade experiences of counting by tens to one hundred, or calendar activities in which they counted beyond one hundred, may make them comfortable enough to bundle and count groups of one hundred.

> **Common Error or Misconception**
> Transition points between counting by different units can be challenging for students. If students miscount (saying 400 instead of 310, for instance), ask them what unit they need to count by. Their answers will help you determine if the error is a casual slip or reflects a misunderstanding.

With your group, use hundreds, tens, and ones to model each number and then count to check. Draw your models in your journal.

Move around the room, observing students as they represent numbers both concretely and pictorially in their journals and listening as they count.

To end the lesson and summarize the important ideas, hold up a bundle of ten.

How many straws do I have in this group? (10.)

Repeat with a bundle of a hundred.

How many straws do I have in this group? (100.)

How do you know? (Because we put bundles of 10 together until we counted to 100. Or, Because it is 10 bundles of 10.)

How many bundles of 10 make up this one bundle of 100? (10.)

> **Common Error or Misconception**
> Watch for student errors modeling and counting any numbers that contain a zero (e.g., representing 407). Guide them in modeling the number accurately, reminding them that the 0 in the tens digit represents no tens.

The Flower Shop Problem SHOW IT!

Students use bundling to further explore place value concepts through a story problem. They explore and decompose numbers using bundles of tens and then extend it in the second part of the problem to think about bundles of hundreds and tens.

Provide students with straws or sticks to use as they solve the problems.

Pose the following:

> The flower shop is getting ready for a wedding. There are 400 flowers that need to be arranged into vases. 10 flowers can fit into each vase. How many vases are needed?

Turn and tell your partner what this problem is about.
How many flowers do they have? What do we need to find out?
Can you visualize the problem? How many flowers are in each vase?
So, we need to know how many tens there are. How could we do that? Work together to solve the problem with your straws.

Allow students time to work out the problem together, and share solutions with other nearby partners.

How did you show the problem with the straws?
What do the straws represent?
What was the solution? How many vases does the flower shop need? How do you know?

Record on the board:

> 400 flowers
> 10 flowers in each vase
> 40 vases

> Having students turn and talk about the problem with partners prior to the class discussion allows them to process the problem as they retell it in their own words.

How many tens are in 400? Does that make sense? Why?

Extend the problem:

> The vases are then put into crates to be delivered. 10 vases fit into each crate. How many flowers will be in each crate? How many crates will they need?

Turn and tell your partner what the problem is about.

How many flowers will be in each crate? How do you know?

Work with your partner to decide how many crates they will need for all the vases of flowers.

Circulate, listening to students as they bundle groups of ten into groups of one hundred. As needed, question students to move their thinking:

How can we use what we know about 10 tens?

How many crates will they need? How do you know?

How many flowers will be in those 4 crates altogether? How do you know?

Have partners draw a model showing the crates of flowers, then have them share their models and describe how they solved the problem.

Change the data in the problem for additional explorations, suggesting there might be 300 or 500 flowers being delivered. Then, pose data like 360 flowers or 420 flowers to start discussions about full crates (hundreds) and leftover vases (tens).

> Remind students that their pictorial model should focus on the math rather than the art. Encourage students to draw simple models.

FORMATIVE ASSESSMENT

Pose the following:

> Yarden had 340 playing cards. They were organized in sets of 10. How many sets of 10 playing cards did he have? Justify your thinking using place value models.

This student shows 34 tens sticks, grouped into sets of 10. His model shows 340, represented as 34 tens, showing an understanding of the connection between tens and hundreds, that 340 can be thought of as 34 tens.

> If a student is not able to show sets of ten with pictures, provide bundles of ten. Ask:
>
> *How can we count these bundles of 10 to get to 340?*
> *How many bundles of 10 do we need?*

Counting to 1,000 Using Tens and Hundreds

Students count up and down between ninety and one thousand by ones, tens, and hundreds. Students model a given number in different ways using base-ten blocks to one thousand.

Provide pairs of students with base-ten blocks and place value mats.

Introduce the base-ten blocks to students. Many may have had exposure to these models in previous grades.

Talk to your partner about the similarities and differences between base-ten blocks and the straw bundles we made.

Allow students time to compare ten units to a rod, and ten rods to a hundreds flat.

As a whole class, practice skip counting forward and backward by tens, while modeling with base-ten rods. Repeat with hundreds flats.

Pose the following:

> The cooks are making sandwiches for a school picnic. 50 sandwiches have been made so far. If they need to make 200 sandwiches, how many more will they need to make?

Turn and talk to your partner about the important information in this problem.
Can you picture the sandwiches that the cooks have already made? What do you see?
Can you imagine how that would look with your base-ten blocks?

Ask students to model fifty using base-ten blocks.

How many tens would you need to model 50?
How do you know?
We can keep counting by tens to 200. Because we know we have 50, we can start counting by saying 50, and continue 60, 70. . .

Model counting with base-ten rods to two hundred.

Turn and talk to your partner about a different way we might count from 50 to 200.

Have students share their ideas. They might suggest counting by tens to 100, then adding another hundred to get to 200. Observe for students who are counting 50 ones units rather than 5 tens. Use questions such as the following to help them understand more efficient strategies.

Would counting by ones be a quick way to get to 200?

Which ways of counting are quicker? Explain.

Base-ten blocks and place value mats support students as they count up and back by tens and hundreds.

Provide students with other sequences to count:

    70 to 450

    190 to 500

    230 to 420

    100 to 340

    150 to 450

As students become ready for a greater challenge, use numbers such as 47 to 257.

To end the lesson, ask:

How are base-ten blocks and bundles of straws similar?

How are they different?

How do our place value tools help us think about our counting?

> If using base-ten blocks to model and count these sequences, the numbers have to remain fairly low because of the limitations of the number of rods and flats in a base-ten classroom set. If additional blocks are available, increase the numbers to include counting sequences like 430–650 or 670–1,000. This also presents the opportunity to encourage students to find ways to count that use the fewest blocks (e.g., by hundreds whenever possible, rather than tens or ones).

Pencils in Boxes

Students explore adding 100 to and subtracting 100 from 3-digit numbers.

Provide students with base-ten blocks.

Pose the following:

> Your class has 245 pencils. Your teacher finds another box of 100 pencils. How many pencils are there?

Model this with your base-ten blocks. Work with your partner to come up with an addition sentence that shows this story.

Have partners share their equations.

Add to the problem:

> Your principal brings your class another box of 100.

Model, using your blocks. Write an addition sentence to match.

Have students share their equations, then ask them to predict what would happen to the number if one more box of pencils were added.

Use your base-ten blocks to help.
What pattern do you notice?

Discuss students' observations, then pose the following:

> We have 545 pencils. Your teacher gives a box of 100 pencils to the other second-grade teacher.

Tell your partner what is happening with the pencils. Model, using your base-ten blocks.
Write a subtraction number sentence that would show this.

Have partners share their subtraction equations.

Add to the problem:

> Now, your teacher gives a box of 100 pencils to a third-grade teacher.

Model this with your blocks and write a number sentence.
What pattern do you notice?
What happens to a number each time you add 100 pencils? Does that make sense? Why?
What happens to a number each time you subtract 100 pencils? Does that make sense? Why?

Pose some 3-digit numbers and have students predict 100 more or 100 less. Have them use base-ten blocks to check their predictions.

To end the lesson, ask partners to discuss:

What rules can help us to add and subtract 100 without using blocks?

Repeat this lesson on a different day, using tens to add and subtract.

Pose a variety of 3-digit numbers, having students explore with models and then predict 10 more or less.

Begin with simpler numbers like 340 and 275, but increase the complexity as students gain confidence, posing numbers like 295 or 305.

Adding and Subtracting 10 and 100

Students investigate adding and subtracting ten and one hundred. They observe patterns and then create rules.

Write the number *235* on the board.

Have students use base-ten blocks to build 235.

> *Turn and tell your partner how many hundreds, tens, and ones you have.*
> *What will happen if we add one flat (one hundred) to this number? Tell your partner what your new number will be.*

Record the number *335* on the board.

> *What will happen if we add another flat? Tell your partner what you think the new number will be.*

Record *435* on the board.

Do this several more times.

> *Observe the numbers we recorded. What do you notice is happening?*
> *Why is the hundreds digit increasing by one each time?*
> *What do you think the next number will be if we add 100 more?*
> *Work with your partner to come up with a rule for how to add 100 to a number without using the blocks.*

Counting up by Hundreds, Tens, and Ones

Students use place value strategies to count by hundreds, tens, and ones. They apply strategies used for smaller numbers to count larger quantities more efficiently.

Have students skip count by tens to one hundred.

Repeat with counting by hundreds to one thousand.

Provide pairs with pre-grouped bundles (hundreds, tens, and ones) of straws or craft sticks and place value mats.

> *Turn to your partner and talk about the groupings of sticks. What is important to know about the bundles?*

Pose the number 134.

> *Use your bundles to model this number.*
> *If we wanted to count these straws, what would we count first? What would we count next?*
> *Why do you think we count in this order?*
> *Count them out loud with your partner.*

Finding 10 more than 295 or 10 less than 305 can be problematic for some students. Exploring this idea with concrete materials will help them visualize why 305 is 10 more than 295 and why 295 is 10 less than 305.

Differentiation
Display a hundreds number line for those students who struggle with identifying the hundred before and after a given number. Have students use the number line to identify benchmark numbers to use when skip counting by tens and hundreds.

Repeat this process with subtracting one hundred, and then with adding and subtracting ten.

> If students have difficulty with the counting sequence, ask them to think about, and tell you, whether they are counting by hundreds, tens, or ones.

Observe and listen as students count "100, 110, 120, 130, 131, 132, 133, 134."

Pose the following:

> A company sells pencils in boxes of 100. The second-grade teachers notice that they have 2 full boxes and 41 loose pencils. If they order 1 more box, how many pencils will they have?

> *Turn and talk with your partner about the important information in this problem.*
> *Can you imagine what a box of 100 pencils might look like?*
> *What can we use to represent the pencils they already have?*

Have students represent the pencils using their bundled sticks.

Circulate around the room, observing students. Are students representing the full boxes with ten bundles of ten each? Can students represent the 41 loose pencils with 4 bundles and 1 more?

As students show an understanding of 2 boxes of 100 and 41 loose pencils, draw their attention to the next part of the problem.

> *How can we show the boxes that are being ordered?*
> *How would you count to find out how many pencils the second-grade teachers will have?*

Repeat, asking students to model and count how many pencils there will be if the teachers order 5 more boxes.

Circulate as students work together to count. Listen for students who start at 241 and count on 341, 441, 541, 641, 741. Ask them to be ready to share their thinking.

> *How did you and your partner count?*
> *Why did you choose to count that way?*
> *What do you notice about this counting pattern?*

Pose various 3-digit numbers.

Have students model and count the number using their place value tools.

> Many students may choose to count from zero. Although they will arrive at the answer, support students to move to the counting on strategy. Ask, "How many pencils did we start with? Let's count on from there."

FORMATIVE ASSESSMENT

Pose the following:

> Trent was playing a game and had a score of 327 points. He scored 30 more points.
>
> Use numbers to show how Trent could skip count to find out how many points he has.

327
337
347
357

Then, Trent scored 400 more points. Use numbers or pictures of bundles to show he could skip count to find his total number of points.

357
457
557
657
757

If students are not able to show the skip-counting patterns, have them use base-ten materials to model the problem and then skip count to find the total. Ask the student to tell you patterns she notices (e.g., the hundreds digit changes when counting by 100, but the tens and ones digits don't change). Provide additional practice skip counting by tens and hundreds.

> Number lines help students visualize the increase as students count by ones, fives, tens, and hundreds. Students should become more comfortable creating their own number lines. We support this by modeling, using think-alouds, and asking questions about the starting point, ending point, or the units being used.

Additional Ideas for Support and Practice

The following ideas extend students' understanding of place value and provide meaningful practice.

BENCHMARK COUNTING ON NUMBER LINES

Pick two 3-digit numbers.

On a blank number line, students show how they use benchmark numbers to count up or back.

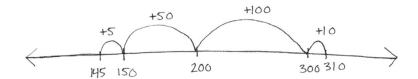

LARGEST/SMALLEST

Give students three digit cards and a place value mat.

Students make the largest number possible and build it using straws or draw a pictorial model.

Students then make the smallest number possible and build or draw it.

Repeat with other digit cards.

ROLL IT, MAKE IT, DRAW IT

Students generate 3-digit numbers with 0–9 dice or 0–9 digit cards.

Have students build their 3-digit number with base-ten blocks or straws.

Then, students draw a picture of their number using squares to represent hundreds, sticks to represent tens, and dots to represent ones.

THE THOUSAND CHART

Create a thousand chart by taping together separate hundreds charts for 1–100, 101–200, 201–300, and so on. Have students use the chart to play the following two games.

4 ON A BOARD

Students take turns using 0–9 dice or 0–9 digit cards to create a 3-digit number, finding and covering their number on the thousand chart.

The first person to cover four numbers on any one of their individual hundred boards (e.g., 1–100, 101–200. . .) wins.

Then, the game starts over.

More-Less 4 on a Board

Students take turns generating 3-digit numbers with 0–9 dice or 0–9 digit cards, and then find 10 and 100 more or 10 and 100 less than their number.

Students cover the two new numbers on the thousand chart.

The first person to cover four numbers on any of their individual hundred boards wins.

Calculator Count

Each student needs a calculator and his math journal.

Have students make a 2-column table in their journals and label one column +10 and the other column +100.

Students pick a 3-digit number and record in both columns.

Type the 3-digit number into the calculator.
Press the buttons '+', '1', and '0' to add 10.
Press the '=' button.
What number appears? Record that number in the +10 column.
Press the '=' button again.
What number appears? Record that number in the same column.
Continue to press '=' and record the new number several more times.
Clear the calculator, type in the original number, and press the buttons '+', '1', '0', and '0' to add 100.
Press the '=' button.
What number appears? Record that number in the +100 column.
Press the '=' button again.
What number appears? Record that number below the last one in the +100 column.
Continue to press '=' and record the new number several more times.

> Most calculators have an equals function that will allow for this activity, but there are some that do not. Double-check your class calculators.

+10	+100
328	328
338	428
348	528
358	628
368	728
378	828

Ask students:

What patterns do you notice?

What happens to the hundreds place in each column? The tens place? The ones place?

Can you predict what comes next in each column?

Talk About It/Write About It 😊✏️

Are 7 hundreds, 3 tens, and 5 ones the same as 5 hundreds, 3 tens, and 7 ones? How do you know?

Oscar used 7 base-ten blocks to create a number. What are some different numbers he may have created?

Explain how to solve this equation 300 + 10 = __.

Is 270 ones the same as 27 tens? Explain.

Skip Count by Tens and Hundreds

Pose counting tasks like the following:

Begin at 53 and count up by tens to 253. Then count back.

Begin at 245 and count up by hundreds to 945. Then count back.

Build a Number

Give each student an envelope with 0–9 digit cards.

Each student selects three random digits and does the following:

- creates a 3-digit number
- tells how many hundreds, tens, and ones are in their number
- shows their number with base-ten blocks
- records the number that is 10 more, 100 more, 10 less, and 100 less than their number.

Students can select three more digit cards and repeat the activities.

DECOMPOSE 3-DIGIT NUMBERS

Students relate place value models to expanded form and extend their understanding of place value to find different ways to decompose numbers.

Comparing Place Value Models

Students use number disks and base-ten blocks to represent numbers and compare the models.

Provide groups of four students with a set of base-ten blocks and number disks, along with accompanying work mats.

With your group, talk about the similarities and differences between the base-ten blocks and the number disks.

For additional ideas on using models to build math understanding, see Math in Practice: A Guide for Teachers, Chapter 3.

Some students may have worked with number disks in first grade. Make note of students who seem familiar with the model and those for whom the model is new.

Have students share their ideas. Look for students to recognize that the number disks are the same size regardless of the value, but the size of the base-ten blocks corresponds to the value.

Provide each group with a different 3-digit number written on an index card.

Have half of each group (one pair) model their number using base-ten blocks, and the other pair model it with the number disks. Then have them compare their number models.

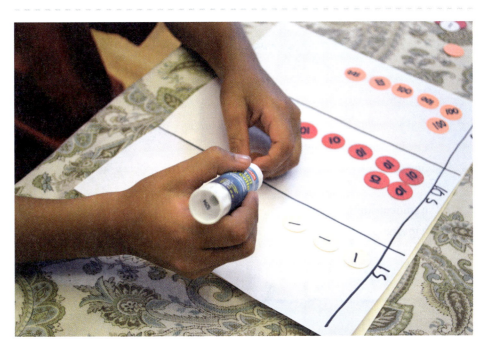

Students can glue paper number disks to a place value chart to display various combinations of numbers.

When all groups feel their models reflect the value of their number, have students do a gallery walk to see the models for different 3-digit numbers.

During your gallery walk, decide if you agree or disagree with each group. Be ready to share your ideas.

Have a class discussion about what students noticed.

What are some things that you notice about the different tools you used?

Is there anything you like more about the base-ten blocks?

What are some advantages to using the number disks?

Pose the following:

Brian counted the play money that came with his new board game. He counted 18 ten-dollar bills, 4 hundred-dollar bills, and 16 one-dollar bills. How much play money came with his board game?

Turn and talk to your partner about the important information in this problem.

The place values are intentionally ordered tens, hundreds, and ones to ensure that students are thinking about the values of each and not simply following the anticipated order of hundreds, tens, and ones.

What kind of math models could we use to represent the bills that Brian had?

Invite students to share ideas, making connections between the play money and base-ten materials.

Work with your partner to represent the values on your work mat, using base-ten blocks or number disks.

Circulate around the room, listening and watching students as they model the ones, tens, and hundreds. As students arrive at a consensus with their partners, ask them to draw a representation of the model in their math journals.

How could we figure out how much money Brian has?

Turn to your partner and share your ideas.

Work with your partner so that each place has fewer than 10 units. Remember that the total value must stay the same.

How many hundreds, tens, and ones do you have now?

How much money came with the game board?

How do you know your new amount of money is the same as what you had before?

Have students draw a pictorial representation of their model in their math journals.

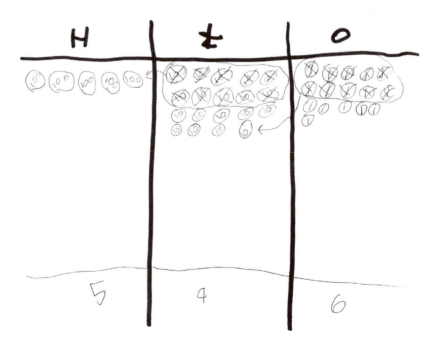

Repeat the process for 12 ten-dollar bills, 14 one-dollar bills, and 3 hundred-dollar bills. To end the lesson, ask students:

What did you do to make counting the money easier?

Have them share their ideas about regrouping.

FORMATIVE ASSESSMENT

Pose the following problem:

> Lucius and Sarah were using place value materials to model numbers. Lucius used 3 hundreds, 2 tens, and 4 ones. Sara used 2 hundreds, 12 tens, and 4 ones. Did Lucius and Sarah show the same number? Justify your answer using pictures.

[Student work: Lucius shown with H|T|O chart with 3 dots, 2 dots, 4 dots labeled 3, 2, 4. Sarah shown with H|T|O chart with 2 dots in hundreds, 12 dots in tens (10 circled), 4 dots in ones, labeled 3, 2, 4. Written response: "Yes, Sarah and Lucius both ended up with 324."]

This student uses dots to represent hundreds, tens, and ones and correctly shows both values. The student shows 10 tens being regrouped as 1 hundred. She identifies that Sarah and Lucius both have 324.

If a student does not identify that Lucius and Sarah have the same value, check to see if he modeled both values accurately. Ask the student if there is another way to name 12 tens. Provide more practice with regrouping 10 ones as 1 ten and 10 tens as 1 hundred.

Representing Numbers in Different Ways

Students connect their understanding of place value to different representations of numbers.

Provide students with number disks, place value mats, and individual dry erase boards.

Pose the number 274.

Work with your partner to show the number 274 on your place value mat, using number disks.

Together, count how many hundreds, tens, and ones there are in 274.

How many hundreds are there?

What are some different ways we can write 200?

Let's make a chart to show how we could write 200 using just numbers, using numbers and place values, and then with only words.

How do we show this value with numbers? Write it on your dry erase board.

Record *200* in the first column.

How many hundreds is that?

Write *2 hundreds* in the second column and have students write it on their boards.

How can we write that in words?

Write *two hundred* in the third column.

> Make a class anchor chart as students create charts in their math journals.

Number	Place Value	Word
200	2 hundreds	two hundred

How many tens are in our number 274?

Talk with your partner: Can you write that using only numbers and then write it a different way using both numbers and place values?

Have students use their dry erase boards to write it both ways.

Invite students to share their ideas as you record *70* and *7 tens* on the chart. Add the word form to show students what it looks like in words.

> The emphasis at this level is not on students being able to write 3-digit numbers in words, but on being able to say the 3-digit number in words.

Number	Place Value	Word
200	2 hundreds	two hundred
70	7 tens	seventy

How many ones are in our number 274?

Can you write that using only numbers and using both numbers and place values?

Again, listen and record *4* and *4 ones* as students discuss their thinking. Include the word *four* on the chart.

Number	Place Value	Word
200	2 hundreds	two hundred
70	7 tens	seventy
4	4 ones	four

The hundreds, tens, and ones together form 274.

Sometimes we write 3-digit numbers using numbers and place value words. How could we write 274 using numbers and place value words?

Pose more 3-digit numbers (e.g., 425) and have students show each one on their place value mats with their number disks, then write the number using just numbers (425) and using numbers and place values (4 hundreds, 2 tens, and 5 ones).

> Encourage students to use their charts if needed.

Decomposing in Different Ways

Students use base-ten blocks to decompose a 3-digit number in different ways.

Pose the number 58.

Have students use a place value mat and base-ten blocks to show the number.

Turn and tell your partner how many tens and ones are in 58.

Is there any other way I could show 58 with my blocks? Show me a different way to model 58.

Have students share their ideas (e.g., 4 tens and 18 ones or 3 tens and 28 ones).

Do all of those ways have a value of 58? How do you know?

Pose the number 253.

Have students use a place value mat and base-ten blocks to show the number.

Turn and tell your partner how many hundreds, tens, and ones are in 253.

Can I show 253 with just 1 hundred block? Work with your partner to find a way.

Have students share their thinking (e.g., 1 hundred, 15 tens, and 3 ones).

> Understanding how to rename numbers in different ways reinforces our students' understanding of place value and lays the foundations for subtraction with regrouping.

> Students have experience renaming 2-digit numbers from first grade.

Do both ways have a value of 253? How do you know?

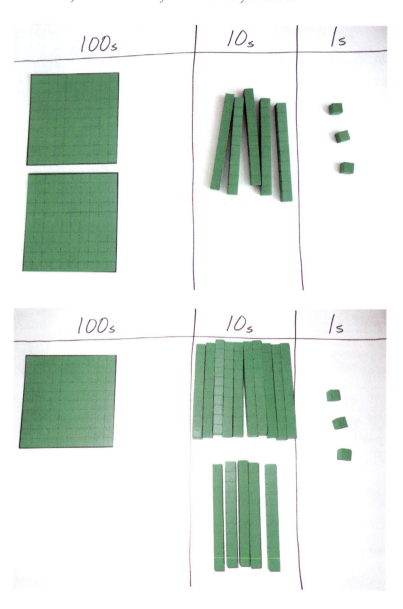

> Sets of base-ten blocks often have a limited number of flats (hundreds), which can make it difficult to do activities like this with the whole class. Consider making some of your own flats by copying a base-ten hundred template on card stock paper.

Record on the board:

    253 = 2 hundreds, 5 tens, 3 ones

    253 = 1 hundred, 15 tens, 3 ones

What do you notice?

Does it make sense?

Have students work with partners to decompose the following numbers into hundreds, tens, and ones and then find a different way to show each one by changing the hundreds digit:

    526

    247

    135

Watch as students work, to be sure they are regrouping accurately.

Have them share their ideas with the class, recording and talking about the patterns in the different ways they decomposed the numbers.

Refer back to the first example of 253 on the board.

> *Could we show 253 in a different way by changing the tens?*
>
> *What if it had 2 hundreds and 4 tens? How many ones would you need to have so it is still 253?*

Have students work with partners using their blocks, then share their thinking.

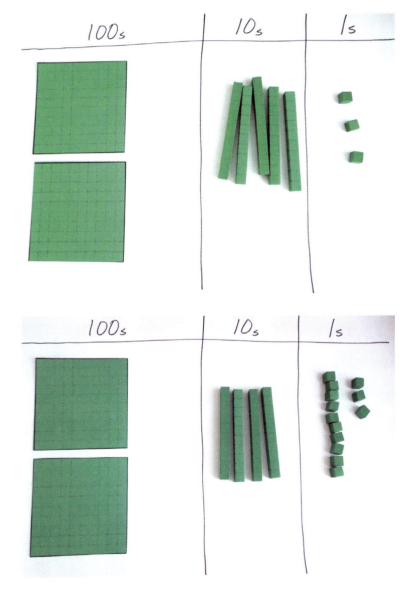

Record:

    253 = 2 hundreds, 5 tens, 3 ones

    253 = 2 hundreds, 4 tens, 13 ones

What do you notice?
Does that make sense? Explain.

Have students work with partners to decompose more numbers into hundreds, tens, and ones and then find a different way to show each one by changing the tens digit.

Have them share their ideas with the class, recording and talking about the patterns in the different ways they decomposed the numbers.

I have some puzzles for you to solve with your partners.
Can you figure out what number goes in each blank? Be ready to justify your answers.

> 382 = 2 hundreds + __ tens + 2 ones
> 491 = 3 hundreds + __ tens + 1 one
> 167 = 1 hundred + __ tens + 17 ones
> 16 tens = 10 tens + __ tens
> 35 tens = __ hundreds + 5 tens
> 7 ones + 6 hundreds = _____

Have students share and justify their answers.

Provide repeated practice with decomposing numbers in different ways.

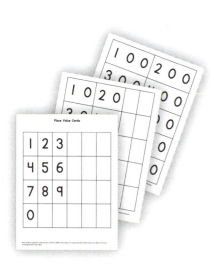

Students can use their base-ten blocks to help them figure out or check their answers.

Introducing Expanded Form

Students are introduced to writing 3-digit numbers in expanded form.

Provide pairs of students with number disks, place value mats, and place value cards that show values 0–9, 10–90 (by tens), and 100–900 (by hundreds).

Pose a 3-digit number: 479

Use your number disks to show 479 on your place value mat.
Tell your partner how many hundreds, tens, and ones are in 479.
Use your place value cards to build the number 479.
What cards do you need?
Lay the tens on top of the hundreds and the ones on top of the tens. What number do you see?

What happens as you pull the cards apart?

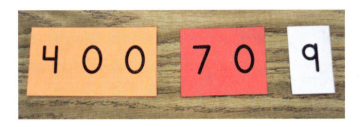

What addition sentence could we write using these numbers to show how 479 is formed?

When we pull something apart, we can say that we are expanding it. When we pull apart our hundreds, tens, and ones, we call this expanded form. We call 400 + 70 + 9 the expanded form of 479.

What happens when we add the parts back together?

Record the words *expanded form* on the word wall or Math Talk chart, along with an example.

Students record the expanded form of 479 in their math journals.

Pose other 3-digit numbers for students to model using number disks and place value cards (e.g., 516). Then, have them record the number form and expanded form (516 = 500 + 10 + 6).

Students create a 3-digit number with place value cards and then use number disks to model their number.

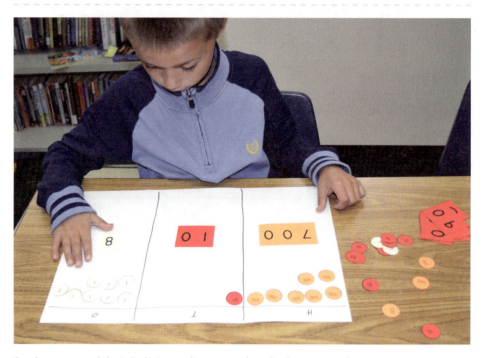

Students expand their 3-digit number to see hundreds, tens, and ones.

Use this question as an exit ticket:

What does it mean to write a number in expanded form?

Additional Ideas for Support and Practice

The following ideas extend students' understanding of decomposing numbers in different ways and provide meaningful practice.

NUMBER BONDS TO SHOW EXPANDED FORM

For students who might benefit from a different visual approach, number bonds can be used to show expanded form or decomposition.

Have students decompose numbers by hundreds, tens, and ones using number bonds and then create expanded form equations.

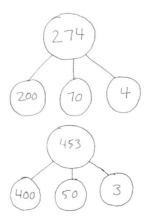

274 = 200 + 70 + 4
453 = 400 + 50 + 3

Or have students use number bonds to show different ways they decompose a number.

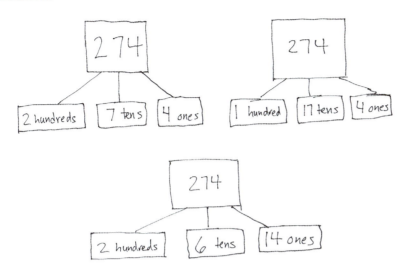

Then, have them list the different ways they decomposed it.

274 = 2 hundreds, 7 tens, 4 ones
274 = 1 hundred, 17 tens, 4 ones
274 = 2 hundreds, 6 tens, 14 ones

Talk About It/Write About It

Name 638 in two different ways.

Naomi said that 2 hundreds and 3 tens was the same as 23 tens. Do you agree or disagree? Prove it.

Morgan said that 1 hundred, 5 tens, and 4 ones was the same as 14 hundreds and 5 ones. Do you agree or disagree? Prove it.

Break 256 into hundreds, tens, and ones in two ways. Explain how they can both equal 256.

Roll and Rename

Partners roll a number cube three times to make a 3-digit number.

Partner A writes the number one way.

Partner B has to write it a different way.

Then, players switch roles and roll again.

Vocabulary Sort

Students work with a team to sort the following words and representations based on their math meanings. Once they have placed the words into groups, they

> There is no one way to sort the words, but the groupings must make sense based on the math meanings of the words and representations.

MODULE 4

Vocabulary

bundle	place value
decompose	regroup
digit	rename
expanded form	tens
hundreds	word form
ones	

Online Resources

General Resources
- 0–9 Digit Cards
- Additional Problems

Resources for Specific Activities
- 1–100 Chart
- 101–200 Chart
- 201–300 Chart
- 301–400 Chart
- 401–500 Chart
- 501–600 Chart
- 601–700 Chart
- 701–800 Chart
- 801–900 Chart
- 901–1000 Chart
- Base-Ten Hundred Template
- Place Value Cards
- Place Value Mat

These resources are available at http://hein.pub/MathinPractice, keycode MIPG2.

---

decide on a title for each group that describes why those words or numbers belong together. Teams then share their groupings with the class or another team and justify their decisions.

> 3 hundreds, 0 tens, and 1 one
> 400 + 60 + 8
> base-ten numerals
> 4 hundreds, 6 tens, and 8 ones
> 300 + 0 + 1
> expanded form
> four hundred sixty-eight
> 301
> number names
> three hundred one
> 468

ELIMINATE IT

Students work with a partner to decide which of the following does not belong with the others, then use math reasoning, numbers, or models to convince their classmates that their thinking makes sense.

810	8 hundreds, 1 ten, and 0 ones
800 + 10 + 0	800 + 0 + 10

MAKE IT RIGHT

Pose statements like the following.

Have students complete each equation to make it correct.

Have them justify their answers with words, pictures, or materials.

> 2 hundreds + 4 tens = _____
> 243 = 2 hundreds + 3 tens + _____ ones
> 16 tens = 10 tens + _____ tens
> 26 tens = _____ hundreds + 6 tens
> 8 ones + 4 hundreds = _____
> 3 tens + 2 hundreds = _____
> _____ = 1 hundred + 2 tens + 5 ones
> 125 = _____ tens + _____ ones

MODULE 5

Comparing Two 3-Digit Numbers

About the Math   2.NBT.4

Everyday life is filled with situations in which we compare numbers. We compare sports statistics, our weights, the distances we travel, and the costs of items we buy. Classes compete to see who sold the most boxes of cookies in the school fundraiser or collected the most coupons for the donation program. We compare numbers regularly.

To effectively compare numbers, our students have to understand the value of those numbers, and their understanding of the value of 3-digit numbers depends on their understanding of place value. In Module 4, we explored strategies for deepening our students' understanding of place value concepts through hands-on experiences and lots of math talk. We used manipulatives and investigations to help our students explore the value of each digit in a 3-digit number, giving them the tools to compare and order 3-digit numbers.

> The key ideas focused on in this module include:
>
> - comparing 3-digit numbers using a variety of strategies like number lines, base-ten models, or benchmarks
>
> - discovering a rule to compare 3-digit numbers based on the value of the digits
>
> - comparing more than two numbers (ordering numbers).

One way to think about the value of a number is to consider how far it is from zero. Visualizing where a number fits on a 0–1,000 number line can help our students understand this concept. Creating a number line with increments of one hundred, and envisioning where a 3-digit number might be placed on the line, provides insight into which number represents a greater quantity, or is farthest from zero (see Figure 5.1).

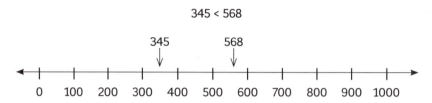

Figure 5.1 Locating the approximate place where each number fits on the number line allows students to visualize which number represents the greater value.

Numbers are compared based on place value. Initially, students might compare numbers by simply creating models of the numbers with base-ten materials (e.g., base-ten blocks) to see which is greater (see Figure 5.2). However, as students build and compare their models, they gain insight into how attention to the digits can streamline the task of comparing numbers. Investigations in which students build numbers using manipulatives, compare the materials to see which represents a greater value, then observe and discuss what they notice about the digits lead to insights and rules based on place value concepts. As students notice that their models show that 345 is more than 257, 561 is more than 394, and 265 is more than 148, they notice that the hundreds digits are greater in all of those examples. Having students verbalize their observations related to the investigation leads to conjectures about comparing numbers based on digits. Students make predictions based on these insights and test their predictions with more number pairs, until they are convinced that their rule works. They discover that numbers are compared based on place value (see Figure 5.3).

Figure 5.2 Building models of the numbers allows students to visualize each number and determine which is greater.

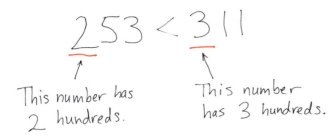

Figure 5.3 As students observe their models and think about their place value understandings, they realize that a look at the digits tells them which number is greater.

Students might also effectively use benchmarks, or friendly numbers, to compare two 3-digit numbers. When comparing 385 and 419, students might simply recognize that 419 is more than 400 and 385 is less than 400. This thinking is simple and effective, and it shows an understanding of numbers.

Students sometimes get confused when comparing two 3-digit numbers that have the same hundreds digit. Revisiting hands-on experiences to build and compare 243 and 221 helps students discover that when the hundreds digits are the same, they compare the digits with the next greatest value, the tens digits (see Figure 5.4), and when both the hundreds and tens digits are the same, they compare the ones digits to determine which number is greater. Being challenged to explain why this is true pushes our students to think about the value of each digit and rely on their place value understanding to justify the process. Students might be asked to write directions for a student who does not understand how to compare 3-digit numbers or to defend why 238 > 236.

243 > 221

Hundreds	Tens	Ones

Figure 5.4 Building models for each number allows students to see why the tens digits in these numbers hold the clue to which is greater.

Learning Goals

I can use my knowledge of place value to compare and order 3-digit numbers.

I can use symbols to show greater than, less than, and equal.

Lessons in This Module

Comparing Numbers Using Place Value Concepts

Comparing 3-Digit Numbers Using a Number Line
Place Value Mats
Expanded Form
What's the Rule?
Ordering Animals

Students compared 2-digit numbers in first grade, but it is recommended that you revisit that skill to be sure students understand the concept with 2-digit numbers before beginning work with 3-digit numbers.

Ordering numbers is simply an extension of comparing numbers, this time with more than two numbers being compared. Once our students recognize the role of place value in comparing numbers, they are challenged with ordering multiple numbers, transferring their insights about comparing two numbers to this new task. Students might begin by using benchmarks to sort the numbers (see Figure 5.5), determining numbers that are greater than 300 or less than 300. This step often happens in their heads now that they are used to comparing numbers by place value. Then, they use their known strategies for comparing numbers to evaluate and determine the exact order (e.g., deciding whether 247 or 295 is greater).

Figure 5.5 Students' understanding of place value allows them to immediately see that some of these numbers are greater than 300 and some are less than 300.

Seeing more than two numbers to compare can feel confusing to students. Helping them see that they are using their known strategies and simply sorting and comparing the numbers helps to simplify the process of ordering numbers and makes it doable for them.

Exploring the Progression

Ideas for Instruction and Assessment

COMPARING NUMBERS USING PLACE VALUE CONCEPTS

Students explore comparing numbers using visual representations and their understanding of place value concepts, recognizing that hundreds have more value than tens, which have more value than ones.

Comparing Two 3-Digit Numbers

MODULE 5

Thinking Through a Lesson

SMP1, SMP2, SMP4, SMP5, SMP7

Comparing 3-Digit Numbers Using a Number Line SHOW IT!

Students create number lines to compare the value of numbers.

Show students the following number line:

Turn and talk to your partners:

What does this number line show? (0 to 50.)

Could I show 35 on this number line? I don't see it on the line. (Yes; it is between 30 and 40, because it is more than 30 but not as much as 40.)

Do number lines have to have all of the numbers shown on them? (No.)

How do you know where a number belongs if it is not shown on the number line? (You think about where it fits if you were counting.)

Show students the following number line:

Turn and talk to your partners:

What does this number line show? (0 to 500.)

Could I show 350 on this number line? I don't see it on the line. (Yes; it is between 300 and 400, because it is more than 300 but not 400.)

How do you know it is more than 300? (Because it is 350, so it is like 300 and 50 more.)

Where would 480 be on this number line? Explain. (It would be between 400 and 500, because it is more than 400 but not 500 yet. Or, It would be almost at 500 because it is closer to 500.)

Write on the board: *290 and 360*

Could you use this number line to decide which number is greater? Tell your partner how you could do it. (We could show where both numbers are and see which is more.)

How would you know which is greater? Where would it be on the number line? Why? (The greater number would be farther from 0 and closer to 500, because it gets more as you go to the right.)

Use your number line to show which is greater.

Have partners show the numbers on a number line and then share their thinking.

> Beginning the lesson with questions that require students to verbalize key ideas about place value concepts and number lines serves as a quick review.

> **Differentiation**
> If students are having a difficult time deciding where a number belongs on the number line, have them think about expanded form from Module 4. Thinking about 480 as 400 + 80 helps them see that it is more than 400, but less than 500.

> This shows a foundational understanding of number lines. Are students seeing that they show numbers in relation to zero? This is especially important later in the lesson when zero may not be labeled on the line.

Which is greater? (360.) *Why? Can you prove it to me?* (It is farther on the number line. *Or,* It is farthest from 0. *Or,* Numbers keeps getting more as you go to the right.)

Pose the following problem:

> Alex's family drove 210 miles during vacation. Mateo's family drove 350 miles. Whose family drove a greater distance?

Retell this problem to your partner.

What are we trying to find out? (We're trying to find out who drove farther: Alex's family or Mateo's family.)

What do we need to do to answer that question? (We need to decide which is more: 210 miles or 350 miles.)

Talk to your partners:

Could using a number line help us solve this problem? How? (We can look at the numbers on a number line and see where they are on the line, and we could see which is farther from 0.)

What numbers are we comparing? (210 and 350.)

Have students work with partners to draw a number line and show the numbers.

Invite a student to locate where 210 would be on the number line.

Invite another student to locate 350 on the number line.

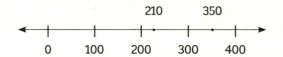

Where is 0 on the number line? (It's on the left side of the number line.)

Which number is farther from 0? (350.)

What does that mean? (You have to count more to get to that number. *Or,* It has a greater value if you have to count more to get to it.)

Which number is greater, 350 or 210? (350.)

Talk to your partners about how you could use numbers and symbols to show which number is greater.

Have students share their ideas, which might include 210 < 350 and 350 > 210.

How would we read 210 < 350? (210 is less than 350.)

How would we read 350 > 210? (350 is greater than 210.)

Which is correct? Why? (They are both right, because if 210 is less than 350, 350 is also greater than 210.)

Record the symbol > and words *greater than* on the word wall or Math Talk chart.

> Do they recognize that the number farthest from zero is greater?

> Students are now applying their strategy to a problem situation.

> Students have been introduced to the comparison symbols in first grade. If needed, remind students that the symbol opens toward the greater number.

Comparing Two 3-Digit Numbers

MODULE 5

Record the symbol < and words *less than* on the word wall or Math Talk chart.

What symbol would we use if the values were the same? (The equal sign.)

Record the symbol = and the words *equal to* on the word wall or Math Talk chart.

What is the answer to our problem? How do you know? (Mateo's family drove farther; 350 is greater than 210.)

Pose the following problem for students to solve with a number line:

> Mark and Isabella were sorting books for the book sale. Mark sorted 375 books. Isabella sorted 545 books. Who sorted more books?

Watch as students create an open number line, show the numbers, and talk about which number is greater.

Was your number line the same as the one you used for the last problem? (No.) *Why?* (Because one number was more than 500.)

So, what did you do so it would work for the problem?

Have students share their ideas and show their number lines. Some may have made a 0–600 number line, while others may have made a 300–600 number line. Talk about why they chose their starting and ending points on the lines.

Where did 375 go on your number line? (It went after 300, but before 400. Or, It went closer to 400 than 300, because it is more than 350.)

Where did 545 go on your number line? (It went between 500 and 600.)

How do you know which is greater when you look at your number line? (The one that is farthest from 0 is greater.)

I don't see 0 on some of your number lines. How do you know where it is? (It is on the left, because you can see the numbers keep getting bigger.)

How could you record the comparison using symbols? (375 < 545. Or, 545 > 375.)

Does it matter how we read these? (Yes; we read left to right.)

How would we read 375 < 545? (375 is less than 545.)

How would we read 545 > 375? (545 is greater than 375.)

Continue with more number pairs for students to compare.

As we compare other numbers, are there any patterns that you've started to notice? (Numbers with more hundreds are farther away from 0.)

> **Differentiation**
> Although many students will be able to create their own number lines, you might choose to provide a number line template with some baseline numbers marked for students who need it (e.g., 0, 100, 200, 300, 400, 500, 600).

> Be sure that students understand that open number lines can be created differently. As long as their number lines show 375 and 545, they would work to show this comparison.

> Make sure students see both forms of the comparison. Both are equally valid.

> A future lesson will have students develop a rule for comparing numbers, but patterns are emerging as students begin comparing on a number line.

> As students get more comfortable using number lines to compare numbers in which the hundreds digits are different, pose some that have the same digit in the hundreds place (e.g., 175 and 125). Encourage students to think about how to create their number lines to help them compare the numbers (e.g., 100, 110, 120, 130, 140, 150, 160, 170, 180, 190, 200).

To summarize key ideas from the lesson, ask:

What happens to our numbers as we move further to the right, away from 0?

How can number lines help us visualize which numbers are greater?

Place Value Mats

Students use place value mats and base-ten materials to visualize and compare 3-digit numbers.

Provide students with base-ten blocks and place value mats.

Which of the base-ten blocks have the greatest value?

Which have the least value?

Pose the following:

Victor and Skylar kept track of the minutes they read for one month. Victor read for 324 minutes. Skylar read for 271 minutes. Who read for a greater length of time?

Retell the problem to your partner.

What do you know?

What could we do to compare these two numbers? How can we find out which number is greater? Share some ideas with your partner.

Have students share their ideas, then have them work with partners to represent each number (one below the other) on a place value mat.

Have them talk with partners about the following:

Which number is greater? How do you know?

What parts of the place value mat are you focusing on when you decide which number is greater? Why?

What are you looking for when you look at the hundreds part of the mat?

Have partners share their ideas with the whole class.

Have students record the two numbers, using the correct symbol to show the comparison.

Pose the following numbers: 178 and 412.

Work with your partner to determine which number is greater.

Which is greater? How do you know?

But 178 has a 7 and an 8. Why doesn't that make it have greater value?

> Students can make their own place value mats. Have students fold an 11 x 17-inch sheet of paper into thirds, open the paper, and draw a line down each fold. Then have them label the sections hundreds, tens, and ones.

Provide more opportunities to practice with additional sets of 3-digit numbers, including numbers with zero in the tens or ones place.

After using base-ten materials, students can draw pictorial models in their journals, using squares, sticks, and dots to show their comparisons.

Continue to remind students of the value of the blocks or drawings so they connect them with the symbolic representation (e.g., 3 flats is more than 2 flats, because 3 hundreds is more than 2 hundreds).

Encourage students to share their work with partners.

To end the lesson, ask students to discuss the following with partners and then with the class:

> In a 3-digit number, which place has the greatest value? Why?
> Is a 9 in the ones place the same as a 9 in the hundreds place?
> How does using blocks help you compare numbers?

Common Error or Misconception

When a zero appears in the tens or ones place, students sometimes get confused about the value of the number (e.g., 209 or 290). Try more specific talk about the value of digits and use models to show 0 tens or 0 ones.

Base-ten blocks support student understanding when comparing numbers. These students see that both numbers have a hundred, but one number has 5 tens while the other number has 2 tens.

For additional formative assessment ideas, see Math in Practice: A Guide for Teachers, Chapter 5.

FORMATIVE ASSESSMENT

Pose the following:

Compare the following numbers using <, >, or =.

357   329

Justify your thinking using base-ten drawings and a number line.

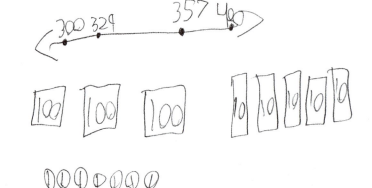

This student correctly uses the greater than symbol to identify that 357 is greater than 329. She shows her thinking with a number line and place value representations.

If students do not use the correct symbol, refer to their work to determine if the error is in understanding the concept or selecting the appropriate symbol. Many students at this level continue to confuse the greater than and less than symbols, although they understand which number is greater.

You might ask:

Compare your hundreds. What do you notice?
Compare your tens. What do you notice?
What does that mean?

Expanded Form

Students use expanded form to compare numbers, emphasizing the importance of comparing hundreds to hundreds, tens to tens, and ones to ones.

Pose the following problem:

> Brian's family went on a trip. On Monday, they drove 321 miles. On Tuesday, they drove 275 miles. Which day did they drive farther?

Retell the problem to your partner.
What do we need to find out?
Turn and tell your partner the ways you know to compare numbers.

Allow students to share ideas.

Record the numbers *275* and *321* on the board.

Ask students to talk to partners about other ways they might write 275 other than the standard, number form.

Have them show you both numbers in expanded form.

Write the following on the board:

$321 = 300 + 20 + 1$
$275 = 200 + 70 + 5$

How could this help us compare the numbers?
Why are you looking at the hundreds?
What is the answer to our problem?

Write *456* and *472* on the board.

What about these two numbers? Which one is greater?
How can we write these in expanded form?

Have students write each number in expanded form and compare them.

Invite students to tell you the expanded form as you write it on the board:

$456 = 400 + 50 + 6$
$472 = 400 + 70 + 2$

What did you look at first to compare them?
What did you find out?
What did you do next? Explain.
Which number is greater? Why?

Continue to pose more number pairs, including ones in which the hundreds and tens digits are the same.

Have partners show the numbers in expanded form, compare the numbers, and justify their answers using place value terms.

Have students turn to partners and discuss:

What do you know about comparing numbers based on place value?

Students may be at very different places in their understanding of comparing numbers. Some may still need to build the numbers to see which is greater, but others will have transferred what they learned with 2-digit numbers in first grade to simply compare the hundreds digits. Using expanded form ensures they are thinking about the hundreds digits as hundreds and not simply comparing digits.

Differentiation
Students who need additional support with expanded form can use the place value cards, found in the online resources, to build and expand the numbers.

As you listen to student thinking, identify those students who are ready to work just with numbers, and which students need additional experiences with concrete materials, number lines, or drawings.

> Although students have had many opportunities to compare numbers, they may not have generalized a place value rule for doing it without the need for models. This lesson helps them uncover this rule.

What's the Rule?

Students use a method of their choice (build numbers with base-ten materials, show numbers on a number line, use expanded form) to compare 3-digit numbers, and then develop a rule for comparing them.

Pose the following question:

Which is greater: 648 or 351?

You may use base-ten blocks, a number line, or expanded form to help you decide.

Have students use the method of their choice to visualize the numbers and compare to see which is greater.

How do you know which is greater?

Record the two numbers on the board with the greater value first.

648 > 351

Pose the following numbers: 275 and 428

Again, have students work in pairs to compare the two numbers.

Once students have modeled the numbers, decided which is greater, and justified their thinking, add the two numbers to the board.

Repeat the process with 521 and 428.

Have students look at the data you recorded and discuss their observations with partners.

648 > 351
428 > 275
521 > 428

What do you notice about the numbers that are greater compared to the numbers that are less?

Do you think that is always true? Let's test it!

Repeat with several other combinations, having students first predict which will be greater and then model and prove using the method of their choice. Choose numbers that highlight good discussions and key ideas, such as:

327 and 427

I notice the tens and ones are the same. Does that matter?

219 and 291

What do you notice about the hundreds digits? What does that mean?
What did you do to figure out which is greater?

Have students model both numbers to see that there are more tens in 291 and that it is the greater number.

473 and 474

This time the hundreds digits and tens digits are the same.
What did you do?

Have students model both numbers to see that 474 is one more than 473.

　　398 and 398

The hundreds digits, tens digits, and ones digits are the same. What does that mean?

What symbol would you put between them to show that?

Continue with different numbers.

Have students predict which number is greater, then check their predictions.

Have students discuss the following with partners and then the class:

How can you tell which number is greater without building the numbers? Come up with a rule that helps us figure out which number has a greater value.

FORMATIVE ASSESSMENT

Pose the following problems:

　　Jane has 195 stickers in her collection. Julie has 213. Jane says she has more. Is she right? Prove your answer.

　　Jane gets 20 more stickers for her birthday. Does she have more stickers than Julie now? How do you know?

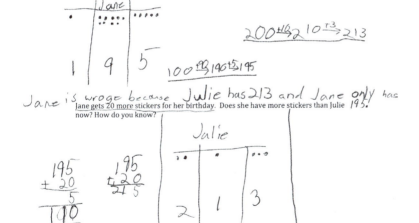

This student places dots on a place value mat to show the number of hundreds, tens, and ones for both Jane's and Julie's numbers. To communicate deeper understanding, the student could draw a similar model for 215.

> You might ask:
>
> *How did you know 215 was greater than 213?*
>
> *What numbers did you compare?*
>
> ---
>
> Jane had 195 stickers in her collection. Julie had 213. Jane says she has more. Is she right? Justify.
>
> *Jane is wrong because Jane has 195 and Julie has 213. I know that 200 is more the 100. So Julie has more.*
>
> Jane gets 20 more stickers for her birthday. Does she have more stickers than Julie now? How do you know?
>
> ```
>   1
>  195
> + 20
> ----
>  215
> ```
>
> *Yes! Jane has more than Julie because Jane now has 215 and Julie still has 213 and 15 is more than 13.*
>
> ---
>
> This student compares 200 and 100 to justify Part A. In Part B, the student compares 15 ones and 13 ones.

Ordering Animals

Students create animals using base-ten materials, find the value of their animal, and order the class or small group's animals from least to greatest values. This task provides a review of comparing numbers and using standard and expanded notation, then challenges students to order numbers.

Have students use base-ten materials (base-ten blocks) to make a model of an animal (real or make-believe).

Your animal should have a total value that is greater than 200 and less than 500.

Once you have made your animal with base-ten blocks and checked its value, you may cut out the 10 ×10 grids and make a picture of your animal.

Students use the full 10 × 10 grid to show hundreds flats, cut a hundred into tens to show the rods, and cut a rod into units to show the ones. Students glue the pieces on construction paper to match their animal.

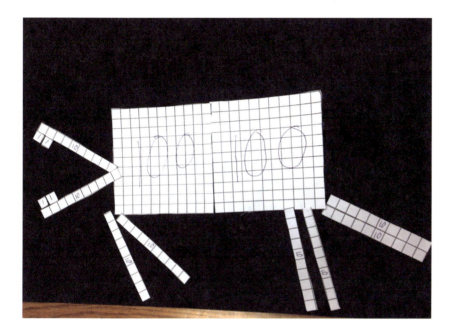

Write the value of your animal in standard and expanded form on the back of the paper.

Then, trade animals with a partner. Have your partner find the value of your animal and you find the value of her animal.

Then, turn over the paper and compare to see if you agree. If not, decide whose value is correct.

When students have found the values and checked them for accuracy, have them decide whose animal has the greater value and be ready to justify it to the class.

Have students share their animals in pairs, telling the value and whose animal has a greater value.

Ask the class to give a thumbs up or thumbs down to show if they agree with the comparison.

MATH IN PRACTICE
Teaching Second-Grade Math

MODULE 5

Differentiation

If ordering the entire class's animals would be overwhelming, have students form small groups and order the animals from their group only.

When all students are done, challenge the class to order the animals made by the entire class from least to greatest value.

Additional Ideas for Support and Practice

The following ideas extend students' understanding of comparing numbers and provide meaningful practice.

SPIN TO WIN

Students build pictures with base-ten blocks, find the value, compare them, and spin a greater than/less than spinner to see who wins.

Partners each make a picture using base-ten blocks, and then calculate its value.

Partner A made a house using 1 hundred, 2 tens, and 8 ones.

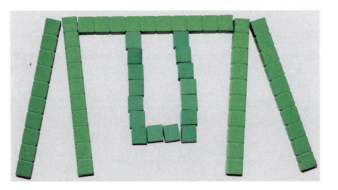

Partner B made a swing set with 5 tens and 16 ones.

Comparing Two 3-Digit Numbers

MODULE 5

Partners spin a greater than/less than spinner to see whether the winner will be the picture with the greater or lesser value.

Students compare the numbers and decide together who wins.

Roll It, Draw It, Beat It

Students fold a paper into four sections and label one *rolled it* and the other three *beat it*.

Students generate a 3-digit number by rolling a 0–9 die three times, then draw their number in the *rolled it* section using squares (hundreds), sticks (tens), and dots (ones).

Students then create three examples of a number that will beat it (has a greater value), drawing each number and labeling each drawing with the number.

Students flip over their paper, roll another 3-digit number, and do it again.

Spin and Compare

Students spin a 1–9 spinner and use their place value understanding to build 3-digit numbers, competing with partners to build the number with the greater value.

Students spin a 1–9 spinner and record the number spun in any space on the game template. Once a number is recorded in a space, it cannot be changed.

When all spaces are filled (three spins per player), students compare their numbers and write the appropriate symbol (>, <, or =) between their number and their partner's.

Talk About It/Write About It

Tara says that 529 and 295 are the same because they have the same digits. Do you agree with her? Why or why not?

What are three numbers greater than 418 but less than 600? How do you know? Place them in order from least to greatest. Justify your order.

Jayla created a number that has 6, 3, and 1 in it. What numbers could she have made?

What is the greatest number? What is the least number?

What is the order of the numbers from least to greatest? Justify your order.

Science Fair

Students explore a problem in which numbers are compared, and are then challenged to find a way to order more than two numbers.

Pose the following problem:

The following data shows the number of students that attend each elementary school.

School	Number of Students
Freeville	291
Buckley	367
Todd	278
Cassavant	349

The students from Freeville, Buckley, Todd, and Cassavant participated in a science fair. Each student did a science fair project. How many more projects were done at Buckley Elementary School than at Freeville Elementary School?

Have partners share their solutions and methods, then pose the following:

The science fair directory listed each school in order from the school that had the most projects to the school that had the fewest projects. In what order did the directory list these four schools?

Talk to your partner about what we are trying to figure out in this problem. What is different about this problem than other ones that we have been doing?

What are some strategies you used when comparing two numbers?

Could you use those strategies to help you order these numbers?

Decide with your partner on a strategy you could use, then put these schools in order.

Circulate, listen, and observe as students work to order the numbers.

Compare your solution to another pair's. Did you have the same results?

How were your strategies similar? How were they different?

To end the lesson, have students share a tip for ordering numbers.

Digit Order Challenge

Students use digit cards to build 3-digit numbers and then order them.

Each student has a set of 0–9 digit cards.

Students arrange the cards to build three 3-digit numbers, recording each one.

Then, students order the numbers from least to greatest.

Students share the order with a partner and explain how they know the order is correct.

Then, they build three more numbers and repeat the task.

Focus on the Question

Use the same problem data each day, but pose a different question for students to discuss. Have them talk with partners to retell the problem, identify the data needed to solve it, and explain how they would solve the problem. This provides students with opportunities to discuss different strategies. They might also be asked to solve it and justify their answers.

> Benfield Elementary School had a cookie sale to raise money for the school. The three top-selling classes each earned extra recess time and got their names posted on the bulletin board outside the office. And the first place class also got a pizza party!
>
> Boxes of Cookies Sold
>
> Mr. Wilson—437
>
> Mrs. Abell—527
>
> Mrs. DiAngelo—523
>
> Mr. Bingham—516
>
> Mr. Meushaw—540
>
> Mrs. Cage—499

1. Which class earned a pizza party? Tell how you would solve it.
2. Who sold more boxes of cookies, Mrs. Bingham's class or Mrs. DiAngelo's class? Tell how you would solve it.
3. Which class sold the fewest boxes of cookies? Tell how you would solve it.
4. Which three classes got their names posted on the bulletin board? What was the order of the first three classes? Tell how you would solve it.
5. If Mrs. Abell's class sold 10 more boxes of cookies, would they have earned the pizza party? Tell how you would solve it.

See Math in Practice: A Guide for Teachers, Chapter 2, for more on this technique.

Card Crazy

Students create 3-digit numbers with digit cards, and then try to find the best number they can make to meet number challenges. This can be played with the whole class, in small groups, or between students as a center activity.

Provide students with the Card Crazy recording sheet.

Students pull three digit cards and make a 3-digit number.

Sometimes a student may not have the digits to be able to meet the criteria. It is important for him to recognize that. His space on the recording sheet will be blank for that section. The student should justify to other players why that section is blank.

Differentiation

Because the online recording sheet is customizable (in a Microsoft Word document), you can modify these challenges to suit your class by changing the difficulty level, or create additional challenges.

Vocabulary

compare   greater than
digits   less than
equal to more than
fewer than order

ONLINE RESOURCES

General Resources

0–9 Digit Cards

1–9 Spinner

10 × 10 Grids

Additional Problems

Open Number Line Template

Place Value Cards

Place Value Mat

Resources for Specific Activities

Card Crazy Recording Sheet

Greater Than/Less Than Spinner

Spin and Compare Game Board

These resources are available at http://hein.pub/MathinPractice, keycode MIPG2.

Prompts on the Card Crazy recording sheet include:

- Make the 3-digit number with the greatest value.
- Make the 3-digit number with the least value.
- Make the number closest to 800.
- Make the even number with the greatest value.
- Make the smallest 3-digit odd number.
- Make the number between 400 and 600 with the greatest value.

Students who win each challenge earn a point for that item. (More than one student can have the same number and thus win a point.)

MODULE 6

Understanding Multidigit Addition

About the Math   2.NBT.5; 2.NBT.6

Students began their study of multidigit addition in first grade. At that level, they explored adding 10 and adding multiples of 10 to 2-digit numbers. In second grade, students extend their understanding of multidigit addition.

> The key ideas focused on in this module include:
> - adding 2-digit numbers using an understanding of place value
> - understanding and explaining varied strategies for adding multidigit numbers
> - adding up to four 2-digit numbers, focusing on place value and the associative property.

In first grade, students created models to show the addition process, using hundred charts, number lines, and base-ten materials. They discussed the process of adding tens to tens and ones to ones. In second grade, we revisit some of these same strategies. Students spend time exploring strategies based on their understanding of place value, rather than memorizing a traditional algorithm for adding 2-digit numbers, because the traditional algorithm focuses on digits and memorized procedures rather than an understanding of the numbers and the process. Students eventually learn the traditional method, but first we focus on helping them understand the process.

Students have experience adding 10 to and subtracting 10 from a 2-digit number. By second grade, their place value understanding allows them to add 10 to a 2-digit number mentally, rather than relying on counting, using hundred charts, or building numbers with manipulatives. Through investigations in first grade, students gained the insight that adding a ten increases the tens digit by one. They are now applying this place value understanding to mentally perform the task.

Posing word problems, so students can explore addition in context, strengthens our students' problem-solving skills. Problem contexts allow students to assess the reasonableness of their answers and gives them repeated exposure to situations in which addition makes sense. Our focus is not just on how to add, but also on when and why we add.

There are multiple strategies for adding 2-digit numbers that are grounded in an understanding of place value and properties of operations. Exploring different ways to add 2-digit numbers provides our students with opportunities to examine methods that work, discuss how they are alike and different, talk about when each might be most effective, and ultimately understand the multidigit addition process more deeply. Some common strategies for adding 2-digit numbers include:

- breaking apart the addends by place value (decomposing), finding partial sums, and then combining them to get the sum
- using open number lines to show the addition process
- compensating by changing one of the addends to simplify the addition process (29 + 54 might be thought of as 30 + 53).

Using these strategies, our students use their understanding of numbers, place value, and properties to find reasonable ways to determine the sum. Students use manipulatives, drawings, and number lines to visualize the addition process as they try the strategies.

DECOMPOSING BY PLACE VALUE

One strategy for 2-digit addition is for students to decompose numbers by place value, then add tens to tens and ones to ones. Once they have found these partial sums, they simply combine them to get the sum (see Figure 6.1). Students might first decompose using manipulatives, later draw sticks and dots, and then transition to simply breaking apart the numbers themselves.

As we pose problems like 35 + 26, students begin to recognize that when they combine the ones, it may add up to more than 10. Using their place value knowledge, they decide when it makes sense to combine (compose) 10 ones as 1 ten.

Adding 2-Digit Numbers

34 + 25 = ____

1. Add the tens.	30 + 20 = 50
2. Add the ones	4 + 5 = 9
3. Add the tens and ones together to find the sum.	50 + 9 = 59

T	O
|||	••••
||	•••••
5	9

Figure 6.1 Students decompose the number and add to find the total.

Adding 2-Digit Numbers
with Regrouping

35 + 26 = ____

1. Add the tens.	30 + 20 = 50
2. Add the ones	5 + 6 = 11
3. Add the tens and ones together to find the sum.	50 + 11 = 61

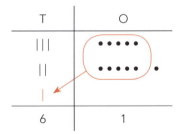

Figure 6.2 Students decompose, add the tens and ones, and then recompose to find the total.

When given more complex problems like 46 + 61, students might notice that they get 10 tens, which can be renamed as 1 hundred. Their place value understandings allow them to make decisions about decomposing and composing numbers. Talking about when each makes sense and asking students to justify their decisions helps them apply their place value understandings to each situation.

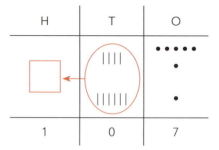

Figure 6.3 Students add the tens, recompose to make a hundred, and then add the ones to find the total.

USING OPEN NUMBER LINES

Showing addition on open number lines allows our students to visualize addition as adding to. Students may need reminders that number lines can begin at any number and that jumps on a number line can be made in ones, tens, or any value they choose. As students record one addend and then break apart the other addend to add it in parts, they are applying their place value understanding (see Figure 6.4). There is not one correct way to decompose or represent the jumps on the number line; as long as students find a starting point (one of the addends) and add all parts of the second addend, the sum will be accurate.

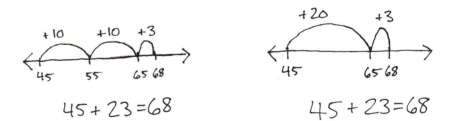

Figure 6.4 Students might begin at 45 on the number line and show adding 23 in different ways as in the figures. Starting at 23 and adding 45 works, too, because the commutative property reminds us that the order of the addends does not affect the sum.

MENTAL COMPENSATION

Some strategies focus on mental math. When considering 28 + 54, what if we simply thought about it as 30 + 52 because that is much easier to do mentally? By adding 2 to one addend and taking 2 from the other addend, we create a simpler task (see Figure 6.5). Now, the computation can be done mentally and doesn't require decomposing into tens and ones, finding the partial sums, and then recomposing the 12 ones to 1 ten and 2 ones. Through number talks, we help our students see how they can use the flexibility of numbers to simplify computations. As long as we take the same amount from one addend that we add to the other, we haven't changed the sum.

$$28 + 54$$
$$(28 + 2) + (54 - 2)$$
$$30 + 52 = 82$$

Figure 6.5 By simply adding 2 to 28 we make a friendlier number, then subtracting 2 from 54 ensures that the sum stays the same.

MULTIPLE ADDENDS

Experiences in which there are more than two addends challenge our students to apply their addition strategies to more complex computations. We continue to emphasize place value understanding but also connect these experiences to the associative property to allow students to add the digits in an order that simplifies the task (see Figure 6.6).

$$26 + 35 + 34$$
$$20 + 30 + 30 = 80$$
$$6 + 5 + 4 = 15 \text{ (I know this because } 6 + 4 = 10 \text{ and } 10 + 5 = 15.)$$
$$80 + 15 = 95$$

Figure 6.6 Students apply their strategies for working with two addends to work with three or four addends. Understanding of the associative property helps them more easily find the sum of three or four numbers; finding the sum of 6 + 5 + 4 as (6 + 4) + 5 leads to seeing the sum as 10 + 5, an easier calculation for many students.

MODELING

Students benefit from using both proportional and non-proportional models to show multidigit addition. Proportional models, such as base-ten blocks, in which the size of 10 unit cubes corresponds exactly to the size of 1 ten rod, enable students to visualize the value of the multidigit numbers, seeing immediately which digits have greater value. As numbers get bigger, however, it can be more difficult to represent them with these models because there is not enough space on place value mats to show large numbers with base-ten materials. Non-proportional models, like number disks, allow students to model larger values in more manageable ways and extend their place value understanding to models in which the size of the disk does not determine its value. Moving to drawings gives students the freedom to create their own models.

MATH IN PRACTICE
Teaching Second-Grade Math

MODULE 6

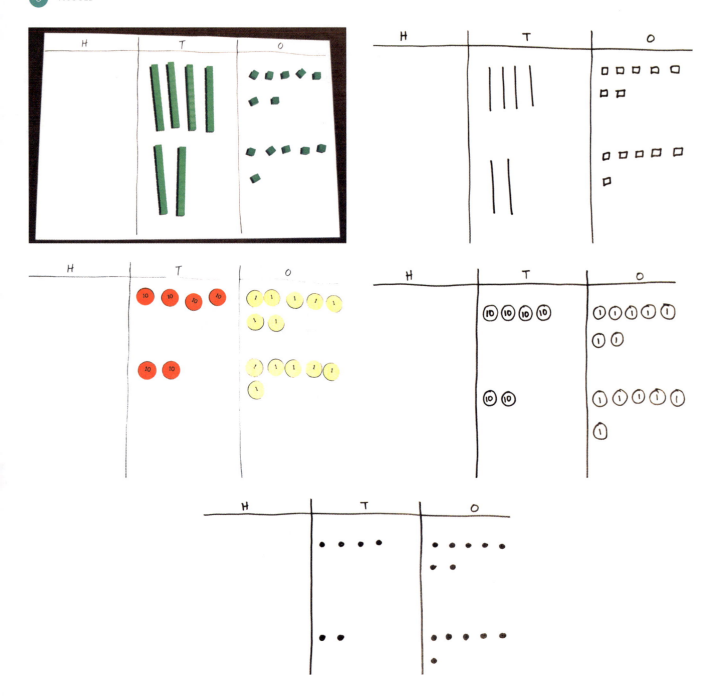

Exploring the Progression

Learning Goals

I can use what I know about place value to add 2-digit numbers.

I can add up to four 2-digit numbers.

PREVIOUS	NOW	NEXT
Grade 1	**Grade 2**	**Grades 2–3**
Adding within 20; adding multiples of 10 to a 2-digit number	Adding 2-digit numbers using place-value-based strategies	Grade 2: Beginning to add 3-digit numbers (see Module 8) Grade 3: Fluently adding within 1,000 using various strategies and place value

Ideas for Instruction and Assessment

USING PLACE VALUE UNDERSTANDING TO ADD 2-DIGIT NUMBERS

These experiences with base-ten materials, number lines, and expanded notation allow students to visualize the addition process and connect place value understanding to the process, building the foundation for understanding 2-digit addition.

Modeling 2-Digit Plus 1-Digit Addition with Base-Ten Blocks *SHOW IT!*

Students use base-ten materials to explore addition with 2-digit and 1-digit numbers, with and without regrouping.

> Provide students with place value mats and base-ten blocks.
>
> Pose the following problem:
>
>> Margo counted 13 red roses in the garden. She also counted 7 pink roses. How many roses did Margo count?
>
> *Retell the problem to your partner. What do you know? What do you need to find out?*
>
> *What could we do to find out how many roses Margo counted?*
>
> *Work with your partner to model this problem with your blocks. Don't solve it yet. Just show what you know about the red and pink roses.*

Circulate as students work, to see if they are able to model the two groups of roses. Then model the situation yourself under a document camera or with digital blocks on an interactive whiteboard.

> *How could you use the blocks to solve the problem?*
>
> *Go ahead and solve it.*

Give time to work. Then invite a pair to come up and use your model to show what they did. Probe their thinking with question such as:

> *What did you do first? What did you do next?*
>
> *How many blocks did you have in all?*
>
> *Did anyone do it a different way?*

The students may have found the sum by counting on or by adding 10 + 10 (thinking about the 7 + 3) to get 20, without regrouping. If you saw a pair that regrouped, have them show what they did. If not, model the process yourself.

> *I have 1 ten and 10 ones. What could I do with the 10 ones? How could I show that with the blocks? What blocks would I have then? Is 2 tens the the same as 1 ten and 10 ones?*
>
> *So how many roses were there?*

Lessons in This Module

Using Place Value Understanding to Add 2-Digit Numbers

Modeling 2-Digit Plus 1-Digit Addition with Base-Ten Blocks

Modeling 2-Digit Plus 2-Digit Addition with Base-Ten Blocks

Drawing Sticks and Dots

Modeling with Number Disks

Drawing Number Disks

Adding with Partial Sums

Adding 2-Digit Numbers on a Number Line

Using Compensation to Add 2-Digit Numbers

Talking About Our Ideas

Adding up to Four 2-Digit Numbers

Exploring Addition with More Than Two Addends

Pose another problem.

> Margo saw some more flowers. There were 26 daisies and 6 tulips in the field. How many flowers were in the field?

Work with your partner. First, tell the problem in your own words.
Then, use your blocks to model the problem and solve it.

Observe and listen to pairs as they model and solve the problem. Facilitate and support as necessary.

What happens if we add our ones?

What should I do with my 12 ones? What is another way to show 12 ones? Are there any ones left over? How many tens do we have now?

So how many flowers were there?

To end the lesson, have students discuss the following with partners and then the class:

Do you think we have to regroup 10 ones for a ten in every problem?
When do you think we would have to make a ten?
When is a time we might not have to make a ten?

Provide additional practice as needed.

> Be sure students understand the term regroup. Ask them to explain what it means to regroup. Be sure they understand that the value is the same (10 ones = 1 ten), but the name is different. That is why we sometimes say we are renaming. Add regroup to your word wall or Math Talk chart.

Modeling 2-Digit Plus 2-Digit Addition with Base-Ten Blocks SHOW IT!

Students use base-ten materials to explore addition with two 2-digit numbers, with and without regrouping.

Provide students with place value mats and base-ten blocks.

Pose the following:

> Rico was having a birthday party. He invited 23 girls and 14 boys. How many children did Rico invite to his party?

Retell the problem to your partner. How is this different from other addition problems we have done?
Use your base-ten blocks to show this problem.
How did you model 23?
How did you show 14?
When you added a 2-digit number and a 1-digit number, what did you do?
How do you think we might add 2-digit numbers? Talk to your partner.
How many tens do we have in all? How many ones?
Did we need to regroup any ones?
Let's try one more. This one is a little different!

> Rico's mom baked cupcakes for the party. She made 24 vanilla cupcakes and 18 chocolate cupcakes. How many cupcakes did she make in all?

Talk to your partner about this problem. How is this problem like the last one we did?

How do you think we will add them?

Using your base-ten blocks, see if you can find the sum of 24 and 18.

Once you have your answer, compare your answer and strategy with your partner's.

Did you get the same answer? If yes, how were your strategies similar or different? If no, work together to find what the mistake was.

Invite students to share their strategies. Check to see if they understand that they combine tens with tens and ones with ones, and whether they are able to regroup the ones correctly.

How many tens do you have when you put them together?

How many ones do you have when you put them together?

What should we do next?

How many tens do you have now? How many ones are left?

How many cupcakes did Rico's mom bake?

> At this introductory level, students should be focused on understanding the process by building and manipulating concrete models. Once students have had multiple experiences using concrete models, they begin to use pictures like sticks and dots to show their work.

Provide additional 2-digit plus 2-digit problems for students to practice. Have students model using their base-ten materials and share their thinking and strategies with their partners.

This is students' first experience with 2-digit addition with regrouping. Be prepared to offer more opportunities for students to explore these ideas with concrete materials before moving to more abstract representations in future lessons.

Have students summarize their learning by talking with partners about the following:

How do we add 2-digit numbers?

Will we always have to regroup the ones?

When do we regroup the ones to make a ten?

What happens to the tens when we regroup 10 ones?

Can you give an example of when we don't have to regroup ones?

Drawing Sticks and Dots

Students represent the expanded form of each number with squares, sticks, and dots similar to what they did with base-ten blocks.

Pose the following problem:

> Collette planted 37 sunflower seeds. Her brother Connor planted 16 marigold seeds. How many seeds did Collette and Connor plant together?

> For additional ideas on building students' problem-solving skills, see Math in Practice: A Guide for Teachers, Chapters 1 and 2.

Retell the problem to your partner. What is happening in this problem? What do we need to find out?

Tell your partner the operation you would use to solve it and why.

Using your base-ten blocks and what you know about place value, add to find out how many seeds were planted.

Be ready to share your answer and your strategy with your partner.

Circulate, observing strategies, and supporting as needed. Have students share their strategies and solutions with partners.

Sometimes we might not have base-ten blocks handy, or we want to show our thinking in our journals. Talk to your partner about how we could represent our addition model using a picture.

Invite students to share their ideas and draw their models. Many students might refer back to sticks and dots that they have used before.

Think about the base-ten blocks that you used to add 37 and 16.

Create a place value mat in your journals. Use sticks and dots to represent the addition.

How can we show the regrouping of the ones?

Share your picture with your partner. How are they similar? How are they different? Does your picture show your thinking?

Pose additional 2-digit addition problems for students to model. Some students may wish to continue using their base-ten blocks and then draw a pictorial model. Other students may be ready to model pictorially without base-ten blocks.

FORMATIVE ASSESSMENT

Give students the following directions:

Draw sticks and dots to show a 2-digit addition problem that would not require regrouping.

Draw sticks and dots to show a 2-digit addition problem that would require regrouping.

Draw sticks and dots to show a two-digit addition problem that would not require regrouping.

Draw sticks and dots to show a two-digit addition problem that would require regrouping.

This student correctly models a problem that does not require regrouping and writes the number sentence 28 + 11 = 39. The student also models a problem that does require regrouping. The student shows a recomposition of 10 ones as a ten. The student writes the number sentence 33 + 49 = 82.

If a student is not able to correctly model these numbers, conduct an interview. Ask the student when we would have to regroup and when it would not be necessary to regroup. Ask what number pairs result in a value of ten or more and need to be recomposed. If a student is having difficulty modeling with sticks and dots, provide base-ten blocks for more hands on practice.

Modeling with Number Disks

Students use number disks to add 2-digit numbers, transitioning from using base-ten materials in which the units are proportional to using more symbolic disks to represent tens and ones.

Copy the ones, tens, and hundreds number disk templates on beige (ones), red (tens), and yellow (hundreds) card-stock paper. Using a 1-inch circle punch, which can be purchased at a craft store, students can punch out number disks to use for models to display on charts or in journals. Teachers might also use a permanent marker to create number disks on circular counters.

Provide students with place value mats and number disks.

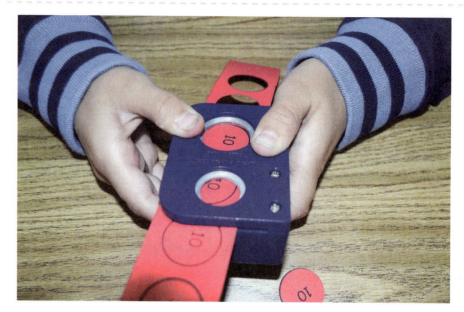

Students use a 1-inch circle punch to punch out number disks to use with various place value activities.

Turn and talk: Where have we used these before?

Talk to your partner about the values printed on the disks. What do they mean? How are they used to represent numbers?

Pose the following problem:

> Mr. Clark's class collected 24 cans for the food drive. They also collected 15 boxes of food. How many items did his class collect?

Turn to your partner and retell the story.

What is the data in the problem and how should we solve it?

How could we use these disks to model the problem? Work with your partner to create a model of the problem with your disks.

Observe pairs as they represent the problem data (24 + 15) with the disks.

If needed, compare the place value disks to base-ten blocks to show how each represents tens and ones. See Module 4 for more on using disks to represent place value.

With your partner, find the sum. Be ready to tell us what you did.

Listen as students solve the problem. Observe to see if they combine ones with ones and tens with tens.

Once students have solutions, ask some pairs to share. Have them demonstrate their work under a document camera or using virtual disks on an interactive whiteboard.

How many items did they collect? How did you figure that out?

How does using the place value mat and the number disks help you?

What is different when we use the number disks instead of base-ten blocks?

Are they the same value?

How are the number disks and base-ten blocks the same?

Write the following equation on the board.

$47 + 36 =$

With your partner, use your number disks to model and solve the equation. Be ready to tell us what you did.

Observe and listen as pairs solve the problem.

What did you notice when you put these two numbers together?

How many ones did you have altogether?

What did you do with all of those ones? Why?

Common Error or Misconception

Students may initially see the 1 and 10 disks as having equal value because they are the same size. Discussions about what it means to represent 1 and 10 are important.

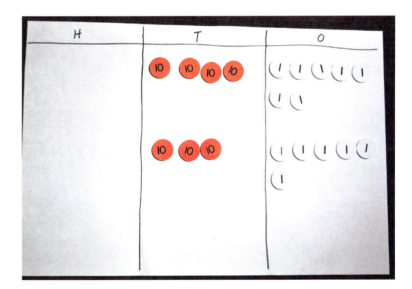

Continue having partners model and find solutions to the following problems. Be sure to discuss their methods and strategies.

37 + 17
28 + 26
37 + 23

Drawing Number Disks

Students use number disks to record their thinking about adding 2-digit numbers.

> Write the following equation on the board:
>
> 47 + 36 =
>
> *Turn and share: What if we didn't have disks? How could you draw a picture to show this?*

Let students share some possibilities and demonstrate them for the class. Be sure to probe their thinking as they do so, asking them to explain why they did what they did. You can also encourage students to ask each other questions about their work. You can give sentence starters such as the following to support discussion:

> *Why did you draw _____?*
> *How did you show _____?*
> *I don't understand _____. Could you say that again?*

Depending on what strategies students show, you may want to use a think-aloud to show the following option.

> *I am just going to draw each number with circles to show the disks.*
>
> *I was thinking I could just circle 10 of the ones. I'll put an arrow to show that they are a ten now. What do you think? Does that show what we did with the disks?*

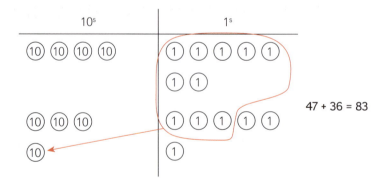

Ask students to find 35 + 27 using a picture of the disks.

Then, have them share their pictures with a partner.

> *How did drawing disks help you show your thinking?*

FORMATIVE ASSESSMENT

Give the following directions:

> 28 + 54 = ___
>
> Solve, using a picture model of sticks and dots.
>
> Solve, using a picture model of number disks.

Understanding Multidigit Addition

MODULE 6

If you had to choose which model you would use, what would it be? Why?

28 + 54 =
Solve using a picture model of sticks and dots.

Solve using a picture model of number disks.

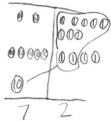

If you had to choose which model you would use, what would it be? Why?

I would choose sticks and dots because it takes less time to draw.

Thinking Through a Lesson

SMP1, SMP2, SMP4, SMP7

Adding with Partial Sums SHOW IT!

Students use expanded form to decompose 2-digit numbers, so they can add tens to tens and ones to ones.

> Provide students with place value cards.
>
> Pose the following:
>> 23 cats at the animal shelter are waiting to be adopted. There are also 14 dogs at the shelter. How many cats and dogs are waiting to be adopted?
>
> *Retell the problem to your partner.* (Dogs and cats are waiting to be adopted, and we need to find out how many there are.)
>
> *What equation would we use?* (23 + 14, because there are 23 cats and 14 dogs.)

See Module 4 for more on expanded form.

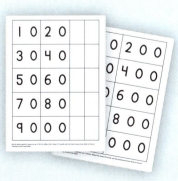

Record *23 + 14* on the board.

Using your place value cards, show the two addends.

As you show the numbers, tell me about the number 23. How many tens are there? How many ones are there? (2 tens and 3 ones.)

How would we write it in expanded form? (23 is 20 + 3.)

Tell me about the number 14. How would we write it in expanded form? (10 + 4.)

What would it look like if we added these two numbers together? What parts of the numbers should we add? (We can add tens to tens and ones to ones.)

We call this partial sums, *because we are finding the sum of the tens and the sum of the ones before we find the whole sum.*

> Students should make connections to previous work with expanded form, decomposing numbers into tens and ones.

Record the word *partial sum* on the word wall or Math Talk chart.

Does it matter what we put together first? (No; we just have to put all the parts back together to find the sum.)

Show 23 as 20 + 3 and 14 as 10 + 4.

$$23 + 14$$
$$20 + 3 \quad 10 + 4$$

How many tens do we have if we put 2 tens and 1 ten together? (3 tens.)
So what is 20 + 10? (30.)

> Using color helps to clarify the place value connections.

$$23 + 14$$
$$20 + 3 \quad 10 + 4$$
$$20 + 10 = 30$$

How many ones do we have if we put 3 ones and 4 ones together? (7 ones.)

Turn to your partner and decide if we need to regroup our ones to make a ten. Be sure to justify your thinking. (No; 7 is less than 10, so there aren't enough ones to regroup.)

How much do we have if we add 3 + 4? (7.)

$$23 + 14$$
$$20 + 3 \quad 10 + 4$$
$$20 + 10 = 30 \quad 3 + 4 = 7$$

Do we know how many dogs and cats need to be adopted? (Not yet; we need to add 30 + 7.)

$$23 + 14$$
$$20 + 3 \quad 10 + 4$$
$$20 + 10 = \boxed{30} \quad 3 + 4 = \boxed{7}$$
$$30 + 7 = 37$$

> For first experiences, showing addition equations in horizontal form allows students to focus on place value. In some cases, however, a vertical format helps students organize their notations and visualize the process in a different way. The goal at this level is not to perform a standard algorithm but to build an understanding of using place value to add 2-digit numbers. It is not necessary for all students to show their thinking in the same way.

Alternate way of recording the process:

$$\begin{array}{r} 23 = 20 + 3 \\ +\underline{14 = 10 + 4} \\ 37 = 30 + 7 \end{array}$$

Direct students back to the problem.

How many cats and dogs are waiting to be adopted? (37.)

Does our answer make sense? Why or why not? (Yes, because it is more than 23 and it is more than 10 more, so it makes sense that it is in the thirties.)

Pose the following:

37 + 18 =

Have students work with partners to solve the problem using expanded form.

Have them show the way they decomposed and recomposed the numbers to find the sum.

> These lesson ideas may be spread across several days to give students time to process the ideas and practice the procedure.

Have them share their solutions and explain their methods.

How does your understanding of expanded form help you to add? (When you expand a number, you can add tens to tens and ones to ones.)

Is there anything you found tricky?

> Asking students what confused them, what was hard, or where they got stuck helps us determine their confusions and figure out ways to support them as they make sense of multidigit addition.

FORMATIVE ASSESSMENT

Option 1 (no regrouping)

52 + 34 =

Use expanded form to decompose (break apart) the numbers, and then add to find the sum.

50+2   30+4

50+30=80   2+4=6

80+6=86

This student correctly expands both numbers, combines tens with tens, and ones with ones. The student then combines the tens and the ones to find the total.

Option 2 (with regrouping)

56 + 38 =

Use expanded form to decompose (break apart) the numbers, and then add to find the sum.

50+6   30+8

50+30=80   6+8=14

80+14=94

This student correctly expands each number and then combines accurately.

Adding 2-Digit Numbers on a Number Line SHOW IT!

Students explore the process of addition with an open number line model, using their understanding of place value to determine the jumps on the line.

> Have students draw a number line or provide students with a number line template.
>
> *Show 25 and 36 on your number line. Share your number line with a partner. How are your number lines the same? How are they different?*
>
> Observe students as they place the numbers on an open number line. Invite students to share their number lines with the class. Select students who used different start and end points, to reinforce the idea that there are different ways to represent numbers on the number line.
>
> *What number did you start your number line with? Explain.*
> *How did you know which number was greater?*
> *Where did you place the number with greater value?*
> *Where would zero be on your number line?*
>
> Pose the following:
>
>> The pet store sold 35 goldfish on Monday. They sold 40 more goldfish on Tuesday. How many goldfish were sold in all?
>
> *Turn to your partner and talk about what is happening in the problem.*
> *Work with your partner to see if you can find a way to show 35 + 40 using a number line. Be ready to tell us what you did.*
>
> Observe pairs as they think about ways to model addition on the number line. Select some students to share their ideas. Ask questions related to their work.
>
> *Why did you start your number line at 30 (or 35 or 25)?*

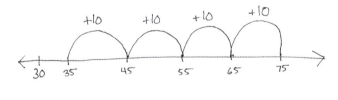

> *Tell us about your jumps. What do they represent?*
> *Why did you find the number 35 first and then show jumps?*
> *I see that Brody showed 4 jumps of 10, but Carlos showed one jump of 40. Does that make sense? Explain.*
> *Do those show equal values?*

Understanding Multidigit Addition — MODULE 6

Although using open number lines may not be a strategy that students rely on for long, consider the benefits of exploring this strategy. Students visualize the addition process, practice decomposing numbers based on place value, see that different decompositions equal the same amount on the line, revisit the commutative property, and discover another way to model the addition process.

Differentiation

Students will most likely be able to draw their own number lines, but you may wish to have templates available for students who need them.

Select students whose work shows key ideas you want to explore and discuss, like the number they chose to begin their number line, the way they showed jumps for addition, or the order of the addends.

> *Kimberly, why did you start with 40 and then show jumps that total 35?*
>
> *Does it matter which addend we started with?*

Pose the following problem. Have students solve individually using a number line, and then share with a partner before discussing with the class.

> Keiko and Paula bought some paper. Keiko bought 20 sheets of paper. Paula bought 54 sheets of paper. How many sheets of paper did they buy?

> *Does it look the same? If not, what's different? Did you get the same answer? See if you can figure out the way your partner added.*
>
> *What number did you choose to start with? Why?* (I chose 20 because it is first. Or, I chose 54 because I only have to do two jumps of 10 or one jump of 20.)

After students have had an opportunity to talk with partners, have them share some ideas with the class.

> *Did we all use the same jumps? Did we get the same answer?*
>
> *Which way did you think was easiest for this problem? Why?*

Pose the following problem for students to solve and discuss.

> My brother collects toy cars. He has 37 on the shelf and 23 in a box. How many does he have in all?

> *Show this using a number line.*

Observe to see if any students move from 37 to 40 by adding 3, and then add 20 more. If so, use their example. If not, you can introduce it as another possible strategy or pose it as "a student last year did it this way."

> *Turn and share: Why might you add 3 to 37?*

Show both examples (jumping 3 first and jumping 20 first) so students can see that the sum is the same.

> *If you break 23 into 20 + 3, does it matter which one you add first?*

Give a few more problems to do with partners.

> *Share your solution with your partner.*
>
> *Do you have the same solution?*
>
> *Did you choose to show it the same way on your number line?*
>
> *If your work looks different, what is the same and different about your work?*

Sidebar:

This discussion allows them to think back on commutative property, remember that the order doesn't matter, and choose a number to start with that makes the most sense to them.

Differentiation

The first expressions had a 2-digit number and a multiple of ten. This example requires students to show ones on the number line. Some students may need more experience with simpler addends, while others are ready to explore more complex addition.

The jumps students use on a number line are flexible. Some students will notice that adding 3 to 37 will take them to 40, allowing for easier addition of the 20. Other students may choose to add the tens first, going from 37 to 47 to 57, and then adding on 3 to get 60.

FORMATIVE ASSESSMENT

Give the following directions:

> Show two different ways to add 28 + 36 using a number line.
>
> Why do both ways get the same answer?

Understanding Multidigit Addition

MODULE 6

> *[Student work showing two number lines:]*
> *First number line: +10, +10, +10, +6 hops from 28 → 38 → 48 → 58 → 64*
> *Second number line: +10, +10, +8 hops from 36 → 46 → 56 → 64*
> *Written explanation: "Beacuse its just swiching thir places."*

This student shows a number line starting at 28, with hops to show skip counting by tens to 38, 48, 58 and then adding 6 to get to 64. The student also shows a number line starting at 36 and hopping to 56 with 2 tens and 8 more to get to 64. The student identifies that he used the commutative property (he switched their places), which would result in the same answer.

If a student does not get 64, consider her number line and the hops that she used. If a student is not able to show a second way, conduct an interview. Ask if the hops must start with 10. Can you hop in a different order? What if you start with the other number?

Using Compensation to Add 2-Digit Numbers

Students think about ways to adjust numbers in order to add them mentally.

Put the following on the board:

29 + 25

Turn to a partner and talk about:
How might you solve this?
Could you do this in your head, without base-ten blocks or even without paper and pencil?
How might you do it?

Listen as students discuss their ideas, listening for students who might be thinking of making the numbers friendlier (e.g., changing 29 to 30). Call on one of those students to share. If no one has the idea, think aloud to share the strategy.

> Compensation can be difficult for some students who are very concrete thinkers, but it is a very important mental math skill and one that is commonly used to simplify mental math tasks. The understanding that numbers are flexible, and that adding to one simply means we take away from the other, allows students to simplify addition tasks. Rather than solving 29 + 25 by decomposing the numbers into tens and ones, then renaming a ten from 14 ones, then putting the tens and ones back together again, students simply solve 30 + 24.

How could you make these numbers easier to work with?

Is 29 close to any number that is easier to think about?

Have students share ideas, then below the *29*, write *30*.

Why would 30 be easier to add to?

We call 30 a friendly number because it is easy to think about and work with.

If we add 30 + 25, will we get the same answer as if we add 29 + 25?

What could we do to fix that and still keep our friendly number? Turn to your partner and share some ideas.

Listen as students discuss. Students may struggle with this idea initially, but that struggle leads to important understanding, so it is important to give students time to wrestle with the idea. If a student comes up with the idea of taking one away from the other addend, invite that student to share; if not, you can introduce the idea.

What did we do to the 29 to get 30?

If you add 1 to a number and then take 1 away, what do you get?

So I was thinking, maybe we could take away 1 from 25 and that would work. Do you think so? Talk about it with your partner.

So if I take 1 from the 25, what would it be? (24.)

Below the *25*, write *24*.

Now what is our equation?

Would that be easy to add?

> Some students benefit from a concrete model of this. Use base-ten blocks or place value disks to model moving a one from one number to the other.

$$29 + 25 = 54$$
$$(+1) \quad\quad (-1)$$
$$30 + 24 = 54$$

What did you do to turn 29 to 30? What did you do to turn 25 to 24?

Use another strategy to solve the problem with blocks, disks, or a number line. Do you get the same answer?

Would it work if we added 2 to one number and subtracted 2 from the other number? Could we do it with any number?

Pose the following equation:

38 + 23

Talk to a partner. See if you can make this easier to do in your head.

Have students try it and then explain their thinking as you record their ideas on the board (e.g., add 2 to 38 and subtract 2 from 23).

Turn and talk: Is it okay to add to a number to make it easier to work with? Explain what you need to do to make it work.

Talking About Our Ideas

This number talk allows students to use their place value understandings to come up with inventive ways to add 2-digit numbers.

Pose the following:

48 + 32 =

Turn and share: How might you solve this problem?

Circulate around the room, listening to students' discussions.

After students have had a few minutes to share their thinking with partners, begin a class discussion with students explaining their methods as you record their ideas on the board.

Look for partners that showed some of the following approaches:

Add tens, add ones
40 + 30 = 70; 8 + 2 = 10; 70 + 10 = 80

Move some to make tens
48 + 2 = 50; 32 − 2 = 30; 50 + 30 = 80

Add on tens and then add the ones
48 + 30 = 78; 78 + 2 = 80

As students share, consider questions like:

How are you using your understanding of place value?
Why does your strategy make sense?

Other expressions for number talks:

25 + 7
42 + 12
35 + 17
67 + 48

To end the lesson, have students share these ideas with partners and then the class:

What is something important to remember when adding 2-digit numbers?
Is there one right way to do it?

> Listen for students using base-ten language. Rather than saying, "4 plus 3 equals 7," say, "4 tens plus 3 tens equals 7 tens" or "40 plus 30 equals 70." This promotes a deeper understanding of the value of each digit.

> Students who are struggling with their understanding might benefit from number talks with simple expressions, like 25 + 4 or 25 + 7. Recording sticks and dots on the board as they explain strategies, or showing the strategies with base-ten materials, helps them visualize the process. For students who would benefit from enrichment, consider number talks with more complex problems, in which they have to regroup both ones and tens.

Additional Ideas for Support and Practice

The following ideas extend students' understanding of adding 2-digit numbers and provide meaningful practice.

Domino Addends

Students pick two dominoes at random.

They use the dominoes to make 2-digit numbers (e.g., they pick a domino that shows 2 and 6 and make 26 or 62).

Students add the two 2-digit numbers, using any method they choose.

Partner Option

The students each pick two dominoes and add to find the sum of the 2-digit numbers they create.

The player with the greater sum wins the round.

Spinning for Sums

Option 1

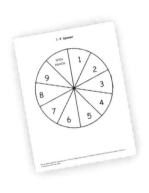

Students take turns spinning a 1–9 spinner and placing the digit anywhere they want on their board.

Tens	Ones

They keep placing numbers in the boxes until both partners have filled the top two rows of the board with tens and ones (four spins each).

Each player then adds to find the sum.

The player whose sum is greater wins the round.

Option 2

Challenge: The player whose sum is closer to 50 wins.

Digit Card Addition

Students draw four cards from a deck of digit cards.

The cards are laid out to form two 2-digit numbers.

Students use these numbers to add.

The student with the greater sum wins the round, then students pick different cards and play again.

Talk About It/Write About It 😊📝

Explain how to add 25 + 47.

Liam says that when you add 45 + 21 on a number line, you have to start at 45. Do you agree or disagree? Justify your answer.

Carmen says that she added 48 + 16 by changing it to 50 + 16. Will she get the right answer? Explain why or why not.

ADDING UP TO FOUR 2-DIGIT NUMBERS

Once students understand the process of adding two 2-digit numbers, they are challenged to find the sum of up to four addends.

Exploring Addition with More Than Two Addends

Students add three 2-digit numbers and connect to their understanding of the addition process.

Give each student a dry erase board. Have tools such as base-ten blocks or number disks available, if needed by some students.

Pose the problem:

Jeremy had 3 bags of candy. How many pieces of candy did he have?

Bag 1—15 pieces
Bag 2—24 pieces
Bag 3—15 pieces

Talk to your partner about the important information in this problem.
How is this problem different from other problems we have done?
Could we use some of the same strategies that we know? Talk to your partner about some ways we could solve this problem.

Circulate, listening to students' ideas. Ask students to think of at least two strategies they could use.

Have pairs share their thinking with the whole class until a variety of possible methods have been identified (e.g., draw a model, add tens and ones, partial sums, open number lines).

Does it matter which numbers we add together first? Why or why not?

Talk about adding tens and ones.

What if we put our tens together first? What could that look like?
Who did it a different way?
Who can tell us how to add the ones?
Now what do we need to do?

Pose the following:

The local pet store has fish for sale. The following chart shows the type of fish and how many the pet store has.

Goldfish	26
Guppy	32
Rainbow Fish	14
Tetra	28

How many fish does the pet store currently have?

Talk to your partner about the important information in this problem.

How is this problem different from the first?

What are some different strategies you could use to solve this?

Invite students to share their strategies. As they do, encourage the class to compare the strategies. Do they see how the strategies relate to each other? Are they thinking flexibly with the numbers? Encourage good listening and productive discussion practices as students share.

To end the lesson, ask:

How is adding three or four 2-digit numbers the same as adding two 2-digit numbers?

How is it different?

What could you do to make it easier?

> Some students might choose to add two sets of fish, then add those totals together. Other students might choose to combine ones and tens separately and may notice the groups of tens that can be made from the ones. The important thing is that students apply what they know about adding, place value, and the associative property to help them find the solution.

FORMATIVE ASSESSMENT

Pose the following:

The table shows how many pennies each person has.

Heather 31	Bob 23	Sue 24	Sean 17

How many pennies do they have in all?

Show or tell how you got the answer.

$$30 + 20 + 20 + 10 = 80$$

$$1 + 3 + 4 + 7 = 15$$
         5   10

$$\begin{array}{r} 80 \\ +15 \\ \hline 95 \end{array}$$

This student decomposes each number into tens and ones. She shows that 30 + 20 + 20 + 10 = 80. The student shows a making-ten strategy by combining 3 and 7. The student also adds 1 + 4 to get 5 and then combines it with the 10 to make 15. Finally, the student combines the 8 tens (80) with the 15 ones to make 95.

> If a student does not correctly solve this problem, consider the model that was used. If the student used place value models, was each number modeled correctly? Did the student recompose 10 ones as a ten? Some students may forget to include the newly recomposed ten. Ask the student what happens when the 10 ones move over to the tens place. How many tens are there now? If the student used expanded form, were numbers correctly expanded? Were all tens added and all ones? How did the student combine the total of tens and ones? If the student used a number line, check to see if hops were accurate. Support students with additional practice using place value models.

Additional Ideas for Support and Practice

The following ideas extend students' understanding of adding more than two 2-digit numbers and provide meaningful practice.

A Fair Bear Share

Provide students with a place value mat and number disks or base-ten blocks.

Before Reading:

Do you like pie? What is your favorite pie?
We are going to read a story about some bear cubs who love pie.
Listen for what they need to make the pie.

During Reading:

Read *A Fair Bear Share* by Stuart J. Murphy.

After Reading:

Have students use their place value tools to model the addition of the nuts, berries, and seeds.

How many nuts, berries, and seeds are needed to make the pie?

Have students share their methods for finding the solution.

Spinning for Sums

Option 1

Students take turns spinning a 1–9 spinner and placing the digit anywhere they want on their board.

Vocabulary

addend regroup
partial sums sum

ONLINE RESOURCES

General Resources

0–9 Digit Cards

1–9 Spinner

Additional Problems

Number Disks

Open Number Line Template

Place Value Cards

Place Value Mat

These resources are available at http://hein.pub/MathinPractice, keycode MIPG2.

Tens	Ones

They keep placing numbers in the first four rows of boxes until both partners have filled their board with tens and ones (8 spins each).

Each player then adds to find the sum and records it in the last row.

The player whose sum is greater wins the round.

Variation: The player whose sum is less wins the round.

Option 2

Challenge: The player whose sum is closest to 100 wins.

TALK ABOUT IT/WRITE ABOUT IT

When adding four numbers, explain why we can add them in any order.

What strategies can you use when adding three or more numbers together?

MODULE 7

Understanding Multidigit Subtraction

About the Math   2.NBT.B.5; 2.NBT.B.9

As we teach 2-digit subtraction, our focus is on helping our students understand the subtraction process and find strategies to subtract 2-digit numbers. When done correctly, our traditional approach to 2-digit subtraction always yields the right answer, but it is not easy for students to understand. Although it is efficient, it focuses on digits and memorized procedures rather than an understanding of the numbers. They will eventually learn the traditional method, but first we help them understand the process.

> The key ideas focused on in this module include:
> - using place value strategies to subtract 2-digit numbers, using different methods (e.g., open number lines, expanded form) to visualize the subtraction process
> - understanding when regrouping is necessary and using place value understanding to regroup, or rename, numbers.

In first grade, students subtracted ten from any 2-digit number and subtracted multiples of ten from multiples of ten. They visualized the subtraction process with manipulatives, number lines, and hundred charts. By second grade, our students' place value understanding allows them to subtract ten from a 2-digit number mentally, rather than relying on counting backward, using hundred charts, or building numbers with manipulatives.

DECOMPOSING NUMBERS

Students' experiences with place value help them see that tens should be subtracted from tens and ones from ones. To find 63 − 42 (Figure 7.1), we simply subtract 60 − 40 = 20 and then 3 − 2 = 1, combining the results to find the difference of 21.

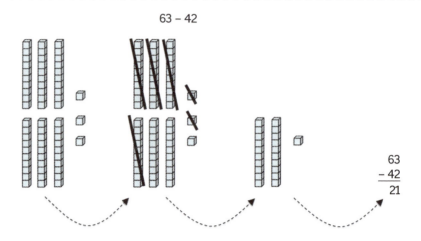

Figure 7.1 Subtracting 42 from 63 does not require regrouping.

But that becomes complicated when the equation is 63 − 45 = n, because simply subtracting tens from tens and ones from ones is less clear. In first grade, students explored place value and talked about ways to decompose a 2-digit number. 63 can be thought of as 6 tens and 3 ones (see Figure 7.2), but might also be thought of as 5 tens and 13 ones (see Figure 7.3). This could be very helpful in this subtraction situation, because it allows us to subtract ones from ones more easily. With this renaming based on place value understanding, the subtraction becomes clear again (see Figure 7.4).

Tens	Ones

Figure 7.2 63 is shown as 6 tens and 3 ones, or 60 + 3.

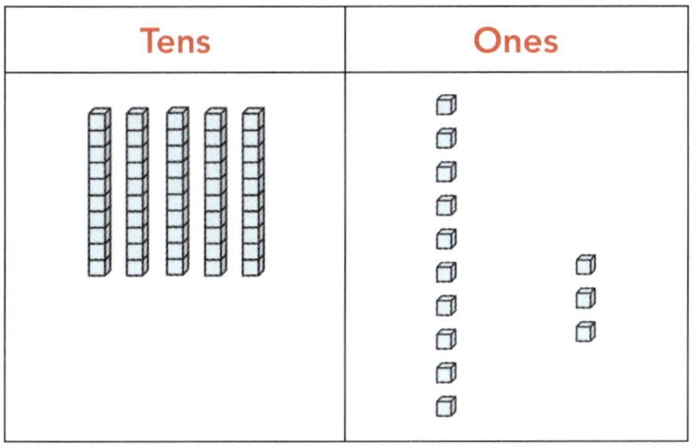

Figure 7.3 63 is renamed as 5 tens and 13 ones, or 50 + 13.

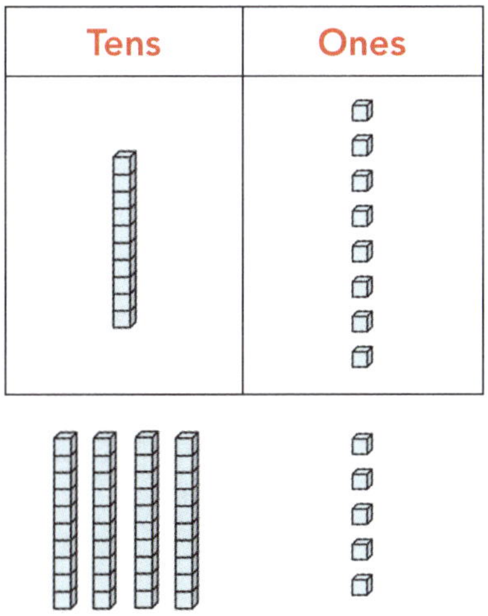

Figure 7.4 Subtraction is shown, with 45 being removed from 63.

Students first visualize this process with manipulatives and then, having internalized the ideas, are able to do the renaming without them. They use their place value understanding to find differences, rather than following rote steps.

COMPENSATION

We have always praised the standard algorithm for being the most efficient way to subtract, but is it? It may be easier to find a difference by just thinking about friendlier numbers. When subtracting 75 – 49, we might use compensation to simplify the task.

Compensation is built on the idea that differences remain constant, but starting and ending points can change. The difference between 9 and 16 on a number line is the same as between 10 and 17, even though the endpoints have changed or shifted. Figure 7.5 shows finding the difference between 75 and 49. The subtraction is immediately simplified by adding 1 to both endpoints (which does not change the difference between them). Now we are finding 76 – 50, which is much easier to solve mentally. This mental math process can be difficult for students to grasp, but using a number line can help students visualize it. The goal is not for students to draw number lines each time they compensate; it is for them to visualize and then internalize the mental math process. With practice, this skill becomes a very efficient way to solve many subtraction problems, and one that many of us use in everyday settings.

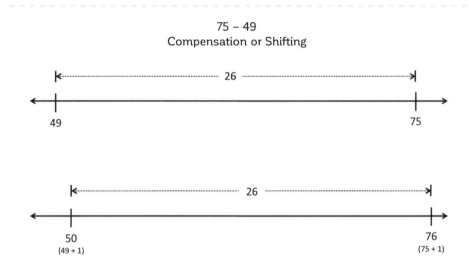

Figure 7.5 By adding 1 to each number, the subtraction is simplified.

Figure 7.6 shows a different example of compensation, this time with the problematic task of subtracting with a zero. We can simplify 70 – 42 by taking 2 from 70 and 2 from 42. Now the expression is 68 – 40, allowing us to subtract without worrying about the zero.

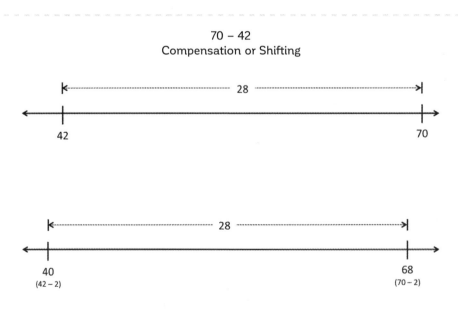

Figure 7.6 This adjustment simplifies the subtraction problem.

OPEN NUMBER LINES

Number lines can help students visualize the subtraction process. Consider these possibilities for showing 72 – 46.

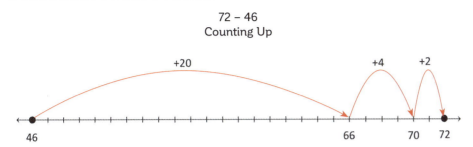

Figure 7.7 Subtraction is the difference between two numbers. Given the choice, many students prefer to count up using friendly numbers. Beginning with 46, we jump 20 to 66, then jump 4 to 70, and then jump 2 to our ending point of 72. We then add the three jumps, 20 + 4 + 2, to find a difference of 26.

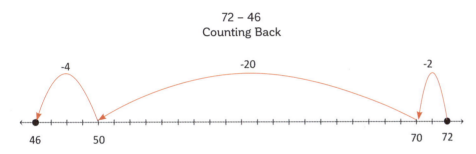

Figure 7.8 Students can find the difference between 72 and 46 by starting at 72 and counting back to 46. The jumps are flexible, with some students jumping 2, then 20, then 4, while others might decide to jump back 10, then 10, then 2, then 4. The difference will be the same.

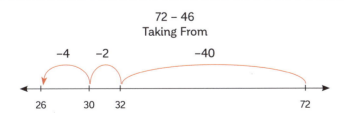

Figure 7.9 Many students think of subtraction as taking from. Beginning at 72 and taking 46 away can also be shown on a number line. Again, the way in which numbers are broken apart is flexible.

Exploration with varied strategies helps our students gain a deeper understanding of numbers and the subtraction process. Students may not master every strategy, but each strategy holds important ideas about numbers that extend our students' understanding and provides more options for computations. As students gain confidence, they may develop preferences for some strategies over others.

We give our students a strong foundation for computational fluency when we choose classroom tasks that encourage them to visualize subtraction with number lines, base-ten materials, drawings, and equations, when we encourage discussions about how strategies work, and when we connect the strategies to big ideas about subtraction. And by exploring subtraction computations through problems, students continue to deepen their understanding of when to subtract and refine their problem-solving skills.

Exploring the Progression

PREVIOUS	NOW	NEXT
Grade 1	Grade 2	Grades 2–3
Fluency with subtracting within ten; exploring subtracting within 20; subtracting multiples of ten from multiples of ten	Subtracting 2-digit numbers with and without regrouping	Grade 2: Exploring subtraction with 3-digit numbers (see Module 9) Grade 3: Subtracting multidigit numbers

Learning Goal
I can use what I know about place value to subtract 2-digit numbers.

Lessons in This Module

Subtraction Without Regrouping
Decomposing Numbers
Subtracting within 100 Using Base-Ten Models
Subtracting within 100 Using Number Disks
Subtracting Using Expanded Form

Subtraction with Regrouping
Decomposing to Subtract
Decomposing Using Number Disks
Subtracting Using an Open Number Line
Subtracting Using Compensation

Ideas for Instruction and Assessment

SUBTRACTION WITHOUT REGROUPING

Students have modeled the process of adding 2-digit numbers, and now explore the subtraction process using similar models. The initial focus is on problems that do not require regrouping.

Decomposing Numbers SHOW IT!

Students use base-ten blocks to explore decomposing numbers.

Pose the following number bond:

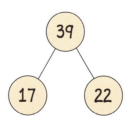

Turn to your partner and talk about what this shows.
Can a number bond show both addition and subtraction? Explain.

> *What addition equations does the number bond show?*
>
> *What subtraction equations does the number bond show?*
>
> *Our number bond shows one way to break apart, or decompose, 39 into 2 parts.*

Give students some base-ten blocks and a blank number bond template (large enough to place the blocks in the sections).

> *Use your blocks to show me 39 as the whole.*

Observe students as they place 3 tens and 9 ones on their number bond.

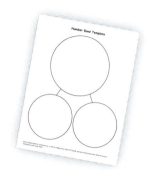

> *How did you show it? Why?*
>
> *Can you find another way to break 39 into two parts? Explore a possibility with your partner.*
>
> *Show it with blocks on your number bond.*
>
> *Then, decide on the subtraction equations that show how you broke 39 into two parts.*
>
> *Be ready to share.*

After they have come up with possible solutions, invite partners to share their ideas with the class.

Record possibilities horizontally (e.g., *39 − 17 = 22, 39 − 22 = 17*).

> *How did you find your solutions? What did you do to find two parts?*
>
> *Is that what everyone did?*
>
> *Did we get all of the possible solutions?*
>
> *Why did you have two subtraction equations for each of your number bonds?*
>
> *Let's use number bonds to model a problem.*

Pose the following:

> Casey's mom made 48 cookies for a party. She decided to make 16 of the cookies chocolate chip. The rest were sugar cookies. Use your place value models to show the problem and to find out how many sugar cookies she made.

> *Turn to your partner and talk about the important information in this problem.*
>
> *What are we trying to find out?*
>
> *How could you use your number bond and base-ten blocks to help you solve it?*

Give students time to work this out either independently or with a partner. Invite students to share their thinking, using the models.

168 MATH IN PRACTICE
Teaching Second-Grade Math

7 MODULE

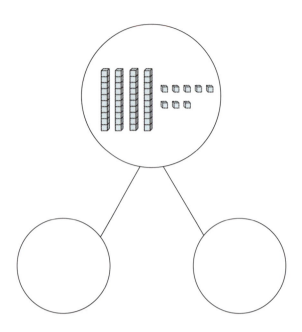

Tell us what you did with your base-ten blocks.
Why did you move 16 to one part?
How many were left to go into the other part?

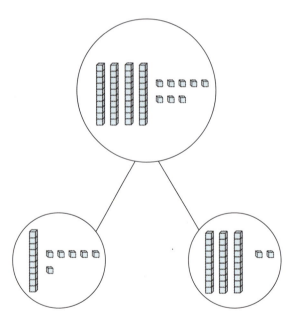

What does the 32 represent?

Pose the problem:

> If Casey's mom had to make 48 cookies, and she wanted to make both chocolate-chip and sugar cookies, what are some other possible combinations she could make?

Provide students with time to use their base-ten blocks and number bonds to find possible solutions and then share with others at their tables.

This open-ended task can be used as an extension or for all students. There are many possible solutions. This problem shows a context for the type of decompositions they did at the start of the lesson, when they were decomposing 39 in several different ways.

For additional practice, have students pick a problem (see the online resources) and solve it with a model and equation.

To end the lesson, have students answer the following question in their journals:

How does a number bond represent subtraction?

> **Differentiation**
> As most students are working on practice problems, pull a small group of students who need additional support. Guide them as they try the practice problems, asking frequent questions to build understanding: "What does your model show?" "What subtraction equation matches this problem?" "What do the numbers represent?"

FORMATIVE ASSESSMENT

Pose the following problem:

> Martin read 37 books over the summer. Some were fiction and the rest were autobiographies. Draw a number bond and base-ten models to show three different possibilities for the number of fiction and autobiographies Martin read.

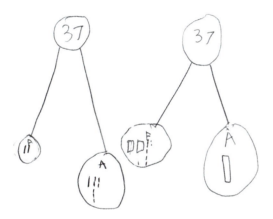

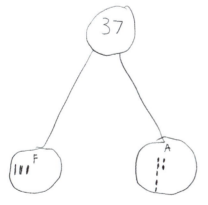

This student shows 37 written as the whole. Although the models drawn are small, the student accurately draws sticks and dots showing 37 as 20 and 17, 27 and 10, and 30 and 7. If you have any questions about the model, interview the student and ask what the pictorial model shows.

> If students cannot represent the number bonds pictorially, have them model with base-ten blocks first. Ask, "How many books did Martin read? How can we show 37 using our base-ten blocks? What's one way we can break 37 apart? Can you think of a different way?"

`SMP4` *Thinking Through a Lesson*

Subtracting within 100 Using Base-Ten Models

Students use base-ten blocks to explore subtraction problems and discuss their strategies.

Provide students with base-ten blocks and a place value mat.

Pose the following problem:

> Tanya had a box with 75 nails. She used 42 of the nails to build a shelf. How many nails does she have left?

Turn and tell your partner, in your own words, what is happening in this problem.

Listen to their retellings of the problem.

What do you know about these numbers? What do they represent? (75 is what she had altogether, or what she started with; 42 is what she used.)

What is happening to the nails? (They are being taken away.)

Subtraction can be thought of as taking away.

How might we use base-ten blocks to show this? (We can show 7 tens and 5 ones; we can take away 4 tens and 2 ones.)

With your partner, solve this problem with base-ten blocks. Talk out loud about what you are doing and why you are doing it.

Circulate, listening, observing, and supporting as needed. Have students share their solutions and how they used the base-ten blocks.

Common Error or Misconception

When students work on this task, they may mistakenly represent both the 75 nails Tanya had as well as the 42 nails she used. It is important for students to understand that they will represent the whole, and remove one part to show the other part.

As with addition, encourage students to use unit vocabulary to deepen their place value understanding. In other words, rather than saying, "Seven minus four equals three," say, "Seven tens minus four tens equals three tens," or "Seventy minus forty equals thirty."

Initially, we start with subtracting the tens first and then ones because that is how we read numbers—left to right. Once we begin introducing problems that require regrouping, we can start asking students if they can begin with subtracting the ones digits. We want them to gain the insight that they could subtract in either way, but sometimes one way may be easier than the other.

Understanding Multidigit Subtraction

MODULE 7

How did you use your understanding of tens and ones to solve this? (I know I can add tens to tens and ones to ones, and I can do the same with subtraction.)

Talk to your partner about a way you can record what you've done in your journal using a picture. Show what you did and be ready to tell us about it.

Invite pairs to share their models. Model recording the subtraction number sentence as *75 – 42 = 33*.

Repeat the discussions with several more examples of 2-digit subtraction that do not require regrouping, having students model the problems with base-ten blocks and record their results in their journals.

56 – 32 =
47 – 25 =
68 – 50 =

To end the lesson, have students discuss this question with partners:

Why do we take ones from ones and tens from tens? (Because tens and ones are different. *Or,* You have to take tens from tens, then you know how many tens are left, and the same with ones.)

> Students might draw 75 using sticks and dots, and cross out 4 tens and 2 ones or a similar representation.

> Recording the problems horizontally, rather than rushing to the vertical format associated with the standard algorithm, keeps the focus on understanding.

FORMATIVE ASSESSMENT

Have students draw a picture of base-ten blocks and write an equation to show how to solve the following problem.

> Elliot found 57 shells at the beach. He decided to give some of them to his sister. If Elliot kept 32 shells, how many shells did he give to his sister?

This student models 57 – 32 using sticks and dots but makes a mistake, subtracting 33 instead of 32. Interviewing the student would help you determine whether he simply miscounted or has a more fundamental misunderstanding.

> If a student is unable to model using a drawing, provide base-ten blocks. Ask:
>
> *How many shells did Elliot find?*
> *How can we show 57 using base-ten blocks?*
> *Do we know how many he gave to his sister? How can we find out?*
> *How many shells did Elliot keep? How can we use our base-ten blocks to model that?*
>
> Provide the student with additional time to work with base-ten blocks to model subtraction. If a student is not able to write a number sentence, ask:
>
> *What number tells us how many shells Elliot found?*
> *What number tells how many he kept?*
> *What symbol do we use for subtraction?*

Subtracting within 100 Using Number Disks

Students will relate their understanding of place value to subtraction. They will explore subtraction concepts, using number disks to show their thinking.

Provide students with a place value mat and number disks.

Pose the following:

> Ashika saved 85 dollars. She spent 24 dollars to buy her brother a birthday present. How much money did Ashika have left?

Tell your partner about this problem.
What type of mathematical situation are we focused on? Why?
On your work mat, show how much money Ashika started with.
Share your thinking with your partner.
Talk about how you might show the money Ashika spent.

Circulate, listening, observing, and supporting. Ask pairs place-value-related questions, focusing on taking ones from ones and tens from tens. Bring students together and have pairs share their thinking.

How could we show this in our journals?

Invite students to help create a pictorial representation as a whole group and in their journals.

What would your picture look like?
What number did you show with your place value disks?
How did you show the 24 dollars?
What is left?
Who thinks they can write a number sentence to model our math?

For more on money skills, see Module 12.

Understanding Multidigit Subtraction

173

MODULE **7**

Pose more examples for students to do in their journals independently, with a partner, or in a small group. Students should represent their thinking with number disk models on their place value mats, then draw a representation in their journals and connect it to a number sentence. As students finish, have them share their thinking with a different partner for each problem.

    52 – 32 =

    75 – 13 =

    97 – 42 =

Have students reflect on the lesson by discussing the following with partners:

How is subtraction with number disks similar to subtraction with base-ten blocks?

What are some key place value ideas that we should remember when subtracting?

Was there anything that made this challenging?

Do you prefer working with base-ten blocks or number disks? Why?

> **Differentiation**
> Whole-class questioning and discussion will surface challenges that students might have, and can be targeted as needed in a small group. Some students may need additional support modeling using place value. Others may need reminders to only take tens from tens and ones from ones.

> 52 – 32 might raise some interesting conversation about the 0 ones.

FORMATIVE ASSESSMENT

Give students the following directions:

> Show how you could use number disks to show 76 – 43. Write a number sentence that goes with your model.

This student accurately models 76 using number disks. The student crosses out 4 tens and 3 ones. The student does not write a subtraction sentence, but does identify the difference as 33.

> If a student is unable to draw number disks to accurately solve this task, offer manipulatives. Ask:
>
> *Which number tells the whole? How do we model this?*
> *How many tens are there? Ones?*
> *How much is being taken away? How can we show this?*
> *How much is left?*
>
> If a student does not write a subtraction sentence, ask them how they might write a sentence to go with their model.

Subtracting Using Expanded Form

Students use their understanding of expanded form to subtract tens from tens and ones from ones.

See Module 4 for activities that support students' understanding of expanded form.

Pose the following:

> Luke picked 56 strawberries. He ate 21 of them. How many strawberries did Luke have left?

Retell this problem to your partner.
How many strawberries did Luke start with?
Can you represent the number 56 in expanded form? What about 21?

Invite students to share their thinking.

Talk with your partner about how we can use expanded form to subtract.

Circulate, listening for discussion about subtracting tens from tens and ones from ones. Invite students to share their ideas as you record.

$50 + 6$ and $20 + 1$
$50 - 20$ and $6 - 1$
$30 + 5 = 35$

How does subtracting with expanded form relate to the work we did with our place value models?
What is the same? Different?

Differentiation
Some students may still need base-ten blocks or number disks to support their thinking around expanded form.

Pose another example for students to tackle with a partner or independently. Circulate and support as needed.

$79 - 37$

Turn to your partner and tell them how to expand 79 and 37.
Then talk about how you could use those answers to help you subtract.

Have students work in pairs to do more examples.

Use a question such as the following to close the lesson:

How does our understanding of place value and expanded form help us when we subtract?

Additional Idea for Support and Practice
The following idea extends students' understanding of subtraction without regrouping and provides meaningful practice.

TALK ABOUT IT/WRITE ABOUT IT

Solve 48 – 25. Explain how you did it.

How could you use your knowledge of 2-digit addition to check your 2-digit subtraction?

SUBTRACTION WITH REGROUPING

Students have modeled the process of subtracting 2-digit numbers in varied ways, and now explore subtraction problems in which regrouping is necessary. Again, our focus is on deep conceptual understanding, not writing and recording using a standard algorithm.

Decomposing to Subtract

As students become more comfortable with 2-digit subtraction that does not require regrouping, we can move deeper to problems that require decomposition.

Provide students with base-ten blocks and a place value mat.

Pose the following:

Silas had 42 golf balls. He hit 15 of them. How many golf balls does Silas have left?

Talk to your partner about the important information.
Use your base-ten blocks to model this problem.
What number will you show?
Do you show both the 42 and 15? Why not?

Observe as students try to solve the task. Allow students time to be challenged with their thinking, but bring the class back together in order to address confusion and refocus their thinking. Some students may apply their place value understanding and think about trading tens for ones, but many may not.

What happened? Why are you looking confused?
Does anyone have an idea of how we could solve this?
Is there a way we could change 42 so we would have enough ones to subtract 5?
Talk with your partner and see if you can come up with a way to do this.

Don't tell students the way to solve the problem; give tips or ideas for them to consider and then have them work with partners again.

Watch and listen as they share ideas.

Who can tell us what you did to be able to subtract?

The goal is for students to apply their place value understanding that a ten can also be thought of as 10 ones. Students have experienced decomposing numbers in different ways and should be familiar with the concept that 42 can also be thought of as 3 tens and 12 ones. Refer students back to previous place value learning if needed.

Common Error or Misconception

With problems like 42 – 15, students often just subtract 5 – 2 for the ones digits without considering which number is being subtracted.

When we exchange a ten for ones, we call this decomposing *or* regrouping.

Write *decompose* and *regroup* on the word wall or Math Talk poster.

How does decomposing 40 help you?

How many ones do you have now?

Do we have enough ones to subtract 5?

Talk to your partner about how 4 tens and 2 ones relates to 3 tens and 12 ones.

As students arrive at a solution, invite them to create a number sentence that communicates their thinking.

Pose the following:

    70 − 41 =

Use your base-ten blocks to model this subtraction situation.

What number will you model?

How can we subtract 41?

I notice there are no ones in the number 70. How can I subtract the ones?

Is 7 tens the same as 6 tens and 10 ones? Explain your thinking to your partner.

Have students use their manipulatives to model the subtraction. Invite students to draw visual models and discuss the connections between the model, the blocks, and the number sentence.

Provide students with additional opportunities to subtract with decomposing, using base-ten blocks, drawing pictures, and writing their equations horizontally.

    61 − 49 =
    35 − 17 =
    80 − 34 =

Use these prompts for exit tickets or student reflections:

How were these subtraction problems different from the ones we've been doing?

Do we always need to decompose a ten or regroup?

How do we know when to decompose a ten?

Can you give an example of when we would need to decompose a ten to subtract?

Can you give an example of when we would not need to decompose a ten?

Remember that the focus in second grade is on building the meaning of decomposing tens and not on the algorithm. For this reason, students should record their number sentences horizontally.

Common Error or Misconception

Students might forget to remove a ten from their mat and just put 10 ones on. Remind students to make that trade, so that they still have 70 and not 80.

Common Error or Misconception

Some students may believe they will always have to decompose to subtract. Have students sort examples into groups of problems that do and do not require decomposing.

FORMATIVE ASSESSMENT

Have students show how they would subtract 72 – 38 using decomposition.

Watch to see if students realize that they need to trade a ten for 10 ones and are able to make the trade correctly. If they do not, provide additional guided practice using questions such as:

Are there enough ones to subtract?
How could you get more ones?

Decomposing Using Number Disks SHOW IT!

Students continue to explore subtraction with decomposing tens as ones, and transition to using number disks to model their thinking.

Pose the following:

The Bears scored 62 points at the basketball game. The Knights scored 47 points. How many more points did the Bears score than the Knights?

Have students retell the problem and identify the type of situation and the important information before solving.

What number would you represent? Why?
Talk to your partner about how you could use number disks to model the problem.
How will you model the subtraction?
Does this pose any problems?
Does anyone have an idea on how we can get enough ones to subtract?

Circulate, listening, observing, and supporting as needed. As students arrive at a solution, have them share their thinking.

Was there anything we needed to do before we could subtract?
How does decomposing a ten help you?
Did we still have 62 after decomposing?

Pose the following:

Terry and Mary both solved the following problem but got different answers. Who is right and who is wrong? What mistake do you think happened?

Terry	Mary
64 – 27 = 43	64 – 27 = 37

Have students represent the problem with their number disks. Invite students to share their thinking with the class.

Who do you agree with?
What mistake do you think Terry made?

> Remind students to use precision when talking about their thinking: "12 ones minus 7 ones equals 5 ones," "5 tens minus 4 tens equals 1 ten."

Pose additional problems that require students to decompose to subtract. Students can use their place value mats and number disks, and can also transition to a pictorial model using number disks and writing their number sentences horizontally. They can share their thinking with different partners as they finish.

To end the lesson, ask students to discuss questions such as these:

Why do we need to decompose?

What happens to our tens place when we decompose?

What happens to our ones place?

Do we still have the same number?

How can we check?

FORMATIVE ASSESSMENT

Pose the following problem:

Caleb solved 73 − 27 = __.

He said the answer is 56. Do you agree with Caleb? Why or why not? Explain your thinking.

Look for students showing evidence to support that Caleb was incorrect because 73 − 27 = 46. Students might show their computations or a model to justify their thinking. Some may explain Caleb's mistake.

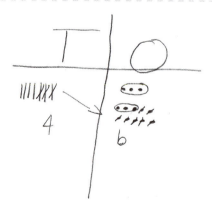

This student shows 73 using sticks and dots. She shows that 73 can be recomposed as 6 tens and 13 ones. She crosses out 2 tens and 7 ones to find the difference of 46. She states that she does not agree with Caleb because she has 4 tens and 6 ones left.

> If a student does agree with Caleb, observe the student's work. Did the student show the decomposition of 1 ten as 10 ones? Did the student cross out 2 tens and 7 ones? Conference with the student to determine where the misunderstanding is. Ask:
>
> *How can we decompose 73?*
>
> *How many tens do we need to take away?*
>
> Provide the student with additional practice subtracting with number disks or base-ten blocks.

Subtracting Using an Open Number Line SHOW IT!

Students have used an open number line to add 2-digit numbers and now explore the same model to show the subtraction process.

Pose 24 + 13 = ____.

How do we use a number line to add these?

What are some tips for using open number lines to add?

Pose 37 − 13.

How could we use a number line to show subtraction?

Work with a partner to solve 37 − 13 using a number line. Record the equation to show your answer. Be ready to tell us what you did.

Have them show and explain their thinking.

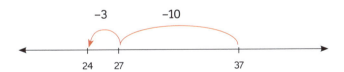

37 − 13 = 24

This model shows subtracting a ten and 3 more to get to 24.

> Some students may begin with 37 and jump back 13, while others might start at 13 and jump to 37. These actually show two different subtraction models—one is taking away, the other is finding the difference.

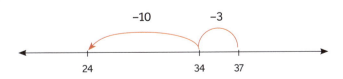

37 − 13 = 24

This model shows subtracting 3 first and then a ten to get to 24.

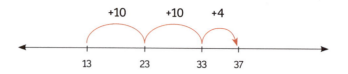

$$10 + 10 + 4 = 24$$

This model shows counting up from 13 by adding 2 tens and 4 more for a total of 24.

Continue with other numbers:

56 − 21

47 − 25

Pose the following:

47 − 28

Talk to your partner. What makes this problem a little more challenging? How can we make it easier?

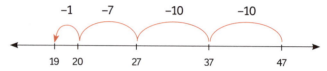

$$47 − 28 = 19$$

Are there ways we could count up?

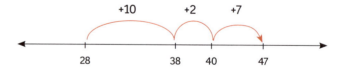

$$10 + 2 + 7 = 19$$

Did anyone think about it a different way?

One possible answer is shown below.

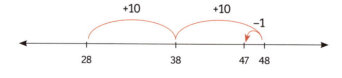

$$10 + 10 − 1 = 19$$

Have students help you make a list of tips for using number lines to subtract.

Subtracting Using Compensation

Students adjust numbers in order to subtract them mentally.

> Desiree picked 50 apples. 23 were red and the rest were green. How many green apples did Desiree pick?

Talk with your partner about this problem.

Why is 50 – 23 hard?

How could we make it easier so that we could do the math in our head?

Listen to all student ideas. If no one suggests compensation as a strategy, ask:

What if Desiree only picked 22 red apples, making her total 49? How did I change those numbers?

Record (–1) under the 50 and 23, showing the new values 49 and 22.

$$50 - 23 = \underline{}$$
$${\scriptstyle(-1)}{\scriptstyle(-1)}$$
$$49 - 22 = \underline{}$$

Can you subtract mentally now? Talk to your partner.

$$50 - 23 = \underline{\ 27\ }$$
$${\scriptstyle(-1)}{\scriptstyle(-1)}$$
$$49 - 22 = \underline{\ 27\ }$$

Have students check using another method.

How does this method work?

Create a number line showing the difference between 23 and 50. Use the same number line to model the difference between 49 and 22. Have students discuss what they notice.

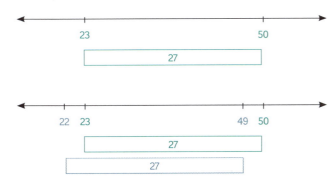

Provide students with additional examples of subtraction from a multiple of 10.

    70 – 34

    40 – 17

    80 – 65

Pose 63 − 29.

This one doesn't have a starting number that ends in zero, but we still have to regroup.

Is there a way we could change these numbers to make them easier to work with?

Listen to student thinking.

Could we add 1 to both numbers? How would they change?

Turn to your partner and tell them how you could subtract in your head now.

63 − 29 = 34

(+1)   (+1)
64 − 30 = 34

Have students check using another method.

Again, model using a number line to show the difference between 63 and 29 as well as the difference between 64 and 30.

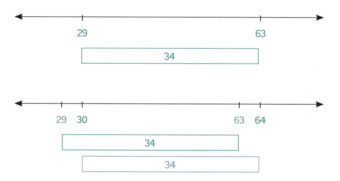

Provide students with additional problems in which they could compensate using a friendlier number.

52 − 19
71 − 38
85 − 49

Additional Ideas for Support and Practice

The following ideas extend students' understanding of subtraction with regrouping and provide meaningful practice.

TO DECOMPOSE OR NOT TO DECOMPOSE

Write various subtraction problems on index cards. Students sort the index cards into problems that require decomposing tens to subtract and problems that do not. Students can create a chart in their journals. For example:

Problems that require regrouping	Problems that do not require regrouping
72 − 35 =	64 − 21 =
46 − 29 =	76 − 40 =
50 − 16 =	89 − 37 =
63 − 44 =	47 − 15 =

Talk About It/Write about it

What does it mean to decompose or regroup a ten? How does it help you to subtract?

Ginger said the answer to 45 − 18 is 33. Is Ginger right? If you agree with her, explain how you found your answer. If you disagree with her, explain what error Ginger made.

Focus on the Question

These Focus on the Question prompts reinforce addition and subtraction with 2-digit numbers. Post the data for a week and ask a different question each day. The goal is for students to determine how they would solve the problem, not jump straight to an answer. Have students talk with partners to retell the problem, identify data that is needed to solve it, and formulate a plan for solving it.

The Egg Hunt
Central Elementary School had an egg hunt.
Number of Eggs Found
Liam—28
Molly—19
Malik—33
Addison—32
Carlos—25

1. Liam and Addison put their eggs in a basket. How many eggs were in the basket?
2. Carlos gave 18 of his eggs to a friend. How many did he have left?
3. How many more eggs did Malik find than Carlos?
4. Molly's sister gave her 12 more eggs. How many does she have now?
5. Malik found 24 pink eggs. The rest of his eggs were blue. How many blue eggs did he find?

Roll and Subtract

Students roll dice to generate two 2-digit numbers. They subtract the lesser 2-digit number from the greater one to find the difference. Players compare their differences. The lesser difference wins each round.

For more on the Focus on the Question technique, see Math in Practice: A Guide for Teachers, Chapter 2.

Vocabulary
compare	regroup
decompose	rename
difference	whole
part	

General Resources
Additional Problems
Number Disks
Place Value Mat

Resources for Specific Activities
Number Bond Template

These resources are available at http://hein.pub/MathinPractice, keycode MIPG2.

ONLINE RESOURCES

MODULE 8

Extending Understanding of Multidigit Addition

About the Math 2.NBT.7

As second graders become more comfortable with adding 2-digit numbers and have had sufficient time to build a deep understanding of the regrouping process, they are ready to extend their knowledge to 3-digit numbers. Continuing with the structure of adding ones to ones and tens to tens, we now add hundreds to hundreds.

> The key idea focused on in this module is:
> - adding 3-digit numbers, using an understanding of place value.

As students transition to adding larger numbers, we revisit the concepts and strategies that we discussed with 2-digit numbers, including:

- decomposing numbers by place value, finding partial sums, and combining to find the total
- open number lines to show the addition process
- compensation to change numbers to friendlier numbers to simplify the task.

By exploring and discussing varied strategies, our students continue to deepen their understanding of the addition process.

Earlier in second grade, students investigated adding 100 to a 3-digit number by building a number with concrete materials, like base-ten blocks, adding 100 to the model that was built, and then recording the new number. As our students observed the numbers they recorded, they gained insights that allowed them to predict what 100 more than a number would be, until they no longer relied on the manipulatives.

Through these investigations, students gained the insight that adding 100 increases the hundreds digit by one, allowing them to perform the task mentally.

Students continue their experiences with multidigit addition, with representational manipulatives once again an essential part of their experiences. As our students use the proportional base-ten blocks to add 3-digit numbers, they begin to notice how quickly the numbers increase as we add. This is an important experience, because the size of numbers often gets lost as students begin to use a standard algorithm if there is not sufficient focus on the value of the digits they are adding. As the hundred flats become more cumbersome to manipulate, students often realize the value of using smaller, non-proportional number disks.

> See Module 4, page 86, for more on this topic.

DECOMPOSING BY PLACE VALUE

Students now decompose 3-digit numbers into expanded form and then add hundreds to hundreds, tens to tens, and ones to ones. From their experiences with 2-digit numbers, they recognize that there will be times when they need to recompose, or rename, 10 ones to be 1 ten, and now 10 tens to be 1 hundred (see Figure 8.1). Students use manipulatives, make drawings with squares, sticks, and dots, and then transition to using numbers alone.

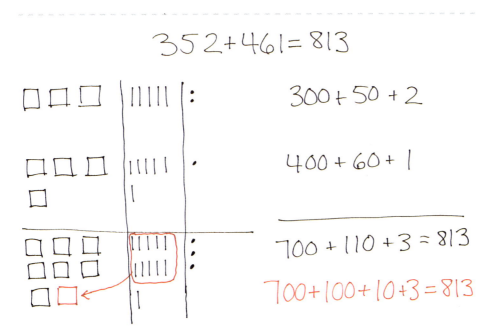

Figure 8.1 Students might use drawings or expanded form to show their thinking as they find the sum.

Students begin to notice that in some situations they need to recompose, or rename, both ones (as tens) and tens (as hundreds) (see Figure 8.2). They also apply their growing place value skills as they find that some sums have 10 hundreds, or 1 thousand.

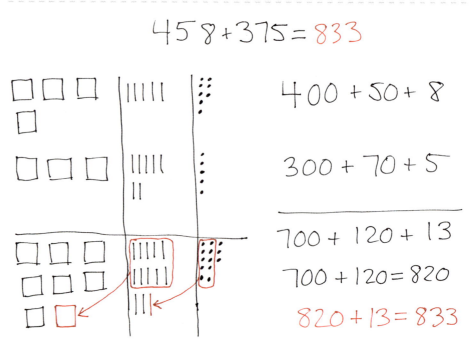

Figure 8.2 Students show regrouping through models and expanded form as they find the sum of 458 + 375.

OPEN NUMBER LINES

Open number lines allow students to visualize addition as *adding to*. As students work with 3-digit numbers, their number lines have different starting points than when they worked with 2-digit numbers, and jumps may have greater value, but the process remains the same. Students record one addend, then break apart the other addend to record the addition in parts (see Figure 8.3). There are varied ways to decompose the number—different jumps to represent on the number line—but as long as students start at one of the addends and add all parts of the second addend, the sum will be accurate. Reminding students that the order in which they add numbers does not change the sum (the commutative property) helps this idea make sense.

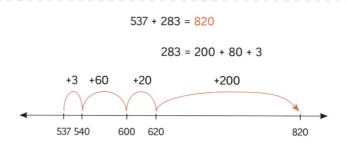

Figure 8.3 Students might choose to first add 3 to make the number friendlier (540), then add 60 to reach 600, then add 20, and then add the remaining 200 to find the sum of 537 + 283 using a number line.

COMPENSATION

Compensation, or shifting the addends to friendlier numbers, simplifies many computations. When posed 539 + 232, we might shift the addends to 540 + 231 (see Figure 8.4). By adding 1 to the first addend and subtracting 1 from the second addend, the expression becomes simpler to solve with no regrouping needed. Talking about our thinking as we explore these strategies, and asking our students to share the ways they adjust the addends, helps our students learn to use numbers flexibly.

$$539 + 232 = \underline{}$$
$$(+1) \quad (-1)$$
$$540 + 231 = \underline{771}$$

Figure 8.4 Students adjust the numbers to make them friendlier, eliminating the need for regrouping.

Compensation is a useful strategy for both addition and subtraction, but the adjustments are different: In addition, the amount taken from one addend must be added to the other, while in subtraction, the same amount must be added to or subtracted from both numbers. Visualizing the strategies with manipulatives or number lines helps students understand why the approach is different.

DISCUSSING STRATEGIES

Discussions about each strategy are an integral part of each math lesson. Asking students to explain how they found the sum, to defend their answer, or to defend their choice of strategies challenges them to choose thoughtfully and allows us to see and assess their thinking. Routinely having students turn and share their processes with partners offers them opportunities to share their thinking and hear the thinking of others, and provides us with important formative assessment data to determine our next teaching steps.

Exploration with varied strategies that focus on place value and making friendlier numbers helps our students gain a deeper understanding of numbers and the addition process. Students may not master every strategy, but each strategy holds important ideas about numbers that extend their understanding and provide more options for computations. As students gain confidence with certain strategies, they may develop preferences for some over others. Understanding varied approaches lays the foundation for working with standard algorithms.

We give our students a strong foundation for computational fluency when we choose classroom tasks that encourage them to visualize addition with number lines, base-ten materials, drawings, and equations, when we encourage discussions about how strategies work, and when we connect the strategies to big ideas about addition and place value. And by exploring addition computations through problems, students continue to deepen their understanding of when to add and refine their problem-solving skills.

Learning Goals

I can add 3-digit numbers using an understanding of place value.

I can use and explain varied strategies for adding 3-digit numbers.

MODULE 8

Lessons in This Module

Using Place Value Models to Add 3-Digit Numbers

- Adding within 1,000 Using Base-Ten Blocks or Number Disks
- Adding Using Partial Sums
- Adding Using Partial Sums with Regrouping
- Using Open Number Lines to Add 3-Digit Numbers
- Using Compensation to Add 3-Digit Numbers

Exploring the Progression

PREVIOUS	NOW	NEXT
Grades 1–2	**Grade 2**	**Grades 3–4**
Building place value understanding to 1,000; adding 2-digit numbers	Exploring adding 3-digit numbers using place value strategies	Grade 3: Fluently adding within 1,000 using place value strategies Grade 4: Fluency with traditional addition algorithms

Ideas for Assessment and Instruction

USING PLACE VALUE MODELS TO ADD 3-DIGIT NUMBERS

Students extend their understanding of place value and adding 2-digit numbers to begin adding 3-digit numbers.

SMP3, SMP4, SMP5, SMP8

Thinking Through a Lesson

Adding within 1,000 Using Base-Ten Blocks or Number Disks SHOW IT!

Students apply their understanding of adding 2-digit numbers to adding 3-digit numbers. Students have used both base-ten blocks and number disks, and apply their knowledge of both to adding 3-digit numbers.

Materials: place value mat for each student, toolbox that includes base-ten blocks, number disks, and paper and a pencil for each pair

Pose the following:

> The animal shelter keeps a record of the adoptions of cats and dogs. Last year, 397 cats and 245 dogs were adopted. How many animals were adopted last year?

Turn to your partner and retell this problem in your own words.

What operation would you use to solve this? (Addition.) *Why?* (We are finding the total of the cats and dogs adopted.)

We've added 2-digit numbers before. What are some things we need to remember when adding 2-digit numbers? (Add tens to tens and ones to ones. Or, If we have more than 9 ones, we make a ten.)

What's different about this problem than others we've done in the past? (This one has 3-digit numbers.)

What do you think we will have to do when adding with hundreds? What strategy can you apply to adding 3-digit numbers? (We add hundreds together, tens together, and ones together. Or, We might have to recompose.)

Have one partner use base-ten blocks and the other use number disks.

Have students work independently on solving the problem, then share their thinking with their partner.

> Facilitate a conversation about putting ones with ones, tens with tens, and now hundreds with hundreds. Students should also apply their understanding of regrouping 10 ones as a ten to regrouping 10 tens as a hundred.

Compare your model with your partner's model.

Did you get the same answer? (Yes.)

How was your thinking similar? (We both combined hundreds with hundreds, tens with tens, and ones with ones.)

Bring the class together to discuss students' strategies for adding the 3-digit numbers. Encourage students to use place value language.

Put your thumb up if you had to compose 10 ones to make a ten. Why? (7 + 5 = 12; there were 12 ones; we had enough ones to make a ten.)

Put your thumb up if you had to compose 10 tens to make a hundred. Why? (9 tens plus 4 tens plus 1 ten is 14 tens.)

Do we always have to compose ones for a ten? When might we not have to do it? (No; if we have fewer than 10 ones, we don't need to make a ten.)

Do you think you will always have to compose 10 tens to make a hundred? Tell your partner your thinking. (No; if we have fewer than 10 tens, we don't need to make a hundred.)

Have students show their solutions in their journals with a model and an equation.

Have partners trade their manipulatives.

> Keeping the addition equation horizontal keeps the focus on place value understanding, rather than an algorithm.

Pose the following:

472 + 241 =

About what will the sum be? Explain your prediction. (It will be about 700, because it is about 500 and about 200. Or, It will be about 750 because it is about 500 and about 250.)

Do you think you will need to compose ones to make a ten? Compose tens? Turn and tell your partner.

Use your tools to solve this problem, then compare your sum with your partner's.

Do you agree with each other? Disagree? Why?

Differentiation

Differentiation of tools is important to build a solid understanding of skills. Some students may make a quick transition from the concrete base-ten blocks to the more abstract number disks, and from the drawn dots to the standard algorithm. Learners should be comfortable with using whatever representation will best support their thinking around the regrouping processes.

Have students show their solutions in their journals with a model and an equation.

As students use place value materials to add, they can physically combine ones, tens, and hundreds, and better visualize when to compose.

Differentiation

Although the goal for second grade is addition within 1,000, some students may need to spend more time with addition to 100 (see Module 6). A solid foundation of 2-digit addition, with concrete and pictorial representations, is essential.

Pose additional problems for practice. Allow students to choose whatever manipulative they prefer.

383 + 149 =

444 + 486 =

507 + 386 =

To end the lesson, have students reflect on questions such as the following:

How is adding 3-digit numbers like adding 2-digit numbers?

What are some important things to keep in mind when we add multiple digits?

How do our base-ten blocks and number disks both show our thinking?

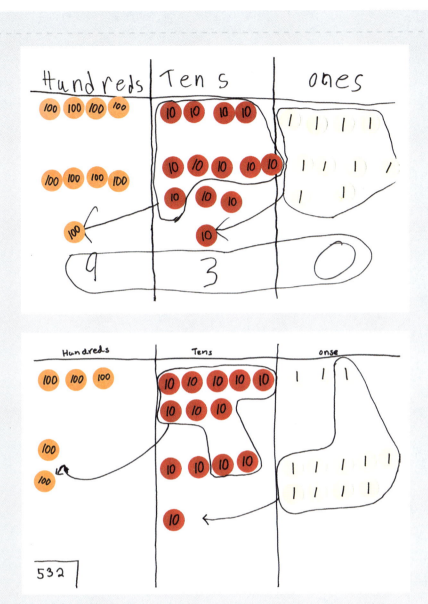

Students use number disks to model the problems 444 + 486 = 930 on the top and 383 + 149 = 532 on the bottom. In both cases, they show composing tens and hundreds.

FORMATIVE ASSESSMENT

Pose the following:

> Mark and Gary built 3-digit numbers using base-ten blocks.
> Mark showed 2 hundreds, 5 tens, and 12 ones.
> Gary showed 3 hundreds, 13 tens, and 6 ones.
> How much do Mark and Gary have altogether?
> Show your thinking with pictures and numbers.

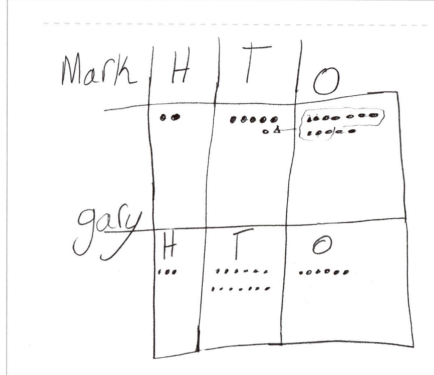

This student correctly models Mark's and Gary's 3-digit numbers. She combines the ones that Mark had to make a ten. She does not complete the task and does not identify how much Mark and Gary have altogether. Conduct and interview with her and ask, "What is the goal of this task? How will we find the answer? What happens when we combine the ones? Tens? Hundreds? Do we need to recompose anything?"

Adding Using Partial Sums

Students use expanded form to decompose 3-digit numbers, so they can add hundreds to hundreds, tens to tens, and ones to ones.

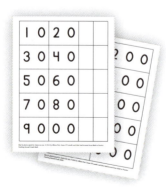

Provide students with place value cards. These cards show numbers 0–9, 10–90, 100–900, and 1,000–9,000.

Pose the problem:

> Jane is playing a digital game. To get to the next level, Jane needs 800 coins. If she already has 372 coins and she collects 426 more coins, will she have enough for the next level?

Retell the problem to your partner. What are we being asked to find out?

Turn and tell your partner an estimate. About how many coins will she have?

Work with your partner and use your place value cards to model the problem.

As you show the number 372 with place value cards, what do you notice?

How many hundreds are there? How many tens are there? How many ones are there?

How would we write it in expanded form?

What about the number 426? How would we write it in expanded form?

What would it look like if we put these two numbers together? What parts of the numbers should we put together?

Does it matter what we put together first?

After we combine our hundreds, tens, and ones, what do we do?

Show 372 as 300 + 70 + 2 and 426 as 400 + 20 + 6. As students explain their methods, show each step on the board.

> Using color helps students distinguish between the steps.

$$372 + 426$$
$$300 + 70 + 2 \quad 400 + 20 + 6$$

How many hundreds do we have if we put 3 hundreds and 4 hundreds together?

What do we have if we put 300 + 400 together?

$$372 + 426$$
$$300 + 70 + 2 \quad 400 + 20 + 6$$
$$300 + 400 = 700$$

How many tens do we have if we put 7 tens and 2 tens together? What number is that?

Turn to your partner and decide if we need to recompose our tens to make a hundred. Be sure to justify your thinking.

$$372 + 426$$
$$300 + 70 + 2 \quad 400 + 20 + 6$$
$$300 + 400 = 700 \quad 70 + 20 = 90$$

How many ones do we have if we put 2 ones and 6 ones together?

Turn to your partner and decide if we need to recompose our ones to make a ten. Be sure to justify your thinking.

$$372 + 426$$

$$300 + 70 + 2 \qquad 400 + 20 + 6$$

$$300 + 400 = 700 \qquad 70 + 20 = 90 \qquad 2 + 6 = 8$$

Do we know how many coins Jane has collected?

$$372 + 426$$

$$300 + 70 + 2 \qquad 400 + 20 + 6$$

$$300 + 400 = \boxed{700} \qquad 70 + 20 = \boxed{90} \qquad 2 + 6 = \boxed{8}$$

$$700 + 90 + 8 = 798$$

Below is an alternate way of recording the process:

$$\begin{array}{r} 372 = 300 + 70 + 2 \\ + \underline{425 = 400 + 20 + 6} \\ 700 + 90 + 8 \end{array}$$

Direct students back to the problem.

How many coins did Jane collect?

Does Jane have enough coins to move to the next level? Why or why not?

Pose the following:

236 + 422 =

Have students work with partners to solve the problem using expanded form.

Have them share their solutions and explain their methods.

Provide additional practice as needed.

To end the lesson, have students answer this question in their journals:

How does your understanding of expanded form help you to add?

Adding Using Partial Sums with Regrouping

Students use their understanding of place value and expanded form to decompose and add 3-digit numbers in problems that require regrouping.

Pose the following:

> The first grade classes donated 237 cans of food for the food drive, and the second grade classes donated 492 cans of food. How many cans of food did they donate together?

Have students retell the problem and decide on an operation and an equation. Then have them use expanded form to solve it.

Observe as students work, paying close attention to what they do to combine their partial sums.

Have them share their solutions and explain their methods.

As students share how they found the partial sums for the hundreds, tens, and ones, show the process on the board, highlighting each step.

$$237 + 492$$
$$200 + 30 + 7 \qquad 400 + 90 + 2$$
$$200 + 400 = 600$$

$$237 + 492$$
$$200 + 30 + 7 \qquad 400 + 90 + 2$$
$$200 + 400 = 600 \qquad 30 + 90 = 120$$

$$237 + 492$$
$$200 + 30 + 7 \qquad 400 + 90 + 2$$
$$200 + 400 = 600 \quad 30 + 90 = 120 \quad 7 + 2 = 9$$

What did you do once you added the hundreds, tens, and ones?

Was anything interesting about doing that? Was anything different than what we have done before? (We had hundreds in two places. Or, We had 600 and 120.)

$$237 + 492$$

$$200 + 30 + 7 \qquad 400 + 90 + 2$$

$$200 + 400 = \boxed{600} \quad 30 + 90 = \boxed{120} \quad 7 + 2 = \boxed{9}$$

$$600 + 120 + 9$$

So what did you do?

$$237 + 492$$

$$200 + 30 + 7 \qquad 400 + 90 + 2$$

$$200 + 400 = \boxed{600} \quad 30 + 90 = \boxed{120} \quad 7 + 2 = \boxed{9}$$

$$600 + 120 + 9$$

$$700 + 20 + 9 = 729$$

> This diagram looks a bit messy and complex, but remember that it is developed in steps with student involvement. The goal is not for them to continue to have to record in this way, but for them to understand the process.

So what was the sum?

Alternate way of recording the process:

$$\begin{array}{r} 237 = 200 + 30 + 7 \\ +\ \underline{492 = 400 + 90 + 2} \\ 600 + 120 + 9 \\ 700 + 20 + 9 = 729 \end{array}$$

Provide additional problems for practice:

348 + 235 = ___
234 + 173 = ___
175 + 238 = ___

To close the lesson, have students turn and talk to a partner about the following question:

How does your understanding of regrouping numbers help you to add?

> Allow students to explore the process over several days if needed, varying the types of regrouping (e.g., regrouping ones to make a ten, or tens to make a hundred, or both).

FORMATIVE ASSESSMENT

Have students use expanded form to solve the following:

384 + 538

$$300 + 80 + 4 \; + \; 500 + 30 + 8$$

$$300 + 500 = 800$$
$$80 + 30 = 110$$
$$4 + 8 = 12$$

$$800 + 110 = 910$$
$$910 + 12 = 922$$

This student accurately decomposes 384 as 300 + 80 + 4 and 538 as 500 + 30 + 8. He combines 300 + 500 = 800, 80 + 30 = 110, and 4 + 8 = 12. He then combines 800 + 110 = 910 and 910 + 12 = 922.

Conduct an interview to assess the student's ability to add using expanded form without regrouping. Some students may get confused adding 800 + 110 + 12. Have them decompose the units further. Offer additional practice with place value cards and number disks.

Using Open Number Lines to Add 3-Digit Numbers

Students use their understanding of number lines and skip counting to show addition.

Pose the following:

> Charlie's family is driving to the city. They plan to stop at his cousin's house along the way. The distance to his cousin's house is 248 miles. The distance from his cousin's house to the city is 192 miles. How many miles will his family travel to get to the city?

> *Talk to your partner about this problem. What do you know? What do we want to find out?*
>
> *What operation should we use? Explain.*
>
> *We've used open number lines to add 2-digit numbers. Let's try them for this problem.*
>
> *What number would you use at the start of your number line? Why?*
>
> *In this problem, they do start by driving 248 miles and then drive 192 more miles, so starting the number line at 248 makes sense. Did anyone think about starting the number line with a different number? Explain.*
>
> *Could we start our number line at 192 and add 248? Why or why not?*
>
> *How will your jumps on the number line be different if you start at 192?*
>
> *Decide on how you want to show this problem. Record your jumps on your number line and compare your answer to your partner's. Did you get the same answer? If not, check each other's work.*
>
> *How many miles did Charlie's family drive to get to the city?*

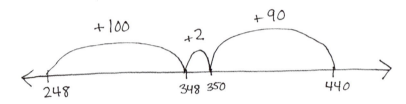

> *What number sentence can we use to show this?*

Pose the following:

> The next day, Charlie's family drove home without stopping. How many miles did they drive round-trip?

> *Turn and talk to your partner. What are we trying to find now?*
>
> *About how many miles did they drive?*
>
> *What equation would you use to model this situation? Why?*
>
> *Use your number line to solve this problem. Compare your solution with your partner's.*

Use this time to circulate and check students' use of the number line. Support students with using benchmark numbers as necessary.

> *How many miles did Charlie's family travel in all?*
>
> *Does that make sense with our estimate?*

Pose additional problems for students to solve using open number lines. More problems can be found in the online resources.

Common Error or Misconception

Students may think they need to begin the number line with 0. Remind students that open number lines can start at any number and that thinking about the problem data helps them determine a good starting point.

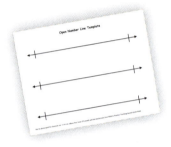

Students might decompose the number in different ways as they show the process on the number line.

Extending Understanding of Multidigit Addition

MODULE 8

FORMATIVE ASSESSMENT

Give students the following directions:

Show how you can add 251 + 364 using an open number line.

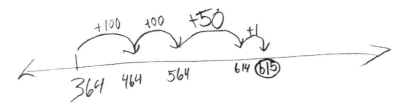

This student starts adding at 364. He shows two jumps of 100 (464, 564). Then he shows a jump of 50 (614) and one more to get to 615.

The jumps should make sense with the addend being decomposed. There is no one right way to decompose the addend. If a student has difficulty adding using the number line, provide number disks to model the second number. Draw connections between skip counting with the number disks and showing the skip counting on the number line.

Using Compensation to Add 3-Digit Numbers

Students think about ways to adjust 3-digit numbers in order to add them mentally.

Pose the following:

302 + 527

Talk to your partner about some of the different ways we could solve this.

When we were adding 2-digit numbers, we found we could make some problems a little easier so that we could do them in our heads. Is there a way we could make this one a little easier so that we could solve it in our heads without using models or pencil and paper?

Listen as students share their thinking with their partners. Listen for pairs who consider using friendly numbers to add.

How could we make the numbers easier to work with?

Model for students, writing *300* below the 302.

How does using 300 make the problem easier?

Can we just change the 302 into 300? Why or why not?

Differentiation
Some students may need a reminder of using compensation to add or subtract 2-digit numbers. Model how this strategy works, using number disks.

Circulate, listening to student thinking. Call on partners to share their ideas.

If we take 2 away from 302, how can we be sure we still get the same sum?

Model for students, writing *529* under the 527.

$$302 + 527 = 829$$
$$(-2) \quad\quad (+2)$$
$$300 + 529 = 829$$

How did we turn 302 into 300?
How did we turn 527 into 529?
How could we check our thinking?
Do we get the same answer?

Pose the following equation:

496 + 235

Think about this problem by yourself. See if you can turn it into an easier problem.
Check your strategy with your partner.

After partners have had a chance to compare their thinking, bring the class together to review strategies and record their thinking.

Offer additional problems. Challenge students to use only mental math, but encourage students to record their thinking if needed. Have students check with their partners or by using an alternate method.

599 + 234
421 + 304
638 + 296

Additional Ideas for Support and Practice

The following ideas extend students' understanding of adding 3-digit numbers and provide meaningful practice.

Two Ways

Using place value dice, students roll two 3-digit numbers.

Students fold a paper in half.

On one side, they draw a model of their numbers, showing the sum.

On the other side, they use a partial sum method to find the sum.

Place value dice are dice showing hundreds, tens, and ones (e.g., rather than 1, 2, 3, 4, 5, 6, they show 100, 200, 300, 400, 500, 600 or 10, 20, 30, 40, 50, 60). Regular dice can be used and designated as the hundreds, tens, and ones digits.

Alternative Number Disk Model

As students continue to gain a deeper understanding of number disks, their relationship to place value, and how they are used to model addition, a modified pictorial model can be used.

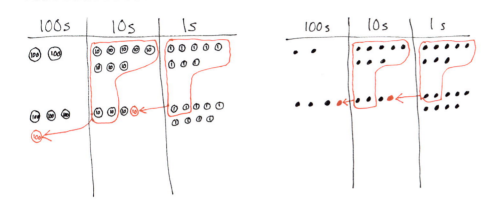

Once students develop a firm grasp of number disks, rather than drawing circles with number values written inside, students can draw dots within the place value chart representing hundreds, tens, and ones, identifiable by their place value location.

Talk About It/Write About It

How does your understanding of place value help you to add multidigit numbers? Explain.

What do you know about adding 2-digit numbers that you can use to add 3-digit numbers?

The sum of two 3-digit numbers is 475. What might the addends be? How do you know?

Use 3, 4, 5, 7, 8, and 9 (or any random set of six digits) to make the greatest sum of two 3-digit addends. Prove that it is the greatest sum.

Dryden Elementary School hosted a book fair. In one week, they sold the following types of books:

| Fiction | 252 | Graphic Novels | 148 |
| Sci-Fi | 389 | Nonfiction | 472 |

Jim says that nonfiction books were more popular than fiction and graphic novels combined. Is he right? How do you know?

For more ideas on generating math talk, see Math in Practice: A Guide for Teachers, Chapter 4.

Multiple Representations

Arrange students into four groups.

Using the following problem, have each group solve using a different representation (e.g., base-ten blocks, number disks, number line, expanded form/partial sums).

258 + 476 = ___

Groups display their thinking on chart paper.

After groups complete their work, have teams share their thinking and models with the class, or have students do a gallery walk.

As a closing, ask students to make connections between the different models and approaches.

Roll and Add It

Students play with partners.

Each student draws a template like the following:

Partners take turns rolling a 10-sided die (or spinning a 0–9 spinner) and filling in the spaces to build two 3-digit numbers (6 rolls or spins each).

Players then add to find the sum.

The greater sum wins the round.

Then, they play again.

Partner-Partner Problem

Students work in teams of four, comprising two pairs. Partners solve the following problem using any strategy and then compare their solutions with the other pair. Students discuss how their methods were similar.

> The Springfield Bird Club recorded the sightings of various birds for the month of January. The chart below shows how many of each bird they saw.

Extending Understanding of Multidigit Addition

MODULE 8

Bird	Number Seen
Cardinal	487
Blue Jay	294
Finch	120
Woodpecker	397
Chickadee	449

Callie's favorite two birds are the chickadee and the blue jay. Devin's favorite two birds are the cardinal and finch. Which grouping of birds was recorded the most: chickadee and blue jay or cardinal and finch? Solve using models, drawing pictures, and using numbers.

Extension:

Pick three or more types of birds and find out how many they saw.
How many birds did they see altogether?

PARTNER ADDITION

Each partner displays a 3-digit number that is less than 500 using a place value model (base-ten blocks or number disks).

What number did you create?
Record your number in your journal.
If you and your partner put your blocks together, what is the total value?
How could you use numbers to find out?
Work together to find the sum.

Observe pairs as they work together to show their thinking with numbers.

Put your base-ten blocks together. With your partner, count to find the value. Were you right?

Vocabulary
addend
addition
compose
decompose
expanded form
open number line
regroup
sum

Differentiation
This goes beyond the grade-level standard and offers a challenge for students who are ready for it.

General Resources
0–9 Spinner
Additional Problems
Open Number Line Template
Place Value Cards
Place Value Mat

ONLINE RESOURCES

These resources are available at http://hein.pub/MathinPractice, keycode MIPG2.

MODULE 9

Extending Understanding of Multidigit Subtraction

About the Math 2.NBT.B.7; 2.NBT.B.9

As our students become more confident with subtracting 2-digit numbers and have had sufficient time to build a deep understanding of place value connections and ways to regroup numbers, they are ready to extend their skills to subtracting 3-digit numbers.

> The key ideas focused on in this module include:
> - applying varied place value strategies to subtract 3-digit numbers
> - explaining strategies to show understanding of the subtraction process.

As students transition to subtracting larger numbers, we revisit the strategies that were discussed with 2-digit numbers: using place value strategies to subtract, using number lines to visualize the subtraction process, and using compensation to make friendlier numbers and simplify the subtraction process. By exploring and discussing these familiar strategies, our students make connections to past learning and continue to deepen their understanding. As with 2-digit numbers, initial computations do not require regrouping, but then we progress to more complex computations that do.

DECOMPOSITION

Understanding place value helps our students recognize that hundreds are subtracted from hundreds, tens from tens, and ones from ones. Breaking numbers apart into expanded form simplifies the subtraction process.

> See Module 4 for more on place value strategies, and Module 7 for more on 2-digit subtraction.

Students find the difference by breaking the number apart (decomposition), subtracting by place value, and then putting the number back together. When subtracting 359 – 146 for example, students might break 359 into 300 + 50 + 9 and 146 into 100 + 40 + 6 and then subtract hundreds from hundreds, tens from tens, and ones from ones. Using manipulatives or drawing diagrams allows students to visualize the process (see Figure 9.1).

$$\begin{array}{r} 359 \\ -\ 146 \\ \hline \end{array} \quad \begin{array}{r} 300 + 50 + 9 \\ 100 + 40 + 6 \\ \hline 200 + 10 + 3\ =\ 213 \end{array}$$

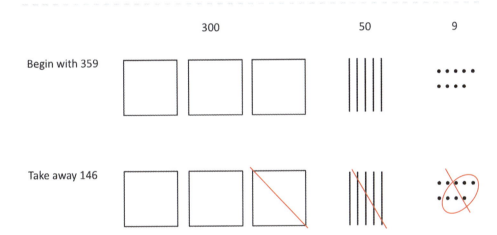

Figure 9.1 Connecting equations and visual representations helps students make sense of subtraction.

From their experiences with 2-digit numbers, students know that regrouping is sometimes needed. They explored renaming numbers by building 2-digit numbers with base-ten blocks, then making trades to rename them (e.g., 43 might be represented with 3 tens rods and 13 ones), allowing them to subtract. Now, they apply this understanding to 3-digit numbers. For 453 – 272, students might rename 453, so 4 hundreds, 5 tens, and 3 ones becomes 3 hundreds, 15 tens, and 3 ones. They might show the renaming using models (e.g., base-ten blocks) or by breaking apart the numbers using expanded form as in Figure 9.2. Understanding this renaming process helps students find differences and will later help them make sense of the standard algorithms.

$$453 = 400 + 50 + 3 \quad \text{or} \quad 300 + 150 + 3$$
$$-272 = 200 + 70 + 2 \quad = \quad 200 + 70 + 2$$
$$ \hspace{8em} 100 + 80 + 1 = 181$$

Figure 9.2 Expanded form can help students decompose numbers using place value.

SUBTRACTING ACROSS ZEROS

The regrouping required for subtracting across zeros can be challenging for students. Their place value understanding and experience renaming 3-digit numbers are invaluable background. Consider 603 − 472. Rather than thinking of 603 as 6 hundreds, 0 tens, and 3 ones, students can rename it as 5 hundreds, 10 tens, and 3 ones, allowing them to subtract (see Figure 9.3). Renaming numbers to subtract is essentially what they will be doing when they transition to the standard algorithm in a later grade (see Figure 9.4).

See place value activities in Module 4.

$$603 = 6 \text{ hundreds} + 0 \text{ tens} + 3 \text{ ones} = 5 \text{ hundreds} + 10 \text{ tens} + 3 \text{ ones}$$
$$-472 = \hspace{12em} 4 \text{ hundreds} + 7 \text{ tens} + 2 \text{ ones}$$
$$\hspace{14em} 1 \text{ hundred} + 3 \text{ tens} + 1 \text{ one}$$

Figure 9.3 Renaming 603 simplifies the process.

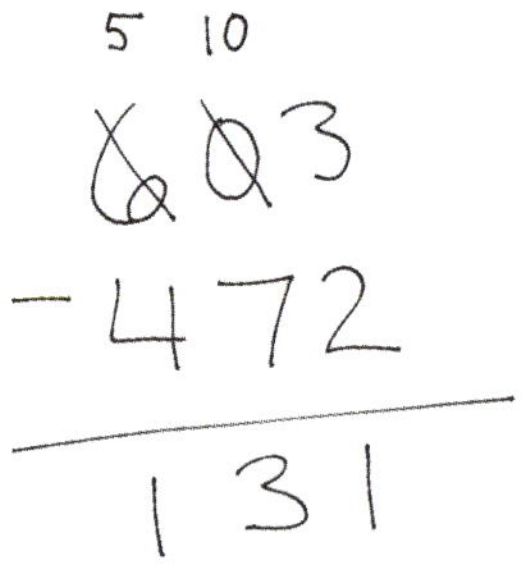

$$\begin{array}{r} \overset{5}{\cancel{6}}\overset{10}{\cancel{0}}3 \\ -472 \\ \hline 131 \end{array}$$

Figure 9.4 When students do transition to the standard algorithm, they will see the connection to renaming by place value.

Using manipulatives can be helpful for students who struggle with renaming numbers across zeros, because the concrete materials allow them to see and manipulate the place value units to show the same number in different ways. When posed with 603 − 195, students might build 603 with 6 hundreds and 3 ones and then decompose a hundred to show 5 hundreds, 10 tens, and 3 ones, and need to regroup again to now show 5 hundreds, 9 tens, and 13 ones (see Figure 9.5). Students see the flexibility of numbers as they decompose them in different ways in order to subtract.

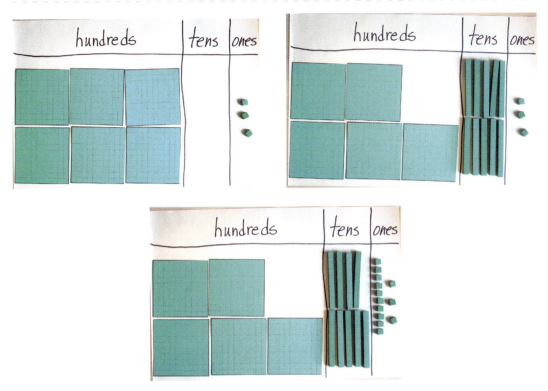

Figure 9.5 Using blocks to model regrouping across zeros can help students visualize a frequently confusing situation.

While we are focusing on subtracting across zeros, consider 500 − 245. Many students struggle with the regrouping needed for this task. And yet, earlier in the year students explored compensation, or shifting numbers to make simpler tasks. What if 500 was shifted to 499 and 245 to 244? Now, the task is 499 − 244—no regrouping needed! It is a simpler and more efficient way to do the computation and is based on students' understanding of numbers. The difference remains the same even if the numbers are each adjusted to be one less. The development of this mental math skill allows students to simplify computations for a lifetime.

OPEN NUMBER LINES

Open number lines can also be used to represent decomposition. Students decompose numbers and represent them as jumps on the number line, helping them visualize subtraction as the difference between two numbers. Students record both numbers on an open number line and then move forward or backward to find the difference between the numbers (see Figure 9.6). There are many ways to decompose the numbers and show the jumps on the number line, but as long as students accurately decompose the number, the difference will be the same.

MODULE 9

Learning Goals

I can subtract 3-digit numbers using an understanding of place value.

I can explain varied strategies for subtracting 3-digit numbers.

Lessons in This Module

Subtracting 3-Digit Numbers

Using Place Value Models to Subtract 3-Digit Numbers

Subtracting Across Zeros

Subtracting 3-Digit Numbers Using Compensation

Subtracting 3-Digit Numbers Using Open Number Lines

For more on using models to build math understanding, see Math in Practice: A Guide for Teachers, *Chapter 3.*

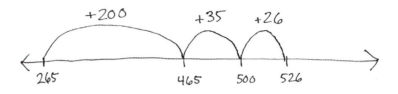

Figure 9.6 Students show the difference by recording jumps on the open number line.

Subtraction on an open number line might also represent taking away. Beginning at 526, students might take away 265 to find the difference.

As numbers get larger and students get more adept with other strategies, their use of open number lines may be replaced by more efficient strategies, which is fine. We give students experience with a variety of strategies to help them gain a deeper understanding of the subtraction process. Classroom tasks that allow our students to visualize the subtraction process with number lines, base-ten blocks, drawings, and equations strengthen their understanding of the process. Facilitating discussions about how strategies work, comparing different place value strategies, and exploring computations through problem contexts all serve to strengthen their understanding and provide a solid foundation for their later transition to a standard algorithm.

Exploring the Progression

PREVIOUS	NOW	NEXT
Grades 1–2	Grade 2	Grades 3–4
Exploring subtraction with 1- and 2-digit numbers with and without regrouping; understanding place value for 3-digit numbers	Exploring subtraction with 3-digit numbers using place value strategies	Grade 3: Fluently subtracting within 1,000 using place value strategies Grade 4: Fluency with traditional subtraction algorithms

Ideas for Instruction and Assessment

SUBTRACTING 3-DIGIT NUMBERS

Students have modeled the process of subtracting 2-digit numbers. Now they will use similar models to explore the subtraction process within 1,000.

Using Place Value Models to Subtract 3-Digit Numbers

Students build from their prior experience subtracting 2-digit numbers and apply their understanding of place value to subtract with and without regrouping.

Provide pairs of students with a toolbox including base-ten blocks, number disks, and place value work mats.

Pose the problem:

> There were 578 students at Central Elementary School. 251 were boys. How many were girls?

Turn and tell your partner what the problem is about.

What equation would show this problem? Why?

When a situation calls for us to subtract, do we model both numbers on our work mat? Why not?

Together, decide which number to model on your work mat. Explain.

Have one student represent 578 with base-ten blocks and the other with number disks.

Tell me what you know about the number 578. How many hundreds, tens, and ones do we have?

Work with your partner to show me how you would subtract 251 from 578.

Observe as students work.

Who can share what you did?

You started with 578. How much did you take away?

How many do you still have?

What does the 327 represent?

Could we show the data in this problem using expanded form? Work with your partner to break each number into expanded form.

Have students share the expanded form as you record it on the board.

$$578 = 500 + 70 + 8$$
$$251 = 200 + 50 + 1$$

How could you use expanded form to find the difference between 578 and 251?

Record the differences for the hundreds, tens, and ones on the board as students share them.

```
   500 + 70 + 8
 − 200 + 50 + 1
   ───────────
   300 + 20 + 7
```

So what is the difference? How did you find it?

Is that what you got when you used your base-ten blocks and number disks? Why does that make sense?

Students benefit from time to explore and discuss these procedures. This lesson addresses multiple skills. The lesson can be spread over multiple sessions to allow students to explore a particular type of model or to separately address problems that do or do not require regrouping.

By using both base-ten blocks and number disks, students bridge the connections between proportional and non-proportional models. Using number disks prepares students for working with larger numbers where base-ten blocks are no longer practical.

Have partners switch place value materials.

> There were 437 students at Benfield Elementary. 282 of them were boys. How many were girls?

Have them retell the problem and identify the equation before subtracting.

Talk with your partner about anything that might make this problem challenging.

How can you decompose 437 so that you can subtract more easily? Once you have a plan, go ahead and try it with your materials and solve the problem.

Circulate and observe students, listening to their thinking.

Have students share their solutions.

How did you decompose 437?

Were you able to subtract then?

Compare the models you used. How did they help you to solve the problem?

What was the difference? What does it represent?

Can you use expanded form to solve this problem? Work with your partner to try it.

Observe as students work, to see how they are handling the regrouping needed to do the subtraction.

Have students tell you the expanded form for each number and record it on the board.

$$437 = 400 + 30 + 7$$
$$282 = 200 + 80 + 2$$

How did you use the expanded form to subtract?

Record on the board as students share:

$$\begin{array}{r} 400 + 30 + 7 = 300 + 130 + 7 \\ -\ 200 + 80 + 2 = 200 + 80 + 2 \\ \hline 100 + 50 + 5 = 155 \end{array}$$

When you rewrote the 400 as 300, and the 30 as 130, did you change the value of the number? Explain.

What was the difference? Was that the same as with the other strategies?

Support students in seeing the connections between the models they made with their place value materials and the expanded form algorithm.

Pose additional problems for students to model and solve.

Extending Understanding of Multidigit Subtraction

MODULE 9

Thinking Through a Lesson

SMP1, SMP3, SMP4, SMP5

Subtracting Across Zeros SHOW IT!

Students use their prior place value understanding to explore problems in which they subtract across zeros.

> Provide students with place value materials.
>
> Explain to students that they will be exploring problems about fruit sold at a farmer's market over the weekend.

Post the following data:

> Fruit Sold at the Farmer's Market
> Apples—232
> Pears—204
> Grapefruit—237
> Oranges—340
> Plums—300
> Peaches—183
> Melons—153
> Bananas—304

> Tell your partner the equation you would use to figure out how many more oranges than apples were sold at the farmer's market. Be ready to explain your equation. (340 − 232 = ? because they sold 340 oranges and 232 apples and we subtract to find the difference.)
>
> Work with your partner to solve the problem. Be ready to share how you did it.

Have students share their solutions and methods, discussing the ways they showed the regrouping.

Pose the following:

> Tell your partner the equation you would use to figure out how many more pears than peaches were sold at the farmer's market. (204 − 183 = ? because we are comparing 204 pears and 183 peaches.)
>
> Work with your partner to solve the problem. Be ready to share how you did it.

Observe as students talk to partners about the problem, watching for how they deal with the zero in the tens place. Have students share their solutions and methods.

> How did you solve this problem? Did you need to regroup? If so, what needed to be regrouped? (There was a zero in the tens place, so we had to regroup a hundred to make it 10 tens, then we could subtract.)

(sidebar) Students benefit from multiple lessons focused on subtracting across zeros. This lesson provides a series of problems in which the task increases in complexity, allowing you to observe students as they explore subtracting across zeros and determine possible tasks and grouping for additional lessons. Spread this material across as many class sessions as makes sense for your students.

(sidebar) Students may have a preference for base-ten blocks or place value disks. Allow students to use the model that works best for them.

(sidebar) Although this initial problem has a zero in the ones place, students already have experience regrouping a ten as 10 ones, so this is not new. Some students may even solve the problem mentally thinking about 40 − 32.

As students share how they modeled the problem, show their regrouping on the board or using a document camera so everyone can visualize the regrouping process.

Pose the following:

Tell your partner the equation you would use to figure out how many more plums than melons were sold at the farmer's market. (300 – 153 = ? because we are comparing 300 plums and 153 melons sold.)

Work with your partner to solve the problem. Be ready to share how you did it.

Observe as students work with partners to solve the problem. Are they able to use the models to show the numbers and then regroup appropriately?

What was different about this problem? (There were 2 zeros.)

Why is that a problem? (We couldn't subtract the tens or ones.)

What did you do?

Have students share their methods and solutions.

How did you regroup? (We made a hundred into 10 tens and then took one of the tens and made it into 10 ones so we had 2 hundreds, 9 tens, and 10 ones.)

Is that the same as 300? Can you use your place value materials to prove they are the same?

Have students discuss their thinking.

How did renaming 300 that way help you solve this problem? (We had enough of everything to subtract.)

Pose the following:

Tell your partner the equation you would use to figure out how many more bananas than grapefruit were sold at the farmer's market? (304 – 237 = ? because we are comparing bananas and grapefruit.)

Work with your partner to solve the problem. Be ready to share how you solved it.

Have students share their solutions and methods. As students share how they modeled the problem and regrouped the hundreds and tens, record their ideas on the board.

Did you have any trouble solving this problem? What did you have to think about? (We took a hundred and made it 10 tens, but then we still couldn't subtract the ones.)

Why not? (There's not enough ones to take away 7.)

So what did you do? Did anyone find a way to solve it? (We regrouped a hundred to make it 10 tens, then we took one of those tens and made it 10 ones, so we had 2 hundreds, 9 tens, and 14 ones.)

How did you get 14 ones? (We already had 4 ones and we added 10 more.)

> **Differentiation**
> If at any point during this lesson students begin to struggle with the regrouping process, pause and provide additional similar subtraction tasks before moving on. For example, you might pause here to explore tasks like 403 – 271 or 305 – 234. The farmer's market context can be revisited the following day, or when students are ready to continue.

> Revisit previous discussions about renaming 3-digit numbers. If needed, provide some additional experience with renaming 3-digit numbers as discussed in Module 4. Asking students to check the renaming with models allows them to validate their thinking.

Model the regrouping on the board as students answer questions about what they did.

Is that still 304? (Yes, because if you add up 2 hundreds, 9 tens, and 14 ones. you get 304.)

How did that help? (Then we could subtract the hundreds, tens, and ones.)

To end the lesson, have students solve 405 – 327 as an exit ticket. Review the exit tickets to determine who understands the process and to identify students who may need additional support.

> Students benefit from repeated opportunities to model and discuss subtracting across zeros, particularly in problems where they regroup multiple times.

> If you paused the lesson at an earlier stage, pose a task that matches the level of task that students were exploring.

FORMATIVE ASSESSMENT

Pose the following:

Use what you know about place value to decompose 600 and then solve 600 – 386.

This student shows 600 using a pictorial representation of number disks. He decomposes a hundred for 9 tens and 10 ones. The student crosses off 386 and correctly identifies the difference of 214.

> If a student has difficulty with this task, provide place value materials. Ask how we can show 600 a different way without changing the value of the number. Can we rename a hundred as some tens and ones?

Subtracting 3-Digit Numbers Using Compensation

Students explore using compensation to subtract.

Pose the following:

> Springwood Elementary School has 600 students. If there are 347 girls, how many students are boys?

Have students retell the problem and identify what they need to find out.

What makes this problem difficult? Why can't we just subtract hundreds, tens, and ones?

Consider if one girl moved away. How would the problem change?

Record *(–1)* and *599* below the 600 for students. Record *(–1)* and *346* below the 347.

$$600 - 347 = 253$$
$$(-1) \qquad (-1)$$
$$599 - 346 = 253$$

Will it be easier to subtract? Why?

Can we do that? Why? Turn and talk to your partner about whether we can change the problem like this.

Invite a student to model the subtraction and share out her thinking.

How can you solve this now?

How many boys go to Springwood Elementary School?

Have students practice with the following:

700 – 328
300 – 134
600 – 512

Pose the following:

> The tiger at the zoo weighs 356 kilograms. The black bear weighs 197 kilograms. How much heavier is the tiger than the black bear?

After students retell the problem and identify key information, ask:

How is this problem different than the ones we just did?

Common Error or Misconception

Students often confuse the rules for using compensation in addition and subtraction. In subtraction, we increase (or decrease) the minuend and subtrahend by the same quantity, keeping the difference the same. In addition, we increase one addend and decrease the other by the same quantity to keep the sum constant. Consider using a number line to represent the difference of simpler expressions (e.g., 11 – 7) and then subtract 1 from each number in the expression to show 10 – 6 on the number line. Students are able to see that the difference is the same.

Does subtracting 1 from each number make this problem easier?

Talk to your partner about how you could change the numbers a different way to make this problem easier.

Circulate and listen for students who suggest adding 3 to both numbers, to make 197 easier to subtract. If no student suggests this, ask:

Is either of these numbers close to a friendly number?

How many more would we need to make 200?

When we add 3 to one number, what do we need to do to the other number?

Model for students a way to record their thinking.

$$356 - 197 = 159$$
$$(+3) \qquad (+3)$$
$$359 - 200 = 159$$

Is it easier to subtract now? Why?

How can we solve the problem now?

Remind students that they are using a strategy called compensation.

To end the lesson, have students discuss the following:

How does compensation help us subtract from multiples of 100?

How does compensation for subtraction differ from compensation for addition?

FORMATIVE ASSESSMENT

Give students the following direction:

Solve 500 − 174 using compensation.

$$\begin{array}{r} 500 \\ -174 \end{array} \begin{array}{r} -1 \\ -1 \end{array} \qquad \begin{array}{r} 499 \\ -173 \\ \hline 326 \end{array}$$

Students may use various compensation strategies, although one appropriate choice is to subtract 1 from both 500 and 174. Then subtraction can take place without regrouping.

> If students have difficulty with the compensation strategy, continue to use models such as base-ten blocks or number lines to help them visualize the thinking process.

Subtracting 3-Digit Numbers Using Open Number Lines SHOW IT!

Students apply their understanding of number lines and counting back by hundreds, tens, and ones to subtract 3-digit numbers.

Provide students with a number line.

Pose the following:

> There were 649 people that visited the zoo over the weekend. 241 were adults. The rest were children. How many children visited the zoo?

Have students retell the problem and identify the operation they would use to solve it.

We've used number lines to subtract 2-digit numbers. Turn and talk to your partner about how you might use one to show subtraction with 3-digit numbers.

Put a dot on your number line where you think 649 should go.

Share with your partner. Where did you place it? Why did you put it there?

Circulate to check students' number lines. Support students who may be unsure of where to place 649.

Talk to your partner about different ways you could use your number line to show subtraction.

How can we count backward and show our skips as we go?

Using your number line, show how you would subtract 241 from 649.

Share with your partner. Are they the same? Different?

Circulate around the room, looking for different examples. Invite students to share with the whole class.

Pose additional problems for students to solve using a number line.

Differentiation

Some students can use a number line without any tick marks. Other students may need a number line with tick marks to better organize their work.

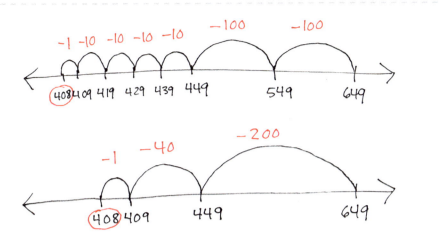

649 − 241 can be shown in different ways, such as counting back by hundreds, tens, and ones, (as seen on the top) or by multiples of hundreds, tens, and ones (as seen on the bottom).

Additional Ideas for Support and Practice

The following ideas extend students' understanding of subtracting 3-digit numbers and provide meaningful practice.

Focus on the Question

Show the following data at the beginning of each week and keep the data posted throughout the week. Each day, ask a different question related to the data.

> The carnival workers kept track of how many people rode the rides on Saturday.
>
> Scrambler—235
>
> Bumper Cars—378
>
> Carousel—263
>
> Pirate Ship—417
>
> Moon Bounce—545

1. How many more people rode the Moon Bounce than the Pirate Ship? Tell how you would solve it.
2. 258 of the people on the bumper cars drove the cars. The others were passengers. How many people were passengers? Tell how you would solve it.
3. How many more people rode the Bumper Cars than the Scrambler? Tell how you would solve it.

Extending Understanding of Multidigit Subtraction — MODULE 9

This lesson focuses on a take-apart subtraction problem in which students count back to find the difference. Do similar lessons with comparison problems in which students find both numbers on the open number line and count forward or backward to find the difference between them.

For more on the Focus on the Question strategy, see *Math in Practice: A Guide for Teachers,* Chapter 2.

Vocabulary

decompose · place value
digits · regroup
expanded form · rename

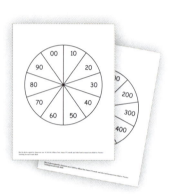

Online Resources

General Resources
- 0–9 Digit Cards
- Additional Problems
- Number Disks
- Place Value Mat

Resources for Specific Activities
- Place Value Spinners

These resources are available at http://hein.pub/MathinPractice, keycode MIPG2.

---

4. 145 people who rode the Carousel were children. How many were not children? Tell how you would solve it.
5. How many fewer people rode the Scrambler than the Pirate Ship? Tell how you would solve it.

Ask students to talk with partners about the following:

Retell the problem.
What information do we need to solve it?
What would you do to solve the problem?
What do you estimate the answer will be?

After students talk with partners, have them share their ideas and planned strategies with the class.

Then, have them find the solution.

Spin It and Show It

Students use place value spinners to generate two 3-digit numbers.

Students model the greater number using drawings of base-ten blocks or number disks.

Students show the subtraction of the lesser number by crossing out as necessary.

Students should include a numerical solution using expanded form, or the standard notation.

Variation: Students can roll place value dice to generate their numbers.

Digit Card Subtraction

Students flip over six digit cards, three on the top and three on the bottom. Students switch the cards in the hundreds place so that the minuend (top number) has more hundreds.

Students use the numbers they generated to create a subtraction problem. They draw a picture and then solve the problem using expanded form.

Diagnose It

Kurt's solution to a subtraction problem is shown below. Is he right? If so, can you prove it using place value models? If not, what do you think Kurt did wrong? How would you fix it?

```
  823
- 397
  574
```

MODULE 10

Understanding Length Measurement

About the Math   2.MD.1; 2.MD.2; 2.MD.3; 2.MD.4; 2.MD.5; 2.MD.6; 2.MD.9

In second grade, students learn to use a standard tool to measure length as they extend their understanding of linear measurement. They also explore line plots as a way to display their measurement data.

The key ideas focused on in this module include:
- measuring and estimating length to the nearest unit
- choosing an appropriate tool and unit of measure depending on the measurement task
- displaying measurement data on a line plot
- adding or subtracting to solve problems about length.

It would be counterproductive to rush through measurement too quickly. Measurement experiences can and should be stretched throughout the school year to allow students to practice skills and internalize concepts.

Students are introduced to using standard units (customary and metric). They measure to the nearest whole unit (inch and centimeter). Although it is important for students to know how to measure objects, it is equally important that they are able to select appropriate measurement tools and measure in appropriate units.

Students are introduced to a ruler as a measurement tool in second grade. Prior to this, they measured with same-sized objects being placed end to end. Having students create their own first rulers helps them understand what this tool represents. By laying square inch tiles end to end, placing a strip of cardstock below the tiles, and

> At this level, students use inches, feet, yards, centimeters, and meters.

making hash marks to show the end of each tile, students transition from measuring with objects to using tools (see Figure 10.1). This allows students to view the ruler as simply a tool that shows the number of end-to-end units.

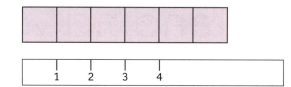

Figure 10.1 As students label each hash mark with a number (indicating the number of tiles), they gain insight into the connection between a ruler and a number line. These handmade tools are perfect first rulers, because students understand their markings.

As students explore a new measurement system, they develop benchmarks in order to visualize units and estimate lengths using those units. As students gather and observe objects that are one inch long or one foot long, they gain a mental image of the measurement unit and are able to use that image to estimate measurements of other objects.

Figure 10.2 Students collect items that are one inch long to get a good sense of that unit of measurement.

Students apply their understanding of addition and subtraction to solve problems related to measurement. They connect subtraction to comparing lengths (finding a difference) and addition to adding to or combining lengths. Exploring addition and subtraction in a measurement context deepens our students' understanding of operations and provides them with additional experience to refine their problem-solving skills.

Because students have heard customary units (inches, feet, yards) in everyday situations, beginning with customary measurement makes sense. Exploring customary measurement units and tools, creating rulers to measure inches, estimating measurements in inches, feet, or yards, and solving problems based on customary measurements will allow students opportunities to become familiar with this system. Once students are comfortable with customary measurement, metric measurement is introduced and explored.

An important understanding in both the U.S. customary and metric measurement systems is that when we measure with different units, we get a different measurement. Although the width of our desk does not change, measuring it in inches yields a different measurement than measuring it in centimeters. Students do not need to convert measurements, but simply to understand that because centimeters are smaller than inches, it takes more of them to measure the same object.

In second grade, students are introduced to line plots as a way of displaying their measurement data. As students record their measurement data above number lines, they are able to visualize a set of measurements. Seeing both a line plot and a ruler as a number line helps students see the connections between number concepts and models (see Figure 10.3).

See the online resources for a table of addition and subtraction story problems related to length. See a similar table with generic addition and subtraction problems in the online resources for Module 1.

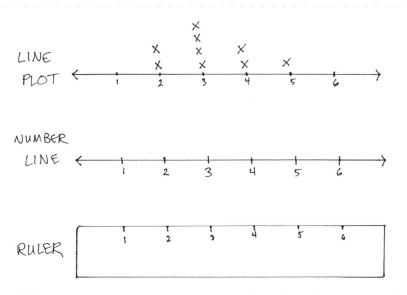

Figure 10.3 Both a ruler and a line plot are number lines. The ruler is a number line that is used as a measurement tool, and a line plot uses the number line to display a set of data.

Learning Goals

I can measure length to the nearest unit.

I can pick a tool and a unit of measure that make sense.

I can add or subtract to solve problems about length.

I can show my measurement data on a line plot.

Lessons in This Module

Understand Customary Measurement Units and Measuring to the Nearest Unit
Inch by Inch
Making Rulers
Inches to Feet
Feet to Yards
Which Tool?
Estimate and Measure

Introduce Metric Units
Making a Centimeter Ruler
Centimeters to Meters
Measuring with Two Standard Units

Solving Measurement Problems
Using Addition and Subtraction to Solve Measurement Problems
What's the Difference?

Creating Line Plots to Display Measurement Data
Displaying Data on Line Plots
Making Line Plots from Measured Data

Exploring the Progression

PREVIOUS	NOW	NEXT
Grade 1	Grade 2	Grade 3
Exploring linear measurement with nonstandard units	Measuring objects to the nearest inch or centimeter; using line plots with whole-number units	Measuring objects to $\frac{1}{2}$ and $\frac{1}{4}$ inch; using line plots marked with whole, half, and quarter units

Ideas for Instruction and Assessment

UNDERSTAND CUSTOMARY MEASUREMENT UNITS AND MEASURING TO THE NEAREST UNIT

Students discover how long one inch is. They estimate and measure objects to the nearest inch.

Inch by Inch

In Leo Lionni's book *Inch by Inch*, students learn what can be measured with inches. Then they identify objects that are one inch in length and make a "One Inch" poster.

Before Reading:

Set a context for reading the book.

> We're going to read a book called *Inch by Inch*. What do you think the title means?
>
> What do you know about an inch?
>
> How long do you think an inch is? Show me with your fingers.
>
> What might be an inch long?

During Reading:

Read *Inch by Inch*.

Ask students to predict what the worm will use to measure the robin's tail.

Make sure students understand the phrases *inch by inch* and *inched out of sight*.

After Reading:

Record the word *inch* on the word wall or Math Talk chart.

> We can abbreviate the word *inch* by using the first two letters plus a period: in.
>
> Why do you think we would want to measure using a standard unit like inches rather than using our fingers, paper clips, or other objects? Share your thinking with your partner.

Understanding Length Measurement

MODULE 10

Provide each student with a 1-inch square tile.

This square tile has sides that are one inch long.
How does the tile compare to your estimate? Is it bigger? Smaller?
What else might be one inch long?

Students explore the classroom using their square tile to find objects that are one inch long.

> Similar activities can be used to explore feet, yards, and, later, centimeters and meters.

Students make a One Inch poster.

We're going to make a poster to show items that are one inch long. What title should we use?
Draw five things that are an inch long.
Use your 1-inch square to check the length of your drawings.
Share your drawings with your partner.

Provide students with items such as strips of paper, string, ribbon, or yarn.

Students cut 1-inch pieces and glue them to their posters.

In-class extension: *Make a list of things in our classroom that are about one inch long.*

At-home extension: *Make a list of things in your house that are about one inch long.*

Thinking Through a Lesson

SMP5, SMP6

Making Rulers

Students create rulers and measure objects with them.

Pose the following:

> Jasmine would like to measure the length of her math journal. What can she use to measure it?

Turn and talk to your partner about what you think Jasmine could use.

Have students share ideas with their classmates.

> Students have been measuring length by placing items end to end. They might suggest a variety of items (paper clips, cubes, etc.) that would work to measure their journals.

Provide students with twelve 1-inch square tiles.

Can you use these tiles to find the length of your journal?
Try it with your partner.

Students line up their tiles and count to find the length.

What if we wanted to measure the length and didn't have these tiles?
How would we know how long 3 tiles or 6 tiles are?

> Watch to see if students remember how to measure: lining up the squares so they touch but do not overlap, and counting how many of the squares make a line the same length as the journal. If some students need more work on this concept, plan to work with them in a small group to review.

> We are beginning to have students think about whether there is a way to measure without having multiple objects to lie end to end.

> Students may come up with the idea of showing the tiles on the strip, but you may need to suggest this in a think-aloud technique as in, "Could we mark the length of each tile on our strip? Would that help us have a tool to remember the length of the tiles?"

Provide students with a 12-inch pre-cut strip of cardstock about an inch wide.

> *How could we use this strip to help us remember the length of 3 or 6 or 9 tiles?*
> *Line up 12 tiles end to end.*
> *How could we make a model to show your tiles?*

Have students put the paper strip under the row of tiles.

> *How could we use the paper strip to make a model?* (We could mark the tiles on our strip.)

Demonstrate on the board how to line up the starting points and make a mark at the end of the first tile. Then, have students do it on their paper strips.

> *Continue making a mark after each tile to show where it ends, all the way to the end of your paper strip.*

Common Error or Misconception

Remind students that there should be no gaps or overlap of tiles, and that the starting points of the tile row and their paper strip must be the same.

Observe as they mark the paper strips.

After students have made a mark on the paper strip after each tile, begin a class discussion, asking students to turn and discuss the ideas with partners.

> *How can this paper strip help you measure the length of something if you don't have tiles?* (We can put it next to what we are measuring and see how many tiles long it is.)

Have students try it to measure the length of a pencil.

How did you know how long the pencil was? (We counted the squares.)

Is there a way we could mark the paper strip so you wouldn't have to count how many squares? (We could put numbers on it.)

Have students number the marks on the paper strip, starting at 1.

Use your paper strip to measure your journal again.

Was the measurement the same?

Did anyone get a different measurement?

(If yes:) What might have caused the measurement to be different? (We didn't start at the beginning of the journal.)

Is our starting point important? (Yes.)

Describe to your partner how you think we should use the paper strip. What part of the strip should we start at? Why? (We should start at the beginning because it is like starting with the first tile.)

Where do we begin on a number line? (0.)

Invite a whole-class discussion as students defend their thinking, making connections between the paper strip and a number line.

You just made a special tool to measure length—you made a ruler.

Does anyone have an idea of how wide each of these parts on your ruler is? Explain. (Each part is an inch—they are like the size of things we put on our posters.)

> Students' previous experience thinking about the size of an inch helps them make sense of the length of the sections on their rulers.

Have students write the word *inch* on their paper strips.

Are inches all the same size? Look at your rulers. Are the spaces all the same size? (Yes, and the tiles were all the same size.)

Have students measure five different objects with tiles and then with the ruler.

Students can make a table in their journals listing the objects, the measurement with tiles, and the measurement with their rulers.

Have students compare their findings with classmates, or as a whole group.

Turn and share: How does a ruler help you measure? (We don't need objects. We can just see the number and know how many inches long something is.)

> An important understanding is that each inch is the same size. With students creating their own rulers from square tiles, they can stack the square tiles, if needed, to prove they all are the same length.

Inches to Feet

Students are introduced to the measurement unit of one foot. Students find objects that are one foot long.

Have students take out their handmade rulers from the previous lesson.

Show me an inch on your ruler.

How many inches long is your whole ruler?

We put 12 inches together to make a longer length. This length has a name as well.

Do you think you know what it is? Turn and tell your partner.

These 12 inches together are called a foot.

Introduce the word *foot* and record it on your word wall or Math Talk chart.

We can abbreviate the word foot *by using the first and last letters plus a period:* ft.

Show students a commercially made 12-inch ruler and have them compare it to the ones they made.

As a class, discuss the term one foot.

How many inches make up one foot?

Is your pencil longer or shorter than an inch?

Is your pencil longer or shorter than a foot?

Have students look around the room and find objects that are less than one foot and more than one foot.

Have them use their rulers to check.

Share some with the class.

Is one foot bigger or smaller than your own foot?

Have students in groups of four place their feet next to each other to compare their lengths.

Why can't we use our own feet as the measurement for one foot?

Are our rulers different sizes? Compare yours with others in your team.

How many inches are in one foot?

Is one inch always the same length?

So, will one foot always be the same length? Why?

So, the feet we measured with our rulers are all the same size?

Why does it help if they are all the same?

Have students use their rulers to measure objects around the classroom, finding objects that are about one foot long. In their journals, students can make a table and list objects that they find. Then have students share results with their classmates.

If you measured a table using inches and measured again using feet, would there be more inches or feet? Why?

Common Error or Misconception

Lots of hash marks on a ruler (e.g., to sixteenths of an inch) can cause confusion at this level. Find rulers with only inches (or centimeters) represented or with a hash mark at the halfway mark between inches (or centimeters). The hash mark at halfway can be helpful when finding the nearer inch. Depending on the rulers you choose, you may need to point out to students where the zero is. Many commercial rulers do not have the zero at the exact end of the ruler, but a short distance away from it. Remind students that they always need to measure from the zero to get an accurate result.

Common Error or Misconception

Some students may mistakenly associate the length of one foot as the length of their own foot.

Differentiation

Have a basket of objects ready at a table to work with a small group of students who need additional support.

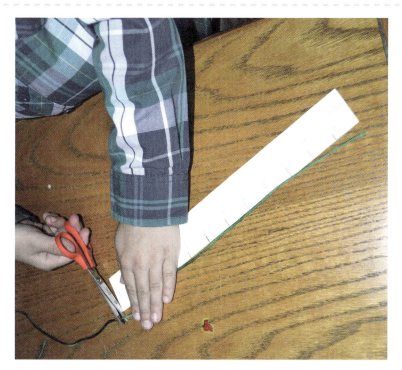

You might have students use their rulers to cut various pieces of string and ribbon at different lengths.

Feet to Yards

Students connect their understanding that twelve inches equals one foot to the discovery that three feet equals one yard. Students find objects that are one yard long.

Pose the following:

> Keith wanted to measure the length of the table in the back of the classroom. It was too long to use his ruler. What could he do?

Turn and talk with your partner about how we might be able to measure objects that are longer than one foot.

What if we wanted to measure all the way across the classroom? Would that be a lot of feet?

We are going to explore a new unit that is even longer than a foot.

Provide students with two more lengths of 12-inch cardstock. Using either their pre-made rulers or 1-inch tiles, students create two more rulers with labeled marks.

Students use tape to connect the three pieces of cardstock.

We discovered how long one inch and one foot are. Now we have a new length.

Tell your partner if you think you know what our new length is called.

Listen for students who identify one yard and invite them to share with the class.

> For precision, it is important that the pieces of cardstock do not overlap when being taped.

Understanding Length Measurement

227

MODULE **10**

Connect to adding three 2-digit numbers.

Some students may be confused by the math-specific meanings of words such as foot and yard, especially if they are just learning English. Discuss the everyday and the math meanings of these words, exploring both meanings with pictures and examples.

How many feet did we use to make one yard?

If 12 inches makes one foot, and 3 feet are one yard, work with your partner to figure out how many inches make one yard.

Invite pairs to share their solutions.

We call your new tools yardsticks.

Record *yard* and *yardstick* on the word wall or Math Talk chart.

We can abbreviate the word yard *by using the first and last letters plus a period: yd.*

Show students a commercially made yardstick and have them compare it to theirs.

Have students use their yardstick strips to measure objects around the classroom.

Have students list objects that are about one yard long in their journals. Then have them compare their findings with their classmates.

Could we measure the length of a pencil with our yardsticks?

So, it is bigger than you need. What tool would be easier to use?

What would we measure with our yardsticks?

Why would we use a yardstick to measure those?

Would the distance across the classroom have more yards, more feet, or more inches? Why?

FORMATIVE ASSESSMENT

Give the following directions:

> Write one object you would measure with a ruler and one object you would measure with a yardstick. Tell why you would choose to measure the objects with the ruler and yardstick.

ruler → Book
yard stick → door
A yardstick is big so I measure biger things.

This student correctly identifies a book to be measured by a ruler and a door to be measured by a yardstick. He demonstrates sufficient understanding that a yardstick would be used to measure something big. Ask the student why a ruler would be best to measure a book.

Which Tool?

Students use their understanding of measurement tools and length to select the appropriate tools for measuring.

Materials: wooden or plastic ruler, wooden or plastic yardstick, and piece of string for each pair

> Ask students to work with partners to measure the distance around their heads any way they want.

> After a few minutes, have them share some ideas with the class.
>> *What is difficult about using the ruler or yardstick?*
>> *Are there any other materials that might help? How?*

> Allow students to continue working, then have them share their strategies with the class.
>> *How did you measure around your head?*
>> *How did you know the measurement? The string doesn't have any numbers.*
>> *What other tools could you have used to measure your heads? Explain.*

> Give each team a measuring tape. Tell them that this is another measurement tool, called a measuring tape. Write *measuring tape* on your word wall or Math Talk chart.

> Ask them to look at the measuring tape and make observations.
>> *What do you notice about the tool I just gave you?*

> Have students place it next to the ruler or yardstick to see if it has the same measurements.
>> *Is 12 inches the same on the yardstick and measuring tape?*
>> *When might you use this tool? When would it make sense to choose a measuring tape?*
>> *What tools have we talked about that you can choose from when you measure?*

If students are figuring out that they may be able to use the string to measure around their heads and then find the measure of the string by placing it on the yardstick, let them keep working. If not, calling a class time-out to share suggestions and possible strategies may help jump-start those who are struggling.

FORMATIVE ASSESSMENT

Pose the following:

Which tool would you use to measure the length of each object?

- the length of a school hallway
- the width of a table
- the height of a chair
- the width of your hand
- the width of a computer screen (or tablet)

> Listen to see if students are able to select reasonable tools and justify their choices.

Estimate and Measure

Students estimate and then find the length of different objects.

Have students turn to partners and estimate the length of a piece of paper in inches (use standard 8.5 × 11-inch paper and have them look at the longer side).

> *How long do you think this is in inches? Tell your partner.*
>
> *How did you know? What did you think about?*
>
> *So, you estimated it was about 12 inches. You didn't know exactly, but you thought that was close.*

Write *estimate* on the word wall or Math Talk chart. Explain that estimates say about what the answer would be. They don't have to be exact.

> *Did anyone else think of something they already knew to estimate how long the paper was?* (We thought it was about 10 inches, because it is as long as my notebook and I measured that before and it was 10 inches.)
>
> *How does it help to think about something you already know when you estimate?*
>
> *You just used what we call a* benchmark*. That means you used something you knew to help you. You knew what was 10 inches long and thought this was about the same.*

Add *benchmark* to the word wall or Math Talk chart.

Have a student measure the length of the paper.

> *Were we close?*

Ask students to talk to a partner and estimate the length of a large paper clip.

> *How long do you think this is in inches? What is your estimate?*
>
> *How do you know it is more than 1 inch?*
>
> *You used a square tile as a benchmark. You knew that length and knew this was longer.*

Have a student measure the length of the paper clip.

> *Were we close?*

Give teams of four a basket of assorted objects and have them estimate, tell how they got their estimate, and then measure each one to see how close their estimate was.

Have students create a table in their math journals, listing each object, their estimate, and the actual measurement.

> *How close were you?*
>
> *What helped you make your estimate?*

Additional Ideas for Support and Practice

The following ideas extend students' understanding of measuring lengths in inches and feet.

TALK ABOUT IT/WRITE ABOUT IT

> Jamie said she is going to measure the length of the school hall in inches. Is that a good idea? Why or why not?
>
> What do the marks on a ruler represent?
>
> How do I decide which tool or unit I use when I am measuring?
>
> What would you use a yardstick to measure? Why?
>
> Explain how to measure a pencil with a ruler.
>
> What might you measure in inches? Why?
>
> What in this room is longer than 1 foot but less than 2 feet? How do you know?

For more on generating math talk, see Math in Practice: A Guide for Teachers, Chapter 4.

BASKET OF STUFF

> Fill a basket with various items.
>
> Students pick an item, estimate its length in inches, and measure to find the exact length.
>
> Students create a table in their journals to record the results.

PICK THE TOOL/PICK THE UNIT

> Students create a table with items listed on the left. Students identify the tool (ruler or yardstick) and unit (inches, feet, yards) they would use to measure each item.

- marker
- width of a window
- eraser
- length of a desk
- tile on the floor
- length of a bookshelf
- crayon
- height of a globe
- width of a doorway
- length of the classroom

> Students share and discuss why they picked each tool and unit.

MEASUREMENT SCAVENGER HUNT

Students find objects of specified lengths. Students record their findings in their math journals.

Have students find something that is each length:

2 inches
5 inches
8 inches
10 inches
1 foot
2 feet
1 yard

Have students share their results with classmates. Make a class chart with all the results.

ESTIMATE AND MEASURE

Students estimate lengths in inches and then measure to see how close they were.

Give students instructions like the following:

Without using a ruler, draw a line that is about 8 inches long. Measure to see how close you were.

Without using a ruler, cut a piece of string that is about 12 inches long. Measure to see how close you were.

Without using a ruler, make a train of connecting cubes that is about 6 inches long. Measure to see how close you were.

JIM AND THE BEANSTALK

Students read about using a measuring tape in *Jim and the Beanstalk* by Raymond Briggs.

Before Reading:

Set a context for reading the book.

What tool would you use to measure the length of a crayon?
What tool would you use to measure the length around your head?
We are going to read a story about a giant. Listen for ideas on how he is measured.

During Reading:

Read *Jim and the Beanstalk.*

What tool did Jim use to measure the giant for eyeglasses?
Why do you think Jim decided to use a measuring tape?

Understanding Length Measurement

MODULE 10

After Reading:

Have students measure the distance around objects in the class that are curved (e.g., globe) and share the results.

INTRODUCE METRIC UNITS

Students create a metric ruler and measure using centimeters and meters.

Making a Centimeter Ruler   SHOW IT!

Students create centimeter rulers and discover a new unit for measuring length.

Give students a set of ten centimeter cubes (such as the unit cubes from a standard base-ten blocks set) to measure some classroom objects by lining them end to end.

Then, give students a strip of cardstock that is 10 centimeters long.

Have them use their cubes to create a centimeter ruler by putting lines between each cube to make the ruler. Follow the same procedure as with the student-made inch rulers (see page 223) and have students mark their new rulers with numbers so they can use them to measure objects.

Have them take out the rulers they made before (inch rulers).

What do you notice about the ruler we just made?
What did we call the units we used on the ruler we made before?
Are these inches?

Tell students that not everyone measures in inches, feet, and yards. There is another way to measure, and we are going to explore these different measurement units and make tools to help us measure with those units.

Add *metric* to the word wall or Math Talk chart and tell students that these new units are called *metric units*, and that they are used a lot in science.

The units on your new ruler are called centimeters.

Add *centimeter* on the word wall or Math Talk chart.

We can abbreviate the word centimeter *using the letters* cm.

Have students write *centimeters* on their rulers.

Which unit is larger: an inch or a centimeter?

Have students go back to the items they measured with cubes and tell what each item measured, using the word *centimeter* (e.g., *5 centimeters*).

What would happen if you told me it measured 5 and did not say centimeters?

Remind students to look at the labels on their rulers to be sure they know which unit they are using when they measure.

These lesson ideas follow the same type of thinking as with customary units. Students make their own centimeter rulers, combine ten centimeter rulers to make a meter stick, and discuss the connections between the measurement units.

Students are making a connection to a number line as they create rulers.

Students from countries that use the metric system might be able to coach their classmates who are less familiar with it.

It is important to emphasize that we are now using different units, and by saying the unit we are making sure our measurements are accurate.

Centimeters to Meters SHOW IT!

Students develop an understanding of meters and measure using a meter stick.

Pose the following:

> Carter wanted to measure the length of the classroom using centimeters. He found that his 10-centimeter ruler was too short to be useful. What could Carter do?
>
> *Have we had similar experiences with measuring longer lengths? What did we do?*
>
> *What could we do to make a longer centimeter ruler?*

Provide students with nine more 10-centimeter-long pieces of cardstock. Using the marks from their centimeter rulers, students create nine more rulers. Students tape their rulers together to form a meter strip. Students number their meter rulers from 11 to 100.

> *How many centimeter rulers did you use?*
>
> *How many centimeters were on each ruler?*
>
> *How many centimeters do you have now? How do you know?*
>
> *One hundred centimeters makes a new unit. Tell your partner if you know what the new unit is called.*

Listen for students who identify *meter*. Record *meter* on the word wall or Math Talk chart.

> *We can abbreviate the word* meter *using* m.
>
> *What are some things in our classroom that are about one meter long? Make a list with your partner and then measure to find the length.*

Students share their results with the class.

Use these questions to close the lesson:

> *We found that 10 groups of 10 centimeters make one meter. Are there other times that we make groups of tens?*
>
> *Have you heard the word* cent *before? What do you know about the word* cent?
>
> *How does that connect to metric measurement?*

Measuring with Two Standard Units

Students measure an item with inches and centimeters to explore the difference in measurement when different units are used.

Students create a chart in their journals with three columns labeled *object*, *inches*, and *centimeters*.

Object	Inches (in.)	Centimeters (cm)

Similar to making the yard strip, students must be sure that their centimeter rulers do not overlap when taping, to preserve the precise length.

Some students may be familiar with other denominations of money that are similarly named. For example, in Mexico, Brazil, and some other countries there are one hundred centavos in one peso.

Choose an object (less than one foot long) from the classroom to measure. Measure it using inches. Record your data in your chart.

You may wish to model and do an example with students.

Circulate and observe students as they measure. Do they use and line up the ruler correctly?

Measure your object a second time using centimeters. Record your data into your chart.

Object	Inches (in.)	Centimeters (cm)
pencil	7 in.	18 cm

What do you notice about your measurements? (There are more centimeters than inches.)

Why would that happen? Did the object get longer?

Choose another object to measure. Measure in both inches and centimeters. What do you think the data will show?

Have students continue measuring other objects using inches and centimeters and recording their data in their tables.

Students can circulate around the room and share their findings with their classmates.

Bring students together and add data to the classroom chart, discussing their insights.

FORMATIVE ASSESSMENT

Put several objects that measure less than one foot in a gallon zipper bag (e.g., crayon, pencil, eraser, glue stick).

Hand the student a ruler with inches on one side and centimeters on the other side.

Have the student measure the items to the nearest inch and then to the nearest centimeter.

Watch the student to see if she:

- chooses the correct side of the ruler for the units she is measuring (e.g., inches or centimeters)
- lines up the ruler at the beginning of the item
- accurately measures to the nearest inch or centimeter
- correctly states the unit measured (e.g., 3 inches).

Additional Ideas for Support and Practice

The following ideas extend students' understanding of measuring length in centimeters and meters.

The activities listed for customary measurement on page 231 (Basket of Stuff and Pick the Tool/Pick the Unit) also work with metric units. The following two activities are variants of activities on page 232.

MEASUREMENT SCAVENGER HUNT

Students find objects at specified lengths. Students record their findings in their math journals.

Have students find something that is each of these lengths:

- 3 centimeters
- 10 centimeters
- 15 centimeters
- 28 centimeters
- 50 centimeters
- 85 centimeters
- 1 meter

Have students share their results with classmates. Make a class chart with all results.

ESTIMATE AND MEASURE

Students estimate lengths in centimeters and then measure to see how close they were.

Give students instructions like the following:

Without using a ruler, draw a line that is about 12 centimeters long. Measure to see how close you were.

Without using a ruler, make a chain of blocks that is about 10 centimeters long. Measure to see how close you were.

Without using a ruler, make a snake with clay that is 20 centimeters long. Measure to see how close you were.

TALK ABOUT IT/WRITE ABOUT IT

If you measured the same object with centimeters and inches, would it measure more centimeters or inches? Why?

Why is the measurement different when you use different units?

Molly said the pencil was 6 inches long and Bailey said it was 15 centimeters long. Could they both be right? Explain.

Vocabulary Sort

Students work with a team to sort the following words and representations based on their math meanings. Once they have placed the words into groups, they decide on a title for each group that describes why those words belong together. Teams then share their groupings with the class or another team and justify their decisions.

> *There is no one way to sort the words, but the groupings must make sense based on the math meanings of the words.*

    centimeter
    difference
    foot
    inch
    length
    longer
    measuring tape
    meter
    meter stick
    ruler
    unit
    yardstick

Eliminate It

Students work with a partner to decide which of the following does not belong with the others, then use math reasoning, numbers, or models to convince their classmates that their thinking makes sense.

ruler	yardstick
inch	centimeter

SOLVING MEASUREMENT PROBLEMS

Students use what they know about measurement units to solve problems using addition and subtraction.

> *It is important to include problem-solving experiences throughout students' work with measurement. And continuing to pose measurement problems throughout the school year is a great way to revisit and review measurement concepts.*

Using Addition and Subtraction to Solve Measurement Problems

Students use measurement contexts to solve addition and subtraction problems, connecting what they already know about these problem structures to the new context.

> Pose the following problem:
>
> Jon had a string that was 56 centimeters long. Albert had a string that was 17 centimeters long. How long were their strings together?

> Make connections to other addition word problems. These are simply about measurement. It is the story structure, adding to or putting together, that tells us when to add. If there is confusion about the operation, suggest a model to show it. Students might refer back to part-part-whole models or bar models to represent the problem.

Turn to your partner and retell the problem in your own words. What do you know? What do you need to find out?

Have you seen a problem with a story like this before? What do you know about solving problems like this? What operation would you use? Talk to your partner.

Have students share their ideas.

Work with your partner to solve the problem. Be prepared to explain your answer.

What about this problem?

> Jerri had a licorice string that was 42 inches long. She ate 13 inches of it. How long is her licorice string now?

Talk with your partner about the problem. What do you need to find out? What other problems like this have you seen? How could you find the answer? Then follow your plan to solve the problem.

After students have time to work, invite pairs to share their answers. Ask questions such as:

How did you know to subtract?

How did you solve the problem?

Pose a couple more problems for students to solve with their partners. You might also encourage them to solve independently and then share their solutions with their partners.

What's the Difference?

Students connect finding difference in length to their experience using bar models.

Show two paper strips of different length.

How would we find the difference between the lengths of these paper strips?

Turn and talk with your partner.

How do we find the difference? What do we need to know?

How does this connect to when we use bar models?

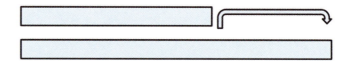

Give partners two strips of paper and have them find the difference.

Did you find the difference by subtracting or by measuring the difference?

Was it the same? Explain.

Try it again with the length of two pieces of ribbon or the height of two towers made from connecting cubes.

Provide students with pairs of objects that have different lengths.

Pose the following problem:

> Jeannie built a tower that is 26 inches tall, and Bobby built a tower that is 19 inches tall. How much taller is Bobby's tower?

This time we know the measurements. How can we use what we know about subtraction to find the difference?

Can we use a bar model to show this?

Invite student volunteers to create a bar model and show the difference.

Additional Ideas for Support and Practice

The following ideas extend students' understanding of solving measurement problems.

Stretch and Compare

Students compare the lengths of objects at rest and when stretched to find the differences in length.

Collect some items that have flexibility and can be stretched (e.g., balloons, springs, gummy worms, rubbery toys, rubber bands).

Give each pair of students an unstretched object and have them lay it on their desk and then measure it.

Students measure stretchable objects at rest and when stretched.

If students have trouble with this, encourage them to have one partner hold the stretched object in place while the other student measures it.

Ask partners to stretch the object and measure it again.

What is the difference in length between the object when you started and when you stretched it?

How did you find the difference?

Place a bag of stretchable items at each table and have several pairs share the items in the bag, taking turns measuring the items at rest and when stretched and then finding the differences.

Have students compare their findings. You may want to probe their problem-solving understanding with questions such as:

What does it mean to find a difference?

What operation do you use to find the difference?

Talk About It/Write About It

Which operation do you use when you want to compare two measurements? Why?

Exploring Problems

Pose the following problems for students to solve. Give each student a +/− pinch card and ask the students to pinch the operation they would use to solve the problem. Have them justify their choice.

I have one very long licorice strip that is 32 inches long.
I have another licorice strip that is just 14 inches long.
How long are my licorice strips together?

The second-grade hallway is 52 feet long.
The cafeteria is 37 feet long.
How far must I walk if I walk down the second-grade hallway and all the way across the cafeteria?

A ribbon was 50 inches long.
After I cut some off, 37 inches were left.
How much did I cut off?

Rita's yard is 19 meters long.
Joe's yard is 25 meters long.
How much longer is Joe's yard?

A snail crawled 25 centimeters.
Then he crawled 16 more centimeters.
How far did he crawl altogether?

For additional strategies to build students' problem-solving skills, see Math in Practice: A Guide for Teachers, Chapter 1.

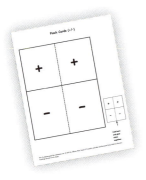

CREATING LINE PLOTS TO DISPLAY MEASUREMENT DATA

Students use measurement data to create line plots, and answer questions about the data.

Understanding Length Measurement
MODULE 10

Displaying Data on Line Plots SHOW IT!

Students create a line plot to display measurement data.

Pose the following problem:

> Mrs. Partin's class was growing bean plants in science. The students measured the plants to see how tall they were. Here are the measurements:
>
> 5 inches
>
> 6 inches
>
> 4 inches
>
> 3 inches
>
> 6 inches
>
> 7 inches
>
> 4 inches
>
> 6 inches
>
> They want to share their data with their parents to show how the plants are growing.

Draw a number line on the board. Label it with numbers *1–10*.

> How could we use this to show the length of each of their plants?

After a few minutes of partner talk, begin putting Xs above numbers on the plot to represent the data.

> What did I just do? What are those Xs? Talk to your partner about what you think I have done.
>
> What do you think the Xs show? How do you know?
>
> Why are there no Xs above 1 and 2?
>
> Why are there 3 Xs above the 6?
>
> How many Xs are above the number line altogether? Why?
>
> We've just made a special kind of graph called a line plot.
>
> What is our line plot about?
>
> What should we call our line plot?
>
> What unit did we measure them in?
>
> Should we put that somewhere on our line plot? Explain.
>
> Let's label the number line *inches*.

Record the title on the line plot on the board. Record *inches* below the number line.

Move slowly through this line of questioning so students are able to count and talk to partners about each question.

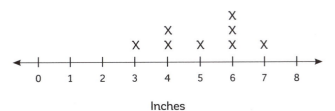

Write *line plot* and *number line* on the word wall or Math Talk chart.

Give each pair the following data about a group of plants.

    3 inches
    4 inches
    4 inches
    3 inches
    5 inches
    4 inches
    2 inches
    4 inches

Have them draw a number line in their math journals and mark Xs to show the data.

> *Put a title on your line plot. What should you call it?*
> *How should you label your number line?*

Have them compare their line plots with a partner's to see if they look the same. If they don't, have them recheck their data to figure out which line plot is accurate.

After they are done, draw a number line on the board and have students come up and add the data to create the line plot, then ask students to turn and share answers for questions like the following:

> *How many plants were 4 inches tall? How do you know?*
> *What was the height of the shortest plant?*
> *What was the height of the tallest plant?*
> *How much taller was the tallest plant than the shortest?*
> *Which height has the most number of plants?*
> *What do you notice about this line plot compared to the last one we made?*

To end the lesson, have students answer this prompt as an exit ticket or in their journals:

> *Tell me two things you know from looking at the line plot we just made.*

Making Line Plots from Measured Data [SHOW IT]

Students generate a set of data by measuring strips of paper and then display their data on line plots.

Create envelopes that have eight strips of cardstock inside. Strips should be cut in varying lengths from three centimeters to ten centimeters, with a width of about one centimeter. Be sure that some are the same length (e.g.,

> By creating multiple envelopes, each with different-length strips, different groups will have different sets of data. Additional envelopes can be used for centers. You might label each envelope so that students can choose a different envelope when doing the center.

strips might be 3 cm, 4 cm, 4 cm, 6 cm, 6 cm, 6 cm, 7 cm, 9 cm). Label the strips *1–8*.

Provide groups of four students with an envelope.

Inside each envelope are strips of paper cut to different lengths. As a group, take out the strips of paper and examine them.

Talk with your group about how you could find the lengths of the strips of paper and display the data you collect.

Have groups share their ideas.

In your journals, create a table to record your measurements.

Take turns measuring each strip of paper using your centimeter ruler.

Complete your table by recording the data you measure. Be sure to label using cm.

Compare your results with those of the other people in your group. Do you agree?

If you don't agree, what do you think you should do?

Circulate and observe students as they measure. Support students who continue to struggle lining up their rulers.

You made a table of the data you collected. How could you display the data so that you can look at patterns?

Turn to your partner and tell them how you would make a line plot using the data.

Work with your group to make the line plot.

Have students create a line plot in their journals. Circulate and support as needed.

Compare your line plot to your partner's.

What should be similar?

What might be different?

Invite students to compare their line plots to those of classmates from other tables.

How are your line plots different? Why?

Use your line plot to write three questions you can ask your classmates.

Invite students to move around the room, sharing their line plots and asking classmates questions about the data they collected.

To end the lesson, use questions such as these to have students reflect on their learning:

How can a line plot be used to display numerical data?

How did you obtain the data for the line plot?

What were some things that made this challenging?

How did you make your line plot and record the data?

Differentiation

If there are multiple students who would benefit from small-group guidance, invite them to a table. Help students line up the ruler with the paper strip and measure to the nearest centimeter.

Understanding Length Measurement

243

MODULE 10

FORMATIVE ASSESSMENT

Have students create a line plot using the data in the table below and then write two questions that could be answered using it.

Bird	Length in Inches
Blue Jay	9 in.
Chickadee	5 in.
Downy Woodpecker	6 in.
Finch	5 in.
Hummingbird	3 in.
Robin	8 in.
Sparrow	6 in.
Wren	5 in.

[Student work: A line plot titled "Length of Birds" with a number line from 0 to 9. X marks are placed at 3 (one X), 5 (three X's), 6 (two X's), 8 (one X), and 9 (one X).]

Write two questions that could be answered using the line plot.

Witch size has the most?

What size is the biggest?

This student accurately represents the data using a line plot. The student has titled the line plot *Length of Birds*. The student does not label the line as *inches*. Ask the student what measurement unit was used to measure the birds. Ask how he can communicate that to his audience. The student asks two appropriate questions that can be answered using the line graph.

If students have difficulty creating a number line, offer a template or encourage them to use their rulers. If students do not represent the data correctly, ask:

How long is a blue jay? Where can we show that on our graph?

How long is a chickadee? How can we show that?

How do you think we would record the data for the length of the downy woodpecker?

> If students struggle to create a question, ask them what information they can see from looking at the line plot. Ask:
>
> *How can you turn that into a question?*

Additional Ideas for Support and Practice

The following ideas extend students' understanding of creating line plots to display measurement data.

BASKET OF STUFF LINE PLOTS

Fill a basket with various items.

Students pick items and measure to find the lengths, using either inches or centimeters.

Students create a table in their journals to record the results.

Using the data collected, students create a line plot.

Students can use data that was previously collected in Basket of Stuff activities.

LINE PLOT QUESTIONS

Students use line plots to answer questions.

Use the following line plots to create cards with a series of questions for students to answer about them.

Height of Sunflowers

Feet

Possible questions:

What is the height of the tallest sunflower?

How tall is the shortest sunflower?

Which height was recorded the most?

How many sunflowers were 6 feet tall?

Vocabulary

benchmark	meter
centimeter	meter stick
compare	number line
estimate	ruler
foot	tools
hash marks	units
height (high)	width (wide)
inch	yard
length (long)	yardstick
line plot	
measuring tape	

ONLINE RESOURCES

General Resources
Additional Problems
Table of Addition and Subtraction Length Problems

- - - - -

Resources for Specific Activities
Pinch Cards

- - - - -

These resources are available at http://hein.pub/MathinPractice, keycode MIPG2.

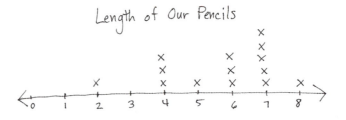

Possible questions:

How many students had a pencil that was 4 inches long?
How long was the shortest pencil?
How long was the longest pencil?
How many pencils were measured?

TALK ABOUT IT/WRITE ABOUT IT

How does a line plot help organize measurement data?

Why is it important to label the line plot with the measurement unit?

MODULE 11

Exploring Time

About the Math 2.MD.7

Prior to second grade, students explored telling time with analog and digital clocks to the hour and half hour. Now they become more precise at telling time.

> The key ideas focused on in this module include:
> - **telling and writing time to the nearest five minutes on a digital and analog clock**
> - **understanding A.M. and P.M.**

An analog clock is basically a circular number line. When students understand this concept, they notice that the 1–12 on the number line represent hours, while the sixty notches along the edge of the clock show minutes. The clock's hour hand works with twelve units (hours), while the minute hand works with sixty units (minutes).

Before moving to telling time to the nearest five minutes, students explore the idea of quarter hours. Folding a clock face into fourths, or quarters, and connecting this to their geometry investigations in which they split circles into fourths, provides insights into the language of telling time (see Figure 11.1). *Quarter after five* or *quarter of nine* become understandable terms. Students connect fifteen minutes to both *quarter after* and *quarter of*.

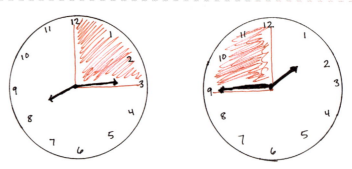

Figure 11.1 Students see quarters on the clock face similar to the quarters they see when partitioning circles in geometry.

See Math in Practice: Teaching First-Grade Math, Module 12 for ideas on teaching time to the hour and half hour.

Students make connections between representing time on digital and analog clocks, recognizing that on a digital clock, the hours are always to the left and the minutes to the right. Having students read and write times on both analog and digital clocks and having them show the time on one when given it on the other help familiarize them with both ways to represent time (see Figure 11.2).

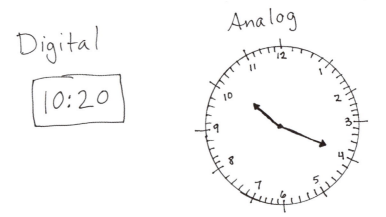

Figure 11.2 Posing a digital time and having students show the time on an analog clock, or vice versa, helps them make connections between these two representations of time.

When telling time to five minutes, students use their understanding of skip counting to determine how to say and write the time when looking at an analog clock. When the minute hand is pointing at the 5, it indicates twenty-five minutes, because each number on the clock face indicates the end of a 5-minute interval (see Figure 11.3). As students revisit the analog clock, think about it as a number line that is split into sixty units, and skip count by fives as they touch the numbers on the clock face, they are connecting number ideas to telling time.

Figure 11.3 Students explore the numbers on the clock face as indicating intervals of five minutes and use skip counting to find the accurate time.

Reflecting on the idea that there are twenty-four hours in a day, but only twelve numbers on a clock face, helps our students understand the need for A.M. and P.M. Exploring examples of what we do during different times of day helps them make sense of the difference between 6:00 A.M. and 6:00 P.M.

Exploring the Progression

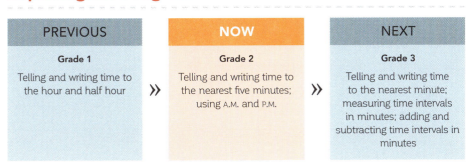

Ideas for Instruction and Assessment

TELLING TIME

Students build on their understanding of time to the hour and half hour to now tell time to 5-minute intervals. Students explore the meaning of A.M. and P.M.

Characteristics of an Analog Clock

This quick review helps determine what students know about telling time and precedes other lessons on telling time.

> Display a model of an analog clock and review its parts with students.
>
> *What do you already know about the analog clock?*

Learning Goals

I can tell time to the nearest five minutes.

I can tell the difference between A.M. and P.M.

Lessons in This Module

Telling Time

Characteristics of an Analog Clock

Make a Human Clock

Telling Time to the Quarter and Half Hour

Splitting the Clock

Understanding A.M. and P.M.

Differentiation

If students are having trouble telling time to the hour, consider focusing only on the hour hand. Although we tend to rely on the hour hand to simply denote the hour and the minute hand to denote the minutes, a closer inspection of the hour hand shows that it can provide information about the approximate time, as students discover they can use just the hour hand to determine if the time is "about," "a little past," or "almost to" the nearest hour. Once students get the idea of telling time from the hour hand, the minute hand can be introduced. See Math in Practice: Teaching First-Grade Math, Module 12.

> What do the numbers 1–12 represent?
> What do the "hands" of the clock tell us?
> Describe how the hands move as time passes.

Give each pair an individual clock with moveable hands. Have one partner start by showing 2:00. Their partner checks to be sure they agree. If they disagree, partners decide how they want to show it and then all pairs show their clocks to the teacher.

> Where did you place the hour hand? Why?
> Where did you place the minute hand? Why?

Have partners switch roles.

> Show me 5:00.
> Where did you place the hour hand? Why?
> Where did you place the minute hand? Why?
> Show me 4:30.
> Where did you place the hour hand? Why?
> Where did you place the minute hand? Why?
> What is another way to say 4:30?
> Why?

Have students use the clocks to practice showing other times with partners.

Make a Human Clock

Students build the connection between a number line and an analog clock.

Begin this lesson by asking students how the analog clock is like a number line.

> How is a clock like a number line? How is it different? Talk to your partner.

Invite twelve students to line up in the front of the classroom.

Give each one an index card with a number 1–12 and ask them to line up in order from 1–12.

> How is our number line like a clock face?
> What would these numbers represent on a clock?
> What do you think we could do to turn our human number line into a clock?
> Is our order important? Should we stay in the same order? Why?

This simple demonstration helps students visualize the clock face as a circular number line. Although they have not explored telling time to five minutes yet, they have explored telling time to the half hour and have talked about sixty minutes being an hour and thirty minutes as being half of an hour. This activity reminds them of those key ideas as they begin to explore time to 5-minute intervals.

Have the students form a circle. Be sure that the person holding the 6 card is across from the 12, and the 3 and 9 are across from each other.

> Which number is halfway around our circle?
> What do you say when the minute hand is on the six?

Give each of the students a second index card that shows skip counting by fives, so the first student gets 5, the second 10, and so on.

Have students count by fives as you point to each person in the circle.

What is the last number?

If we were telling time, what would we be counting with these numbers?

Why do you say that?

Invite students to share ideas about how the clock face is a circular number line that can be counted by hours (1–12) or minutes (1–60).

How can we use our understanding of the number line to help us better understand the clock?

Telling Time to the Quarter and Half Hour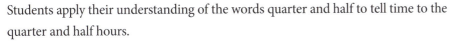

Students apply their understanding of the words quarter and half to tell time to the quarter and half hours.

Write the words *half* and *quarter* on the board or Math Talk chart.

Tell your partner what these words are. Have you seen these words before? When? What do they mean?

Listen to students talk about the words *quarter* and *half*. Listen for connections to money, time, and geometry. Invite students to share their different thinking.

How many halves are in one whole?

How many half-dollars are in one dollar?

How many half hours are in one hour?

On an analog clock, display the time 3:00.

Tell your partner what time my clock says.

Model for students by beginning at 3:00 and moving the minute hand until it reaches 3:30.

Be sure to also move the hour hand to between the 3 and 4 to indicate half past 3:00.

When the minute hand points to the 6, how far around the clock has the minute hand traveled?

We say it is "half past the hour." Why do you think we say that?

How many minutes have passed? How do you know?

How many minutes are in half of an hour?

I've shown 3:30 on my clock. What's another way to say that?

Turn and talk to your partner. How does thinking about halves help you to understand this as half past three?

Where is the hour hand when it is 3:30? Explain.

Listen to students as they discuss geometry and the clock face.

> It's important to explicitly point out that both the hour and minute hands move, though at different rates. Students need to be aware of this when they read and show time on an analog clock.

Move on to *quarter*, following a similar questioning pattern using the time 8:15 and introducing the term *quarter past*.

Then continue:

> If the minute hand moves 15 more minutes, what time will it be?

Move the minute hand so the clock displays 8:30.

> Some people call 8:30 "30 minutes before 9." Does that make sense? Why?
> What do you notice about the hour hand? Why?
> If the minute hand moves 15 more minutes again, what time will it be?

Move the minute hand so the clock displays 8:45.

> What do you notice about the hour hand?
> How many more minutes are there before the next hour? How do you know?
> What do we know about 15 minutes?
> Some people call this time "a quarter to 9." Does that make sense? Why?

Continue this pattern of questioning with other hours.

Have students show partners a time with 15-minute intervals and practice using the language *quarter after*, *half past*, and *quarter to*.

Have students answer the following questions in their journals:

> How does our understanding of the word *quarter* help us tell time? How many minutes are in a quarter of an hour?
> How many minutes are in half of an hour?

Differentiation
While students practice with partners, you might choose to work with a small group of students, supporting their use of the language. Help students make connections to quarters and halves within geometry.

SMP2, SMP4, SMP6, SMP7

Thinking Through a Lesson

Splitting the Clock

Students partition circles into halves and quarters, and then twelfths, as they create a clock face.

Provide each student with an 8-inch circle template. Have students cut their circle out.

> What shape is the face of an analog clock? (It's a circle.)
> We are going to use our circles to create a clock face. How many hours does our clock face display? (12.)
> How many partitions should we make on our circle? (12.)

Begin by having students fold their circles in half and then open them back up.

> How many parts do we have after folding our circle? (Two.)
> What do we call two parts? (Halves.)

For more on partitioning shapes, see Module 15.

Although second-grade students do not need to master twelfths, they can apply their understanding of halves and quarters as they complete their clocks.

In first grade, students partitioned circles into two and four equal shares. Students will connect their understanding of geometry and circles to understanding time.

Have students place their circles so that the fold is vertical.

> *Let's begin labeling our clock face. Is there a clock in the classroom that we can use to help us?*

Direct students' attention to an analog clock in the classroom.

> *What number goes at the top?* (12.)
>
> *What number goes at the bottom?* (6.)

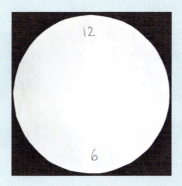

Have students write *12* at the top of their circle and *6* at the bottom of their circle, but not too close to the edge.

> *Let's continue to partition our circle.*

Have students re-fold their circle into halves and fold in half again, then open it back up.

> *How many parts do we have now?* (Four.)
>
> *When we split a circle into four parts, what do we call each part?* (Fourths or quarters.)
>
> *When we tell time, we think of an hour being split into four sections. We call each one a quarter of an hour.*
>
> *Turn and talk to your partner about what numbers we can add to our clock now. How do you know?* (We can add 3 and 9, because when I look at a clock, I see the 3 on the right side and a 9 on the left side.)

Have students label the *3* and the *9* on their clock faces.

> This is important, as students will also be labeling the minutes later on.

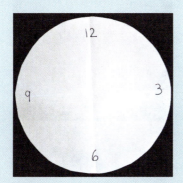

> Make connections to the term quarters from students' experiences partitioning circles in geometry. Quarters might also be connected to the monetary term in which four quarters equal one dollar.

> *Let's partition our circle again. Re-fold your circle two times. Now we need to fold our quarter into thirds.*

Demonstrate to students how to fold the quarter into thirds, as in the picture below.

> Because folding thirds can be challenging for this age, modeling is critical. As students are folding, circulate and support as needed.

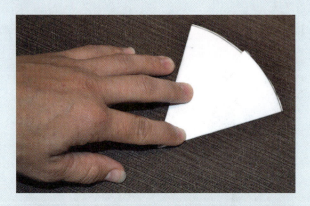

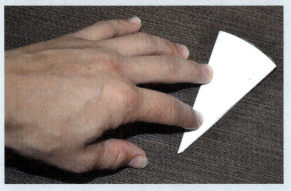

After students have completed their folds, have them open their circles up again.

> *What do you notice? How many parts do we have?* (Twelve.)
> *Fill in the missing hours and compare your clock face with your partner's.*
> *What part of the clock have we shown?* (Hours.)

> *Clocks usually show each number for the hours but not for the minutes. Why not?* (There are sixty minutes—that's too many to label.)
> *What do we see on a clock that shows the minutes?* (We see hash marks. Or, We see little lines.)

Count by fives as you touch each number on the clock. What do you notice? (There are sixty minutes.)

Have students count by fives a second time, this time writing the numbers they skip count in smaller print around the outside edge and circling them.

> **Differentiation**
> If you have students who still need work on skip counting by five, do the counting all together now and then work with a small group later to strengthen this skill.

> You may also opt to have students make hash marks to represent each minute. Model for students how to do this.

Ask students a series of questions related to their clock faces.

How many minutes are in one hour? (60 minutes.)

How many minutes are in half of an hour? How do you know? (30 minutes, because 30 + 30 = 60. Or, 30 is halfway around the clock.)

When we partitioned the clock into fourths, how many minutes were in each fourth or quarter? How do you know? (There were 15 minutes; I counted 5, 10, 15. Or, I did 5 + 5 + 5.)

How many groups of 5 minutes are in each quarter? How do you know? What do you notice on a clock that shows this? (There are 3 groups of 5 minutes; there are 3 sections.)

What number do you say when you touch 3? Why? (15; there are 15 minutes in a quarter hour.)

What number do you say when you touch 6? Why? (30; there are 30 minutes in a half hour.)

What number do you say when you touch 11? What does that mean when we read the time? (55; 55 minutes have passed.)

Have students slide their paper clocks into page protectors and use a wipe-off marker to show different times.

Show the time 3:05.

Talk to your partner about the hour and minute hands on the clock. Which one is shorter? Which one is longer?

Show 8:30.

Where should the hour hand point? Why? (It should point between the 8 and 9, because the time is halfway between 8:00 and 9:00.)

Pose a variety of other times.

Students take turns showing different times on their clocks to their partners, counting by fives aloud.

> As students work with partners to display times to the nearest five minutes, pull a small group to the side to address any skip-counting support needed.

Modify the times to 5-minute intervals as students are ready.

FORMATIVE ASSESSMENT

Have students show the time on each clock face and write two different ways they could say each time in words.

  4:15
  10:30

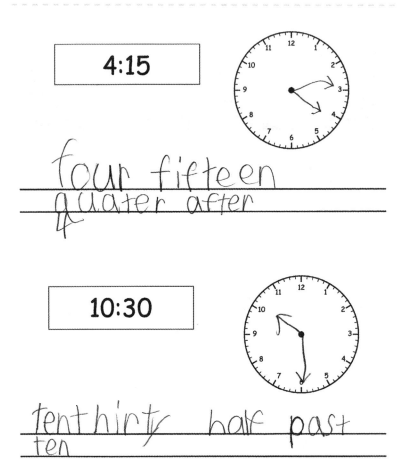

The student shows both times sufficiently on the analog clocks. On the top clock, the curved minute hand showing 4:15 indicates a self-correction on the part of the student, who curved it so it would point to the 3. The student correctly expresses 4:15 as *four fifteen* and then as *quarter after 4*. On the bottom clock, the hour hand points to the 10. Follow up by asking, "How much of the hour has gone by? Where would halfway between 10 and 11 be?" The student correctly expresses 10:30 as *ten thirty* and *half past ten*.

Understanding A.M. and P.M.

Students build their understanding that there are twenty-four hours in one day and that our 12-hour analog clock can be used with A.M. and P.M. to identify the time of day.

> *When do you think a new day begins?*

Display a clock face showing 12:00.

> *12:00 is midnight. It is the start of a new day.*
> *How many complete hours are in one day?*
> *How many hours does the clock face show?*
> *How can we tell time with a clock that only has twelve hours, if we have twenty-four hours in a day?*

Allow students to discuss the idea. Listen for students who might say that 2 twelves make twenty-four hours, or that we would have to have the clock go all the way around twice to go through a whole day.

> *What do you do at 8:00? (I have breakfast. Or, I go to bed.)*
> *How can that be? Some people have breakfast at 8:00 and some go to bed? Does that make sense?*
> *What do you do at 12:00? (I eat lunch. Or, I sleep.)*
> *What's another way to say 12:00 when we are at school?*
> *We use A.M. to label times between midnight and noon.*
> *We use P.M. to label times between noon and midnight.*
> *Tell your partner if you would do these activities in the A.M. or the P.M. Be sure to justify your thinking.*

> - Eat breakfast
> - Go home from school
> - Watch the sunset
> - Put your pajamas on
> - Eat dinner
> - Watch the sunrise
> - Go to P.E. class
> - Do your homework

Have students share their thinking as a whole class.

Then pose different times, labeled A.M. or P.M., and have students identify what they might be doing at that time.

As an exit ticket, have students answer the following question:

> *Why is it important to identify A.M. or P.M.?*

Common Error or Misconception

A.M. and P.M. can be challenging for students, particularly noon and midnight. Some students are confused as to when A.M. and P.M. start and stop. Remind students that the transition between A.M. and P.M. always occurs at 12:00.

Students will likely think a day begins in the morning or when the sun rises, or may be familiar with religious or other systems in which the day begins at other times such as sunset. Explain that in this system, people have agreed that the day will start at midnight.

Although not expected vocabulary for second grade, many students are curious what the abbreviations A.M. and P.M. stand for. Many will have an incorrect belief that A.M. stands for after midnight. Although this can be a useful way to remember, it is not factual. The abbreviations come from the Latin *ante meridiem* (before noon) and *post meridiem* (after noon).

FORMATIVE ASSESSMENT

Give students the following three situations:

- the time I go to school
- the time I go to bed
- the time I eat lunch

For each, have them show the time in both analog and digital form and indicate whether it would happen in the A.M. or P.M.

My Day

This is the time I go to school.

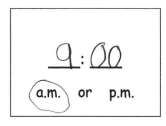

This is the time I go to bed.

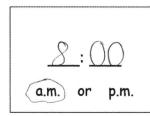

This is the time I eat lunch.

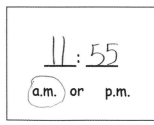

This student demonstrates some understanding of representing both analog and digital time, but has some errors in the second and third clocks that should be addressed. In the second clock, the student shows 8 A.M. as the digital time for bed, which is unreasonable. It's possible that he simply circled the same thing for each response, but you'll want to ask questions (e.g., Do you wake up in the A.M. or the P.M.?) to check his understanding of A.M. and P.M. The third clock shows some misunderstanding about the time 11:55. He may need some additional support around the movement of the hour hand.

Additional Ideas for Support and Practice

The following ideas extend students' understanding of telling time to the nearest five minutes and provide meaningful practice.

WHAT TIME IS IT?

Have students pick a time card, then show the time on a clock face.

> They write what they do at that time of day and label their clock face with the time, including whether it is A.M. or P.M.
>
> Then, they pick another time card and repeat.

RODEO TIME

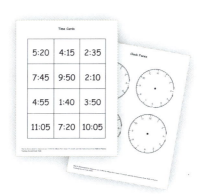

Before Reading:

> *What is a rodeo? What might you see at a rodeo?* (People ride bulls at a rodeo. *Or,* We might see horses and cowboys.)

Give students clocks with moveable hands.

During Reading:

Read *Rodeo Time* by Stuart Murphy.

As you read the story to the class, alternate between students reading the times on the pages or displaying the times on their clocks.

After Reading:

Go back through the clocks in the book and use them to explore the times.

Show the clock on page 9.

> *What time does the clock show? How do you know?*
> *After getting lunch, Katie yells that, "It's way past 2:00!"*
> *What time does the clock show on page 10?*
> *How many minutes past 2:00 is it?*
> *What's another way to say that?*
> *Do you think it's 2:30 A.M. or P.M.? Why?*

Show the clock on page 13.

> *What time did Katie and Cameron get to the holding pen?*
> *What time were they supposed to get there?*
> *Were they early or late? Explain.*

Show the clock on page 20.

> *Show me 4:45 on your clock.*
> *What's another way to say 4:45?*

Many class activities and centers require students to record times using an analog model. There are commercial ink stamps available that make recording in journals easier, or you might copy some clock faces from the template in the online resources and have students glue them into journals.

For more ideas on integrating children's literature into math lessons, see Math in Practice: A Guide for Teachers, Chapter 2.

Differentiation

Clocks can be copied on different colors of paper. Blue clocks may show time to five minutes, while yellow clocks show time to the hour and half hour for students who may still need practice with those. Tell partners which color they are focusing on for the day. Blank clock face templates are provided in the online resources.

Similar questioning can be used on other pages where the clocks are shown and times are referred to.

TIME SCAVENGER HUNT

Tape twelve clock faces showing different times in various places on the classroom walls.

Students create a recording sheet by writing the letters A–L in a column on their papers.

Students then work with partners to find each clock and say the time to their partners.

Then, they record the time shown on the clock, in digital form, next to that letter on their recording sheets.

When students are done, have them share their times with the class.

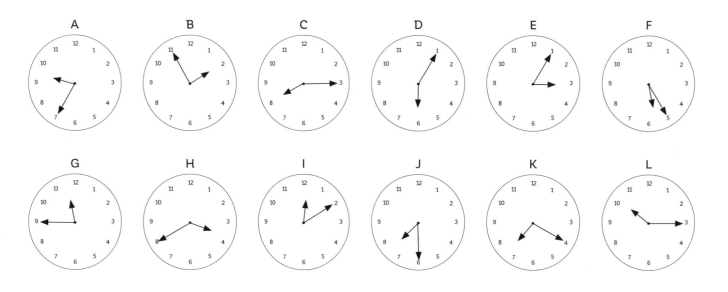

TALK ABOUT IT/WRITE ABOUT IT

Brendan said he ate breakfast at 7:30 P.M. Do you agree or disagree? Explain why.

Allison said she goes home from school at 3:00 P.M. Do you agree or disagree? Explain why.

Blake says she is sleeping at 12:00 A.M. Do you agree or disagree? Explain why.

Students use clocks to show various times to the nearest five minutes.

TELLING TIME MEMORY

Students match cards with digital times and cards with corresponding analog times.

Copy each set of cards (analog and digital) on a different color of cardstock paper.

Have students lay the analog clock cards in three rows of five facedown, then lay the digital time cards in three rows of five facedown.

Have students turn over two cards to see if they match (one analog and one digital).

If the cards match, the student keeps the cards. If not, she returns them to their place on the desk.

The student who makes the most matches wins.

Differentiation

You could limit the number of cards to eight digital time cards and eight analog clock face cards. Or play a simple matching game in which students lay one set of cards (e.g., clock faces) face up, and then take turns picking a digital time card and finding its match.

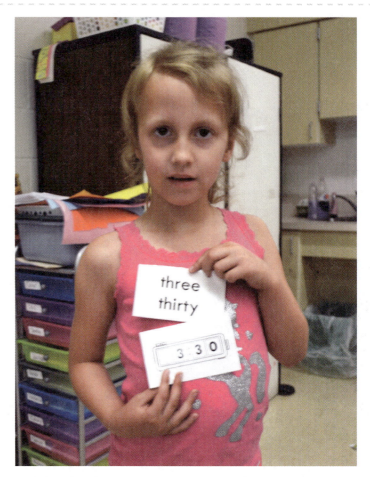

Students match digital and analog times to the written form.

For an added challenge, create a similar game that includes times written in word form.

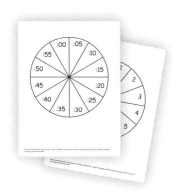

Time Spin

Students spin two spinners, one with hours (1–12) and one with minutes (00, 05, 10, 15 . . . 55).

Students record the time in their journals, in digital and analog time.

Variation: Include a third spinner with A.M. and P.M. Students write about what they might be doing at that time of day.

Daily Schedule Sort

Students create a daily schedule in their journals.

Record the times for various class events on strips.

Although most school schedules work for this activity, if your schedule has times to the minute (e.g., 1:23 P.M.) you may have to adjust the times to be the nearest five minutes.

Sample Schedule

Morning Meeting	8:25 A.M.
Reading	8:45 A.M.
Math	10:15 A.M.
Writing	11:30 A.M.
Lunch	12:15 P.M.
Recess	12:45 P.M.
Music	1:15 P.M.
Science	1:45 P.M.
Dismissal	2:30 P.M.

Give each team a set of strips and have them work together to order them from earliest to latest in the day.

Then, have them record the various times on analog clock templates and glue them into their journals.

They can label each clock with the activity and the time in digital form.

Analog clocks do not appear in many places outside of school, because most clocks are computerized and show time in a digital format (e.g., cable boxes, microwaves, computers). Rather than posting the time in a digital form on your classroom schedule, consider showing it in an analog format. The more students see the time on analog clocks, the more comfortable they get with that representation of time.

Vocabulary

A.M. o'clock
analog clock P.M.
digital clock quarter after
half past quarter past
hour hand quarter to
minute hand

General Resources
8-Inch Circle Template
Additional Problems
Clock Faces

Resources for Specific Activities
Telling Time Memory Cards
Time Cards
Time Spinners

These resources are available at http://hein.pub/MathinPractice, keycode MIPG2.

ONLINE RESOURCES

Exploring Time 263
MODULE 11

MODULE 12

Exploring Money

About the Math   2.MD.8

First-grade students began exploring coins by identifying them and their values and counting like coins. Second-grade students expand their skills with coins and begin to explore problems about money.

> The key ideas focused on in this module include:
> - counting sets of unlike coins
> - showing monetary amounts using the dollar and cent symbols
> - solving word problems related to money.

To count coins, students learn to organize coins from greatest value to least value to more efficiently count them, using their skip-counting skills to determine the total amount of money. As they count the value of each coin, they learn to shift their skip counting as the denomination changes, as when counting a quarter, two dimes, and two nickels: 25, 35, 45, 50, 55 (see Figure 12.1).

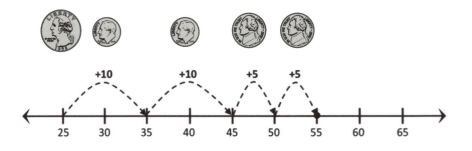

Figure 12.1

Students apply their decomposition skills (breaking numbers apart in different ways) and their addition skills as they investigate different ways to show a value. A dime (10 cents) can be decomposed into two nickels (5 cents + 5 cents = 10 cents) or one nickel and five pennies (5 cents + 1 cent + 1 cent + 1 cent + 1 cent + 1 cent = 10 cents). By using their understanding of the value of coins and their ability to decompose numbers, they change the coin denominations while still keeping the value the same.

1 dime = 10 pennies

1 dime = 2 nickels

1 quarter = 5 nickels

1 quarter = 25 pennies

Understanding the relationship between coins and bills is foundational for the problem-solving tasks that follow. Hundred charts are a helpful tool for exploring the connections between various coins and one dollar, and making connections to place value concepts (10 tens equal one hundred like 10 dimes equal one dollar). In Figures 12.2 and 12.3, the hundred chart represents $1.00, or 100 cents.

For some students, a review of skip counting by fives and tens may be necessary to allow them to efficiently count coins.

Figure 12.2 The hundred chart on the left shows $1.00 as the value of ten dimes, while the hundred chart on the right shows $1.00 as the value of twenty nickels.

Figure 12.3 This hundred chart shows $1.00 as the value of four quarters.

Students learn the symbols for dollars and cents (see Figure 12.4). Although they have not studied decimals, they learn that a decimal point separates dollars from cents and become familiar with the way dollars and cents are represented, with $1.25 meaning one dollar and twenty-five cents.

Figure 12.4 Students become familiar with expressing monetary amounts with dollar and cent symbols.

Students apply their problem-solving skills to money situations as they use addition and subtraction to solve money problems.

Katie had 40 cents. She found 25 cents. How much money did she have? (adding to)

Kyle had 40 cents. He found 1 dime and 3 nickels. How much money did he have? (adding to)

Molly had 3 dimes in her pocket and 4 nickels in her purse. How much money did she have? (putting together)

Cruz had 75 cents in his piggy bank. He took out 40 cents to buy a toy. How much was left in the bank? (taking from)

Genevieve had 40 cents. She had 2 dimes. The rest were nickels. How much money did she have in nickels? (taking apart)

Liam had 85 cents and Bailey had 35 cents. How much more money did Liam have? (comparing)

Problem situations continue to challenge students with unknowns in different positions:

Jamie had 40 cents in her piggy bank. She put some more money in the bank. Now she has 70 cents in her piggy bank. How much did she put in?

Jamie had some money in her piggy bank. She put 30 cents more in the bank. Now she has 70 cents in her piggy bank. How much did she have to start?

Brendan had 55 cents in his hand. He dropped some money. Now he has 32 cents. How much money did he drop?

Brendan had some money in his hand. He dropped 23 cents. Now he has 32 cents. How much money did he have in his hand to start?

As their confidence and abilities with money increase, students apply their understanding of decomposition and their knowledge of the value of coins to solve problems in which multiple answers are possible. These problems can be simple (How many ways can you make 15 cents?) or more complex (Patrick paid $1.00 to ride the bumper cars. He paid in coins. How might he have paid?).

Number bonds (Figure 12.5) can be very useful to model the relationships of parts to wholes within monetary values.

Ellen bought a game token for 25 cents. What coins could she have used to pay for the token?

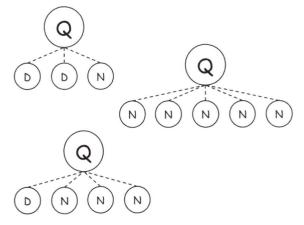

Figure 12.5 As second graders work to understand different ways to make specific amounts of money, this type of model may be helpful to organize their thinking.

Rich problems with multiple answers require students to apply their understanding of decomposition and their knowledge of the value of coins, to use appropriate operations (addition or subtraction), and to rely on their perseverance to find multiple solutions.

> See Module 1 for additional ideas on helping students identify addition and subtraction story structures when solving word problems. A table of money-related problems is available in the online resources.

> The emphasis in Common Core standards is on problem solving related to money. Counting money is included here to strengthen students' background with coins and bills, to make connections to skip counting, decomposition, and place value concepts, and to support students in everyday tasks like counting amounts and making change.

Learning Goals

I can count coins and dollar bills.

I can show money amounts using the dollar and cent signs.

I can solve problems about money.

Lessons in This Module

Counting Money
Ten Frame Pennies
Counting the Value of Unlike Coins
Exploring Monetary Symbols
Exploring Coin Combinations with Number Lines
Using Number Bonds to Explore Coin Combinations
Making Trades

Solving Problems About Money
Solving Problems with Number Lines
Who Has More?
Solving Problems with Number Bonds

Sam had 50 cents. He found some coins. Now he has 85 cents. What coins might he have found?

Allison bought a cookie at the school fair for 35 cents. What coins could she have used to pay for her cookie? Find as many ways as you can.

Jason bought a book for $4.00. He used 2 dollar bills and some coins. All of the coins were the same. How might he have paid for the book?

Students apply a variety of number skills as they explore money in second grade. Problems that ask students to find change can be connected to finding the difference, with coins or number lines being helpful visuals. They apply their understanding of skip counting and decomposition as they combine coin amounts to find a total: counting 2 dimes, a nickel and 2 pennies as 10, 20, 25, 26, 27 cents. They use subtraction and decomposition skills to separate monetary amounts into more coins with lesser values (e.g., 35 cents might become 1 dime, 2 nickels, and 15 pennies). They use place value understanding to add tens to tens and ones to ones. And they extend their problem-solving skills as they revisit problem structures and refine their skills, applying the operations of addition and subtraction to money problems.

Exploring the Progression

PREVIOUS	NOW	NEXT
Grade 1	**Grade 2**	**Grade 3**
Identifying coins and values; skip counting to count groups of like coins	Counting groups of unlike coins; showing money values with dollar and cent signs; solving addition/subtraction problems with money	Solving more complex problems related to money

Ideas for Instruction and Assessment

COUNTING MONEY

Students use skip-counting strategies to find the value of different sets of coins.

Ten Frame Pennies [SHOW IT!]

Students use ten frames to review the values of pennies, nickels, dimes, and quarters.

Students need ten frames (or double ten frames) and coins.

Have students use pennies to fill one row of a ten frame.

How much money do we have? Let's count the pennies.

Tell your partner which coin has a value of 5 cents?

Have students find a nickel in their coins. Record *penny* and *nickel* on the word wall or Math Talk chart, including a drawing of a ten frame with 1 counter by *penny* and a ten frame with 5 counters by *nickel*.

Use pennies to fill a ten frame.

How much money do we have now?

Tell your partner which coin has the same value as 10 cents?

Have students find a dime in their coins. Record *dime* on the word wall or Math Talk chart, including a drawing of a ten frame with 10 counters.

Is there a different way that we can make 10 cents?

Will thinking about your ten frame help?

Have students share ways to make 10 cents using their understanding of one, five, and ten, making connections to the ten frames.

Then, have partners work together to fill their two ten frames with 20 pennies.

Students can also use double ten frames.

> *How many pennies filled both frames?*

As a group, use the ten frames to skip count by fives and tens to 20.

Give partners another ten frame. Have them add 5 more pennies.

As a group, skip count by fives to 25.

> *There's a coin that has a value of 25 cents.*
> *Turn and talk to your partner and see if you know what it's called.*

Have students find a quarter in their coins. Record *quarter* on the word wall or Math Talk chart, including a drawing of two full ten frames and one more frame with 5 counters.

> *Is there another way you could make 25 cents besides 25 pennies or a quarter?*
> *Could looking at your ten frames help you find a way?*

Have students share their ideas.

To end the lesson, have students answer the following question in their journals:

> *Is there another way to make 20 cents besides 20 pennies? How?*

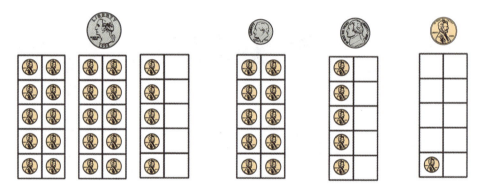

Counting the Value of Unlike Coins

Students use skip-counting strategies to count unlike coins.

> Provide pairs of students with a cup of coins.

Pose the following problem:

> Quinn had 9 pennies.
> Carla had 4 dimes.
> Marty had 6 nickels.
> Harper had 2 quarters.
> Who had the most money?

> *Talk to your partner about the information in this problem.*
> *Use your coins to help you solve.*
> *Tell your partner what the total value of each set is.*

Circulate around the room, observing students and listening to their counting. Support students as necessary. Watch for students who may be unable to identify the coins or their values.

> *What strategies could you use to count the coins?*
> *How did you know 4 dimes equal 40 cents?*

As a whole class, have partners share their thinking.

> *Did anyone think about it differently?*
> *Who had the most money? Why?*

Randomly display 4 dimes and 3 nickels on an interactive whiteboard or document camera.

> *Talk with your partner about how you could find the total.*
> *What is the total?*
> *Why was it hard to skip count this time?*
> *What could you do to make it easier?*

Have a student rearrange the coins on the whiteboard from greatest to least value.

> *Work with your partner to count the total now.*
> *Was it easier? Why?*
> *How does it change the way you skip counted?*

Have students take turns skip counting the coins out loud to their partners.

Repeat this with 3 dimes, 2 nickels, and 2 pennies.

Student pairs should put any 6 coins into their cups.

> *Tip out the coins in your cup and arrange them from greatest to least value.*
> *Why are we ordering the coins? How will it help us to count?*

Have students work with partners to find the value of the coins in their cups.

> *Was there anything that made counting difficult?*
> *What strategies did you use?*

In their math journals, have students draw pictures of the coins and record the total value.

> *Compare your picture to your partner's. What's the same? Is there anything that's different?*

Have students repeat the activity with 6 different coins.

As an exit ticket, have students answer these questions to reflect on their work:

> *What did you find challenging?*
> *What strategies helped you?*

Common Error or Misconception
Some students might count the number of coins and say the total is seven. Revisit the concept that each coin has a value, and we are counting the value of the coins, not the number of coins.

Ask pairs who had values greater than $1.00 to talk about their thinking.

For students who need a transitional model between concrete coins (either real or plastic) and drawn images, rubber ink stamps that depict both the heads and tails sides of coins can be used as an aid.

MATH IN PRACTICE
Teaching Second-Grade Math

MODULE 12

FORMATIVE ASSESSMENT

Pose the following:

> Ann has 3 dimes, 5 nickels, and 1 quarter. She wants to buy a pencil that costs 75 cents. Does she have enough money? Show your thinking using pictures and numbers.

If the student does not correctly add the values, conduct an interview to determine where the confusion is. Ask the student what the value of each coin is and how he could find the total amount for each type of coin.

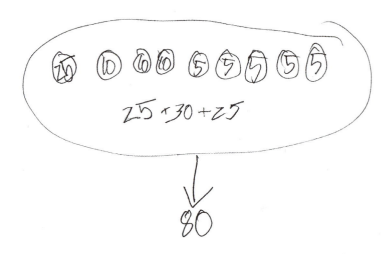

This student shows a representation for each coin. The student adds the value of the quarter (25 cents), plus the value of the dimes (30 cents), plus that value of the nickels (25 cents) to get a total of 80 cents.

Exploring Monetary Symbols

Students are introduced to the symbols for dollars and cents.

When you tell someone you have 5 cents or 5 dollars, they understand what you mean.

How does someone know if you mean cents or dollars if you write the amount?

Introduce the symbol for cents, recording it on the word wall or Math Talk chart.

Ask students to write the value of 3, 7, and 12 dimes, using the cents symbol.

Have them share what they have written.

What do you know about 120¢?

What do you know about 100¢?

What's another name for 120¢?

What if I showed it like this: $1.20. What part do you think shows the dollars? What shows the cents?

What do you think the point (decimal point) tells us?

Have students identify the number of dollars and cents in more examples, such as $4.13 or $6.35.

Record the dollar sign on the word wall or Math Talk chart with a couple of examples.

Pose $0.65.

What if I showed you this? What do you think it means? Why?

How do you know there aren't any dollars?

Have students work with partners to show various amounts of money using money notation.

    2 dollars and 34 cents

    3 dollars and 14 cents

    13 dimes

    25 nickels

To end the lesson, have students discuss these questions with partners:

Why are the dollar and cent symbols important to use?

Explain why we use the point (decimal point) when writing dollar amounts.

> Although second graders do not understand the concept of decimals yet, using the term *decimal point* just gives them a name for the point and will later make sense to them when they further explore decimals.

SMP1, SMP3, SMP4, SMP5, SMP8

Thinking Through a Lesson

Exploring Coin Combinations with Number Lines `SHOW IT!`

Students use number lines to support their skip counting as they count different sets of coins.

Differentiation
Provide students with access to coins as needed.

Provide students with the number line template.

Pose the following:

> *How could we use a number line to show the value of 3 dimes and a nickel? Talk with your partner.* (We could show skip counting.)
>
> *Think about the value of each coin.*
>
> *Think about how you can show the value with jumps.*
>
> *What would your jump look like for a dime?* (It would be a jump of 10.)
>
> *What would your jump look like for a nickel?* (It would be a jump of 5.)

Although students have had previous experience with number lines, some may need additional guidance when first using them to show monetary values. Make connections to their previous experiences in which each jump on the line showed a part of a quantity.

Observe as students use their number lines to show the amount.

> *How much money do you have if you have 3 dimes and a nickel?* (35 cents.)
>
> *How does the number line show that?* (We landed on 35.)
>
> *What do your jumps represent? Why are some different than others?* (They show the coins. Or, We did a jump of 10 for every dime and a jump of 5 for the nickel, and ended up on 35. Or, A nickel and a dime are worth different cents, so the jumps have to be different.)
>
> *How is this like how we used number lines before?* (We are adding, and we used them to add before. Or, We are adding money instead of just numbers.)
>
> *Skip count with your partner the coins that you modeled.*

You can support flexible skip counting by having students alternate between counting by tens and counting by fives as you give hand signals.

Listen as students count 10, 20, 30, 35 cents.

Pose the following problem:

> *How many ways can we make 35 cents using quarters, dimes, and nickels?*
>
> *You already found one way to make 35 cents. Are there other ways?*
>
> *Use your number lines to find more ways.*

This task opens up conversation for multiple approaches.

> *You can use quarters, dimes, or nickels.*
>
> *Try a few on your own, then share your ways with a partner. See if you found the same ways or different ones.*
>
> *Be ready to share your ways with the class.*

Observe as students explore combinations with the number lines. If some students appear to be struggling with the use of the number line, make note of who they are and pull them into a small group during the next segment of the lesson as the others practice with additional tasks.

Watch for students who do not start with the greatest-value coin. Although not necessary to find the total value, counting coins in this manner is often easier.

Is there only one way to make 35 cents? (No.)

Who can show us one way and explain what your number line shows? (My number line shows nickels. I counted by fives to get to 35.)

Does anyone have a different way? (I used 1 dime and 5 nickels.)

Create a chart showing the number of quarters, dimes, and nickels used.

Continue to make different combinations until all possibilities are found.

How did the number line help you to show your thinking? (I can organize the coins and show how I skip counted.)

Draw attention to the solution with the fewest coins.

Which one of our solutions uses the fewest coins? (1 quarter and 1 dime.)

Why would we want to have fewer coins? (It's easier to carry. Or, It's lighter.)

Have students practice using the number lines to show combinations to make 45 cents using nickels, dimes, and quarters.

Share out solutions as a whole class until all possible combinations have been found.

Which solution used the fewest number of coins? (1 quarter and 2 dimes.)

Students can be challenged with more complex data, like showing the coin combinations for 55 cents or 75 cents or the possible combinations for 58 cents using pennies, too. 🔵🔺

> **Differentiation**
> Providing a guided review for a small group of students, while others continue to practice the task, gives them the additional guidance they need to understand the use of the number line in this context and allows us to take a closer look at them to figure out what they know and what they might be struggling with.

Ways to Get to 75¢

[Number line showing three 25¢ jumps: 25¢, 50¢, 75¢]

[Number line showing 25¢, 25¢, then 10¢, 10¢, 5¢ jumps: 25¢, 50¢, 60¢, 70¢, 75¢]

[Number line showing seven 10¢ jumps and one 5¢ jump: 10¢, 20¢, 30¢, 40¢, 50¢, 60¢, 70¢, 75¢]

To end the lesson, use questions such as the following to facilitate a class discussion:

How do number lines show different ways to make coin values?

Why are there multiple ways to make coin values?

FORMATIVE ASSESSMENT

Pose the following:

> Show how you can use a number line as a way to model counting these coins:
>
> 2 dimes, 3 nickels
>
> 4 dimes, 2 nickels, 2 pennies
>
> Choose 6 coins of your own. Order them from greatest value to least. Use a number line to show how you would count the value of all of the coins together.

---

2 dimes, 3 nickels

[Student work: open number line with jumps of +10¢, +10¢, +5¢, +5¢, +5¢ from 0¢ to 10¢ to 20¢ to 25¢ to 30¢ to 35¢]

4 dimes, 2 nickels, 2 pennies

[Student work: open number line with jumps of +10¢, +10¢, +10¢, +10¢, +5¢, +5¢, +1¢, +1¢ from 0¢ to 10¢ to 20¢ to 30¢ to 40¢ to 45¢ to 50¢ to 51¢ to 52¢]

Choose 6 coins of your own. Order them from greatest value to least. Use the number line to show how you would count the value of all coins together.

3 Pennies, 2 dimes, 1 nickel.

[Student work: open number line with jumps of +1¢, +1¢, +1¢, +10¢, +10¢, +5¢ from 0 to 1¢ to 2¢ to 3¢ to 13¢ to 23¢ to 28¢]

This student shows open number lines with skip counts to find the total. On the third task, she does not order the coins from greatest to least; however, this does not detract from finding the total, and shows deep understanding of skip counts. To emphasize ordering ask: "What would be the order of the coins if they were ordered from greatest to least?" "Would ordering the coins differently change the value?" "Could ordering the coins help you to count easier?"

Number Line Coin Count
Show how you can use a number line as a way to model counting coins.

2 dimes, 3 nickels

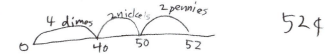

35¢

4 dimes, 2 nickels, 2 pennies

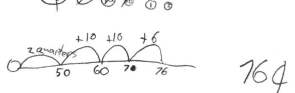

52¢

Choose 6 coins of your own. Order them from greatest value to least. Use the number line to show how you would count the value of all coins together.

76¢

This student uses number lines to show counting groups of coins.

Using Number Bonds to Explore Coin Combinations

Students use number bonds to find different coin combinations with equal values.

See Module 1 for more about number bonds.

Pose the following:

> Kendall has 35 cents. What are some possible coin combinations she could have?

Talk to your partner about different combinations of coins that would equal 35 cents.

Together, see how many possible combinations you can make.

Think about how we used number bonds to show parts and wholes. Could you use number bonds to show your thinking?

Circulate as students work together with their partners to show the possibilities by recording them in their math journals. Look for students who use number bonds to show the combinations. If some students are struggling to

Coins can be represented by writing the value inside of a circle (e.g., a dime could be a circle with the numeral 10 inside it).

represent the coins in an organized way, call a class time-out and have one pair share a number bond to show one possibility, reminding students how they used the bonds to show addition. Then, have the class go back to work finding more possibilities.

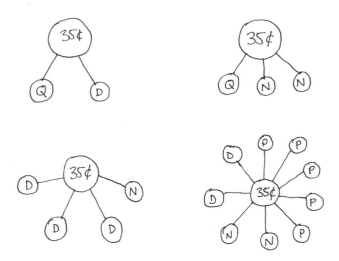

Have pairs share the possibilities they found, using addition or skip counting to show that their coins equal 35 cents.

How did using number bonds help you?

Have students work with partners to use number bonds to show 24 cents.

See how many combinations you can find using number bonds. Be ready to share them.

Have students share the bonds to show varied combinations of coins.

Once students have explored making number bonds with partners, have them try the following on their own:

31 cents

45 cents

56 cents

Use questions such as these as an exit ticket to assess students' understanding:

How does using a number bond help you organize your thinking?
How is this similar to what we do in other areas of math?

Making Trades SHOW IT!

Students apply what they know about coin values to make trades.

Provide students with coins.

Pose the following:

Colin had 25 pennies in his pocket. All of the pennies were very heavy to carry. What could he trade to have the same amount of money, but with fewer coins?

What trades can he make? Try it with your coins.
Talk to your partner about different combinations of coins he could trade.

Have student use their journals to draw picture representations of their coin trades.

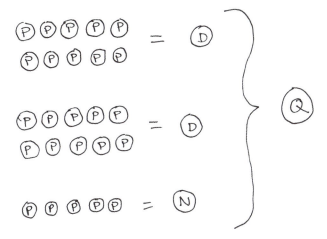

Pose the following:

Trina has 6 nickels, 4 dimes, and 5 pennies. What coins could she trade to have the fewest coins possible?

Try to figure this out on your own. Use your coins, then draw pictures of coins to show your thinking.
How much money does Trina have?
What other coins could she trade for?
What is the fewest coins she could have? Talk to your partner.

For additional practice, students can use spinners or coin dice to collect coins and then practice making trades to show the values in different ways.

Additional Ideas for Support and Practice

The following ideas extend students' understanding of counting coins and provide meaningful practice.

Hundred Penny Charts for Coin Concepts

In a small-group setting, give each student a hundred penny chart in a page protector and an erasable marker.

Tell students that each square in this chart represents 1 cent.

What coin is 1 cent?

> Students may suggest she could use a half-dollar. If not, you may want to introduce this less common coin, explain its value, and add it to your word wall or Math Talk chart.

> **Differentiation**
> Using a hundred penny chart provides another way for students to picture combinations of like coins that make one dollar.

Have students chorally count each row to see how many cents (or pennies) are on the whole chart.

What do we know about 100 cents?

Record on the board: *1 dollar = 100 pennies*

Have students label the chart *1 Dollar*.

What coin is the same as 10 cents?

Have them outline groups of 10 on their charts to see how many dimes are in a dollar.

How many dimes are in dollar? How do you know?

Record on the board: *1 dollar = 10 dimes*

Try it with groups of 5 to see how many nickels are in a dollar or with groups of 25 to see how many quarters are in a dollar.

Money Counts

Write the numbers *25*, *10*, *5*, and *1* on a dry erase board.

Tell students that they will begin by skip counting by one number, and at your signal they will change to counting by a different number.

For example, as you point to 10, students begin by counting by tens, and at your signal (point to 5) they will continue counting, but now by fives.

Initially, have students count within only two patterns, always starting with the larger pattern.

As they become more skilled, you can add more patterns within a count.

Make This Amount

Show a collection of coins and have students work in pairs to figure out how much money is shown.

Have students share their strategies, such as which coins they counted first, or which coins they combined.

Have student pairs make the same amount of money in a different way and draw their way on paper. Then have students share their ideas, so they can see that the same value can be represented using many coin combinations.

Mystery Money

Share with the class that you have a mystery amount of money and you will provide clues to help them figure out what your coins are and how much money you have.

Differentiation

This activity reviews skip counting for students who may need that additional practice.

Provide a clue like this to start:

I have two coins.

Have students offer suggestions. Record their predictions, but don't affirm any correct responses.

Both are silver and both have ridged edges.

Ask if any students want to change their predictions, and have two or three students share their reasons. Again, don't affirm correct responses.

One coin is larger than the other.

Discuss which of the predictions is correct and have one or two students tell how the answer fits all the clues.

Ask for the coins and the total amount. (One dime and one quarter; 35 cents.)

Doing this once a day could become a favorite activity for those 5-minute chunks of time that often occur between activities. Some possibilities include:

> I have three coins.
> Two of the coins are not silver.
> The other coin is the next higher coin in value. (Two pennies, one nickel; 7 cents.)

> I have two coins that are the same.
> Both are silver.
> Together, they equal the value of a coin that is smaller in size. (Two nickels; 10 cents.)

> I have two coins.
> Both are silver, but one has a smooth edge.
> The value of one of the coins is equal to five of the other coin. (One quarter, one nickel; 30 cents.)

MAKE IT THREE WAYS

Students work in pairs for this activity.

> Each student gets an index card and writes a money amount, such as 75 cents.

> Students exchange index cards with their partner and use coins to find three ways to make the amount of money on the card.

> Students can record their three ways in their journals through drawings, coin stamps, or coin stickers.

When finished, students share the three ways they made the money amount with their partner and challenge their partner to find yet another way.

Scoop and Count

Students are provided a loose bucket of coins.

They use a tablespoon or small cup to scoop, write a prediction in their journals for how much money they have scooped, order the coins, and count.

Students record their thinking in their journals, using pictures and numbers.

Money Roll

Students use tens and ones place value dice to roll a value in cents.

In their journals, students show various possibilities to make the value using coins, using number bonds, number lines, or coin stamps.

Spinning for Coins

Option 1

Partners take turns spinning a coin spinner.

Each partner records the amount he collects each turn and adds to find his total.

After three rounds, partners compare to see who has more.

Option 2

The goal is to get to $1.00.

Partners take turns spinning a coin spinner.

The student collects whatever coin is spun and adds it to her total, making trades to make the counting easier.

Students take turns spinning, collecting coins, and finding the total.

The first player to collect one dollar is the winner.

Make the Value

Students spin and count sets of coins that equal the value spun.

Students record the value and coins used in their journals.

Variation: Students find multiple sets of coins that show the value.

Exploring Money
MODULE 12

Students spin and count coins to match the value.

COIN CONTAINER COUNT

Put various coins into small containers labeled *A*, *B*, *C*, and so on.

Students sort and count the coins in each container.

Students then draw the coins and record the amounts in their journals.

TRADING COINS

Students work with a partner to spin a coin spinner six times, taking the coin each time.

Students then count to find their total amount of money.

They then make trades to show the same amount with fewer coins.

Students record both ways to show the amount.

Example: Partners spin a nickel, penny, dime, quarter, dime, and nickel. The students count the coins to find a total of 51 cents. The students then trade two dimes and a nickel for a quarter. They show the two ways with models or equations.

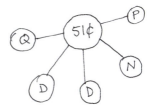   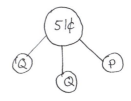

25 + 10 + 10 + 5 + 1 = 51 cents   or   25 + 25 + 1 = 51 cents

> Drawing the coins lets you match students' coin drawings to the value to check for accuracy.

Differentiation
Glue plastic coins onto craft sticks labeled A, B, C, and so on, for students to count. This allows you to place the coins in order and students can practice their counting. Students then record the letter for that stick and the value of the coins on it.

SOLVING PROBLEMS ABOUT MONEY

Students connect their understanding of money and number sense to problem-solving situations.

Solving Problems with Number Lines

Students use a number line to solve various problems involving money concepts.

> Pose the following:
>> Kenneth bought a pencil at the school store for 35 cents. He paid with a 1-dollar bill. How much money should Kenneth get back?
>
>> *Turn and talk with your partner about the important information.*
>> *What is going on in this story? Which operation would you use? Why?*
>> *How would you solve it?*
>> *How could you show your thinking?*
>
> Ask students to set up an equation that represents the problem.
>
> Work with students to solve the problem using a number line.
>
>> *Talk to your partner about how we could use a number line to find the difference.*
>
> Support students as they use a number line to find the difference.
>
>> *What number should I start my number line at? Why?*
>> *What skips should I make? Why?*
>
> Students might start at 35 and then show jumps to 100, or they might start at 100 and count, or jump, back 35.
>
> Review the (inverse) relationship between solving $1.00 − $0.35 = ___ and $0.35 + ___ = $1.00.
>
> Pose the following:
>> Davina has $1.00 to spend at the carnival. She bought a snow cone for 60 cents. She also wants to ride the carousel. Tickets for the carousel are 50 cents. Does Davina have enough money to ride the carousel?
>
>> *Retell the problem to your partner. What do you need to find out?*
>> *Choose a model to show your thinking and solve.*
>> *Compare your solution and strategy with your classmates'.*
>> *Did anyone use a number line?*
>
> Students might have subtracted 60 cents from $1.00 to see how much money Davina had left, or they may have added 60 cents and 50 cents to see how much a snow cone and tickets would cost.
>
> To end the lesson, have students discuss this question with partners:
>
>> *How can a number line be used to help you solve money problems?*

For additional ideas on problem solving, see Module 1.

For additional ideas on strengthening students' problem-solving skills, see Math in Practice: A Guide for Teachers, Chapter 1.

Who Has More?

Students compare the total value of two sets of coins to find which is more.

Provide students with the number line template.

The template can help students have greater accuracy in showing the values and comparing the two amounts.

Pose the following:

> Blake had 1 quarter, 3 dimes, 2 nickels, and 6 pennies. Carly had 2 quarters, 2 dimes, 3 nickels, and 4 pennies. Who had more money? Prove it.

Talk with your partner about this problem.
Who has more coins?
Does that mean Blake has more money than Carly?
What could you do to prove who had more?
Let's use our number lines to show our thinking.

Have students work independently and then share solutions with a partner. Facilitate a whole-class discussion on similarities and differences between different solutions.

What numbers did you start from?
How does the number line prove who had more?
Were there other strategies that helped?

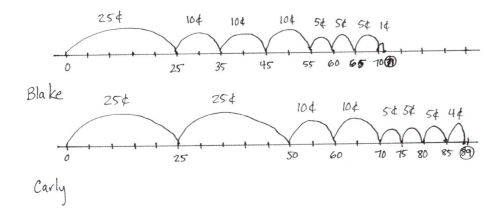

Have students work with partners to solve more comparison problems and share their strategies.

Solving Problems with Number Bonds SHOW IT

Students use coins to show different ways to make money values and then represent the combinations with number bonds.

Provide students with coins.

Pose the following:

> Olivia has 2 coins that total 26 cents. Quinn also has 26 cents, but he has 4 coins. What sets of coins do Olivia and Quinn each have?

Retell the problem to your partner.

What are we trying to find out?

What is important to know?

How can they each have the same amount of money but different coins?

Use your coins and work with your partner to find out what coins Olivia and Quinn have.

Circulate and observe students as they work together to show 26 cents.

Invite the class to share their thinking.

Let's record our thinking using number bonds.

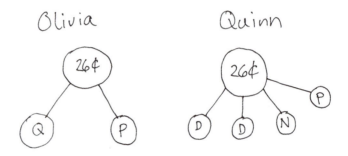

Pose the following:

Three students each have 46 cents.

Paul has 4 coins.

Madison has 5 coins.

Jack has 6 coins.

What coins do Paul, Madison, and Jack each have?

Talk with your partner about the important information in this problem.

How might you be able to figure out the 4 coins that Jack has?

Use your coins to try some different combinations. Compare your thinking with your partner. Be ready to share with the whole class.

Circulate as students work with partners. Observe students as they count different sets of coin combinations to get to 46 cents.

What coins does each of the students have?

As students share their thinking, invite them to create number bond models.

Are there multiple possibilities for any of the students?

Students may have identified a second possibility for Jack. If not, draw student attention to the combination they did not identify.

> **Differentiation**
>
> For students who are struggling with finding different coin combinations, a very basic look at this skill is presented in Monster Money by Grace Maccarone, in which the author presents different ways to make fifteen cents.

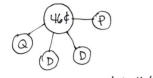
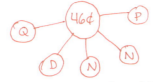
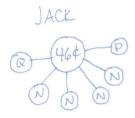
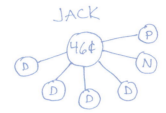

To end the lesson, have the class discuss the following question:

How can number bonds help us think about the value of different coin combinations?

Additional Ideas for Support and Practice

The following ideas extend students' understanding of solving problems with money and provide meaningful practice.

Focus on the Question

Post the following data and have students answer one question about the data each day for a week.

School Store Prices
folder—$1.20
pencil—$0.45
glue stick—$0.75
eraser—$0.25
pen—$0.80

1. Colin bought a folder and a pencil. How much money did it cost? Tell how you would solve it.
2. Molly bought 4 erasers. How much money did it cost? Tell how you would solve it.
3. Liam had 2 quarters and 2 dimes. He bought a pencil. How much money did he have left? Tell how you would solve it.
4. How much more does a pen cost than a pencil? Tell how you would solve it.

For more about the Focus on the Question activity, see Math in Practice: A Guide for Teachers, Chapter 2.

Increase the monetary values in problems as students gain confidence and skills.

Vocabulary

¢	dollar
$	half-dollar
bills	nickel
cent(s)	penny
coins	quarter
decimal point	symbol for decimal point
dime	

ONLINE RESOURCES

General Resources

Additional Problems

Coin Spinners

Money Value Spinners

Number Lines

Table of Addition and Subtraction Money Situations

- - - - - - - - - - - - - - - - - -

Resources for Specific Activities

Double Ten Frame Mat

Hundred Penny Chart

Ten Frame Mat

- - - - - - - - - - - - - - - - - -

These resources are available at http://hein.pub/MathinPractice, keycode MIPG2.

---

5. Blake had 3 quarters, 2 dimes, and a nickel. Could she buy a folder? Tell how you would solve it.

TALK ABOUT IT/WRITE ABOUT IT

Martin had 1 nickel, 2 quarters, and 3 dimes in his pocket. When he counted it, he thought he had 60 cents. Do you agree or disagree? Why?

Senny has 1 quarter, 2 dimes, and 3 pennies. Carly has 2 dimes, 4 nickels, and 8 pennies. Carly thinks she has more money because she has more coins. Senny says he has more money because he has a quarter. Who do you agree with? Explain why.

THE PENNY POT

The face-painting booth at the school fair provides plenty of opportunities to count combinations of coins adding up to fifty cents.

Before Reading:

Briefly introduce the book to set a context. Tell students that you will be reading a story about a little girl who wishes she had more money.

Look at the cover. What do you think the girl wants more money for? How might she get more money?

Ask them to listen to see if she gets the money she wants.

During Reading:

Read *The Penny Pot* by Stuart J. Murphy.

After Reading:

Have students work with a partner. Give each pair a coin spinner and some coins. Each student spins the spinner and takes the coin that he spins. The first student to collect fifty cents wins.

Variation: Partners take turns rolling a die and receive the number of pennies that they roll. Students can trade five pennies for a nickel, two nickels for a dime, and so on. The first person to trade for a quarter wins.

Pose problems related to the face-painting context:

If Jessie had 3 dimes, 3 nickels and 7 pennies, could she have gotten her face painted? Justify your answer.

If Jessie had 2 dimes, 4 nickels, and 3 pennies, how much more money would she have needed? Explain how you figured out your answer.

Jessie decided to buy a cupcake at the school fair. It costs 20 cents. How many different ways could she pay for the cupcake?

MODULE 13

Representing and Interpreting Data

About the Math 2.MD.10

In first grade, students gathered data, organized it, and talked about what the data showed. They might have tallied responses to survey questions about their favorite fruit and then made declarations about the fruit most of their classmates preferred. In second grade, they learn to display this data on bar graphs and picture graphs.

> The key ideas focused on in this module include:
> - interpreting the data shown in simple picture and bar graphs
> - creating simple picture and bar graphs from existing and student-generated data
> - solving addition and subtraction problems based on data gained from picture and bar graphs.

Picture graphs use symbols to show each item, with each symbol representing an item (see Figure 13.1). In bar graphs, students learn to display the data in either vertical or horizontal bars, with each bar representing a category and the height or length of the bar representing the number of items in that category (see Figure 13.2). In both cases, limiting the categories to four or fewer allows students to explore graphs without an overwhelming amount of data.

In second grade, picture and bar graphs have scales to represent single items, but in third grade, students are introduced to scaled picture and bar graphs in which a picture can represent more than one item (specified by a key), and the number intervals on a bar graph might be in fives, tens, and so on.

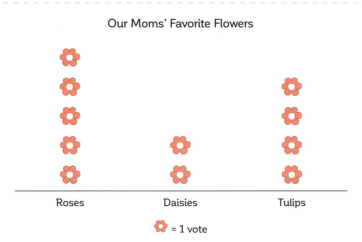

Figure 13.1

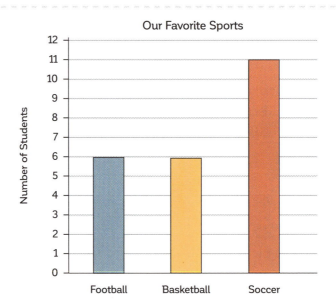

Figure 13.2

Students learn that a graph tells a story about a set of data. The graph title tells the big idea of the graph and the categories, bars, or symbols give us more information. We help our students understand and interpret graphs by reading the titles, reading the labels, and counting the symbols or finding the height or length of bars. Reading and talking about graphs, prior to creating their own, helps our students make sense of these unique representations of data.

As students begin to create their own graphs, we challenge them to tell us the story of their data through the title, labels, and accurate representation of the data. Exposure to both horizontal and vertical picture and bar graphs shows our students that the orientation does not matter when displaying or interpreting graphs (see Figure 13.3).

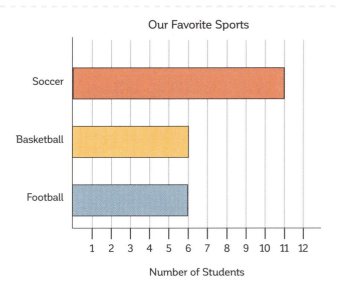

Figure 13.3 This graph shows the same data as in Figure 13.2, but displays the bars in a horizontal format.

Graphing is more meaningful when it connects to our students' lives. Having students answer survey questions, create graphs to show their responses, and then analyze the class data helps them see the usefulness of graphs. They recognize that graphs help us see data more clearly and understand it better. Students might describe graph data to tell us *most* and *least* or to tell us how many classmates prefer chocolate milk or white milk. They might try to explain pieces of data (Why do so few students ride their bikes to school? Do they live too far away? Are there no sidewalks near the school? Is it too cold to ride bikes? Could it be that some students do not have bikes to ride?).

And graphs provide data for problem-solving experiences. Posing problems about graph data challenges our students to apply their understanding of when to add or subtract to solve a problem. Posing problems that ask students to determine *how many more*, *how many fewer*, or *how many in all* provides additional practice with choosing the operation that makes sense for the task. Their graphs become the context for their problem-solving experiences.

Exploring graphs throughout the school year allows us to revisit graphing skills, integrate graphing lessons with problem-solving tasks, and engage our students in the collection of varied data throughout the year.

MATH IN PRACTICE
Teaching Second-Grade Math

MODULE 13

Learning Goals

I can tell what a graph shows.

I can draw a bar graph and a picture graph.

I can solve problems about a graph.

Lessons in This Module

Understanding Picture Graphs
Introducing and Interpreting Picture Graphs
Creating Picture Graphs
Comparing Picture Graphs

Understanding Bar Graphs
Introducing Bar Graphs
Interpreting Bar Graphs
Creating and Using a Bar Graph to Analyze Data
Creating Bar Graphs
Graph and Compare

Exploring the Progression

PREVIOUS	NOW	NEXT
Grade 1	Grade 2	Grade 3
Organizing and interpreting data in charts, tables, and diagrams	Creating and interpreting simple picture and bar graphs	Creating and interpreting scaled bar and picture graphs

Ideas for Instruction and Assessment

UNDERSTANDING PICTURE GRAPHS

Students are introduced to picture graphs as a way to display data and create and interpret picture graphs.

Introducing and Interpreting Picture Graphs

Students are introduced to the picture graph as an organized display that includes a title, labels, and a key.

Display the following picture graph.

Desserts Sold on Monday

Pie

Fruit Cup

Cupcake

Pudding

Turn to your partner and talk about what you see.

What does this show? How do you know?

What do the pictures represent?

We call this a graph. There are not a lot of words like in a paragraph, but it still tells us information.

This kind of graph uses pictures to show information. We call this graph a picture graph.

Add the words *graph* and *picture graph* to the word wall or Math Talk chart.

Have students describe to a partner the story the picture graph tells.

How many different kinds of desserts were sold?
What kinds of desserts were sold?
How many desserts does each picture represent?

Have students talk with their table group about what they notice about the desserts sold.

Have a few students share their ideas. Pose the following questions if not already addressed by students.

How many cupcakes were sold?
Which dessert was most popular on Monday? How do you know?
Which dessert was least popular? How do you know?
Were there more fruit cups sold, or cupcakes? How many more? How do you know?

Show students this second picture graph, similar to the first.

Desserts Sold on Tuesday

Pie	🥧🥧
Fruit Cup	🍓🍓🍓🍓🍓🍓
Cupcake	🧁🧁
Pudding	🍮🍮🍮🍮🍮🍮🍮🍮

Have students talk with a partner to describe the desserts sold on Tuesday. Pose interpretative questions such as these:

How many pudding desserts were sold?
Which dessert was least popular on Tuesday?
What is the difference between the most popular and least popular dessert?
How many total desserts were sold on Tuesday?

> *If your table group added their dessert choice to the picture graph, how would the graph change?*

Show the picture graphs side by side.

Ask table groups to estimate the desserts needed for Wednesday, based on the number of desserts sold on Monday and Tuesday.

> *About how many of each dessert would you suggest the café order for Wednesday?*
> *Which dessert would you order the most of? Why?*
> *Would you order some of each dessert? Why?*

Ask a few students to share their tables' estimates and discuss the reasonableness of the estimates based on the picture graphs.

> Explaining that the data collected on Monday and Tuesday is being used to estimate desserts needed for Wednesday gives a purpose to the data collection and display.

Creating Picture Graphs

Students create their own picture graphs and then observe and describe the data on classmates' graphs.

> *We are going to collect data to learn more about our class.*
> *What is your favorite flavor of ice cream?*

Allow students to suggest their favorite flavors and pick four of them to use for the graph.

> *I wonder what most people like best? How could we see all of your choices?*
> *Let's make a picture graph to show our favorite flavors.*

Provide each student with an ice-cream cone card and a loop of masking tape.

Display a piece of large chart paper, folded to make four columns.

> *Let's label each column, so we know where to place our cones.*
> *How should I label them?*

Label the columns as students name each flavor.

Write the word *label* on the word wall or Math Talk chart, and point to the labels on the graph.

> *Place your cutout in the column to match the flavor of ice cream you prefer. Look for the label to help you decide where to put it.*

The picture graph may look something like the one shown on page 295, and will serve as a model as groups work to create their own picture graphs.

When all cones have been added to the graph, discuss the data collected.

> *What is our graph about? How could we let someone else know what it is about?*

Representing and Interpreting Data

MODULE 13

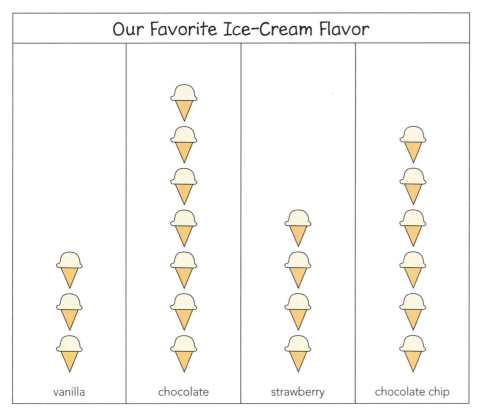

= 1 person

What would be a good title to tell the story of our data?

Why do we need the labels on our graph?

What does one ice-cream cone picture represent?

Create a key on the graph to show that 1 ice-cream cone = 1 person's choice by placing a cutout on the graph and writing = *1 person* next to it.

What does this key show?

Turn and tell your partner something you know about our favorite flavors by looking at the graph.

Use a number to tell me something our graph shows.

How did you know that?

What flavor did most people choose? How do you know?

Can you tell me how many more people chose one flavor over another? How do you know?

Provide each group with one of the data charts from the online resources. Have them create a picture graph to display the data.

Remind students to include a title, labels, and a key.

A key is not particularly helpful when introducing picture graphs where each picture represents one data point, but will be important in third grade when each cone might represent five or ten people. Having it here helps students get used to it as a part of a picture graph.

Be sure that students see examples of both horizontal and vertical graphs. It is important for students to see that data can be displayed either way.

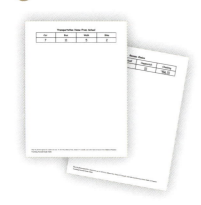

Students might benefit from a review of tally marks and how they represent groups of five.

Common Error or Misconception

When creating picture graphs, students may draw the pictures different sizes or space them irregularly resulting in the pictures not lining up across rows. Remind students to try to draw the data with consistent spacing and, most importantly, to interpret the data based on the number of pictures in rows rather than the length of the rows.

You may provide a template for the picture graph symbols, or groups may create their own symbols.

It is beneficial if two or more groups are using the same data. This enables students to see that the same data could be represented differently, such as horizontally or vertically, or by using different symbols.

As students work to create their picture graphs, circulate around the room to gauge progress and pose questions.

What symbol makes sense for this data?
How will you choose a title?
What labels are needed?
How will you show the key?

Display the completed picture graphs around the room.

Have groups circulate to each picture graph and record two observations about each graph.

Review and discuss the observations during a whole-class discussion.

Comparing Picture Graphs

Students create and compare picture graphs.

Pose the following:

> Mr. Klein is purchasing more books for the class library. He surveys his class to find out their favorite genre. After the survey, he organizes the following data:

Genre	Tally	Count
Mystery	IIII	4
Science	ʟʜʇ IIII	9
Poetry	III	3
Historical	ʟʜʇ I	6

Turn and talk to your partner. Why would Mr. Klein want this information?

How can we organize the data so that it's easier to understand? (We can make a graph.)

What symbol might you use?

How will you use the tally chart to help complete the picture graph?

Is there any other information we should include?

As students create picture graphs, circulate and support them as needed.

Share your picture graph with your partner.

How are they the same?

How are they different?

Have students write three questions that could be answered using their picture graph. Students can ask their questions in whole group or with partners.

> **FORMATIVE ASSESSMENT**
>
> Give students the Number of Books Read picture graph.
>
> Have them answer the following questions about the graph:
>
> > How many books did Cooper read?
> >
> > How many more books did Ryan read than Madison? How do you know?
> >
> > How many books did Ryan and Cooper read together? How do you know?
> >
> > If Abby reads 2 more books, how many will she have read? How do you know?
>
> Look for students who are able to find the correct answers and show how they got the answers with either an equation or an explanation.
>
> For students who struggle, conduct an interview to assess their understanding. Ask:
>
> > *What information would tell us how many books Cooper read?*
> >
> > *How many books did Ryan read? How many books did Madison read? What would we do to find out how many more books Ryan read than Madison?*
> >
> > *How many books did Ryan read? How many books did Cooper read? How would we find out how many they have read together?*
> >
> > *How many books did Abby read? What is 2 more than 5?*

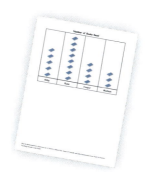

Additional Ideas for Support and Practice

The following ideas extend students' understanding of picture graphs and provide meaningful practice.

USING EQUATIONS TO JUSTIFY REASONING

Students analyze a picture graph and use equations to justify their thinking.

Display the following picture graph:

Plants in the Garden	
Daisy	✿
Marigold	✿ ✿ ✿ ✿
Sunflower	✿ ✿ ✿ ✿ ✿ ✿ ✿ ✿
Snapdragon	✿ ✿ ✿ ✿ ✿

What information does the graph tell us?

Were more daisies planted than snapdragons? How do you know?

How many more sunflowers were planted than marigolds? Write an equation to show your thinking.

How many flowers were planted in all? Write an equation to show your thinking.

Scoop and Graph It

Students work with partners to scoop colored cubes or counters and create a graph to show the colors scooped.

Provide a small (bathroom-sized) paper cup and a bowl of colored cubes or counters.

One partner scoops a cup of counters.

Partners sort the counters by color and then create a picture graph to show their counters.

After the graph is complete, they work together to write three sentences describing what their graph shows.

What Is It Saying?

Give students a picture graph and have them answer these prompts:

Write a sentence to tell what the graph is about.

Use a number to tell me something about this graph.

Write a problem that could be solved using this graph.

Tell me something about this graph that shows a comparison (something that is more or less than something else).

Another way to do this activity is to have students fold a paper into four parts and write about the graph using the following prompts:

The graph is about . . .	I noticed . . .
Use a number to tell about your graph.	What is more or less?

Differentiation

For students who struggle with constructing descriptive sentences, try sentence starters like:
This graph is about . . .
I see that more people picked ___ than ___.
Most people chose . . .

Representing and Interpreting Data   299

MODULE 13

TALK ABOUT IT/WRITE ABOUT IT

Explain how to make a picture graph.

What are some important parts of a picture graph? Explain each one and why it is needed.

ROLL AND PICTURE IT

Students create a picture graph by rolling a number cube and graphing the results.

- Place data cards in an envelope (see Roll and Picture It cards in the online resources).

- Students pick a data card that names three categories of data (e.g., 3 types of sports balls: baseballs, footballs, and basketballs).

- They roll a number cube three times to determine how many of each item they have (e.g., 3 baseballs, 4 footballs, 6 basketballs).

- They then create a picture graph to show their data.

- Students write an addition or subtraction problem that can be solved by looking at the graph (e.g., How many more basketballs than footballs are there?).

UNDERSTANDING BAR GRAPHS

Students are introduced to bar graphs as a way to display data and create and interpret graphs.

Thinking Through a Lesson

SMP2, SMP4, SMP5, SMP6

Introducing Bar Graphs

Students work together to create a bar graph and share insights about the information displayed.

> This will be students' first exposure to bar graphs. Students should apply what they already know about picture graphs to guide their understanding of bar graphs.

Prepare a chart with the title Our Favorite Seasons. Label the bottom of the chart *winter*, *spring*, *summer*, and *autumn*. Label numbers up the side, spaced out to allow for sticky notes to be added to the graph.

> Chart paper with inch grid lines can be especially useful. If you do not have grid chart paper, measure out the scale based on the size of the sticky notes you will use.

> You might choose to survey anything that might interest your students, such as favorite animal, favorite school lunch, favorite sport, or favorite author.

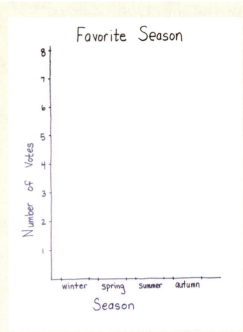

Turn to the person next to you and tell them your favorite season. Why is it your favorite season?

Before, we used pictures to represent our data. Instead of a picture, this time we will each use a sticky note.

Give each student a sticky note. Model for students how to line up and place their sticky notes as they cast their votes. One at a time, invite each student to place her sticky note in the column that corresponds with her favorite season, starting at the bottom.

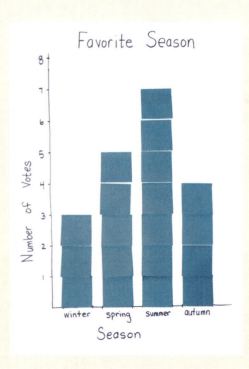

Once all students have placed their sticky notes:

What do our sticky notes represent? (They are our votes for our favorite season.)

Let's trace around all our sticky notes and then take the sticky notes off.

> Although sticky notes are separate squares, they form the bar as they are stuck to the chart paper. This can help students see how each sticky note makes its bar longer and taller.

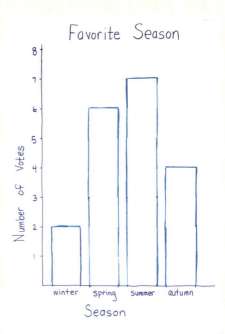 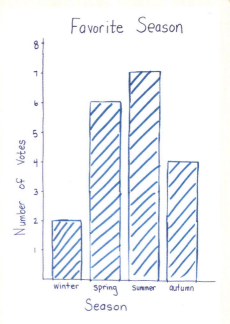

What kind of shape did they make? (A tall rectangle.)

Our rectangles look like long bars. We call this kind of graph a bar graph.

Add the words *bar graph* to the word wall or Math Talk chart.

How do the title and season labels help us understand the graph? Are they important? (They tell us what the graph is about. *Or*, We know what season the votes are for.)

Now that we don't have pictures to count, how will we figure out how many people liked each season? (The numbers up the side show how many.)

How do we use those numbers? (We can see how high the bar goes and look at the number by the top of the bar.)

Turn and talk to your partner about some things you notice. (Summer has the most. *Or*, Only 2 people like winter.)

What questions can we answer from our graph? (What got the most votes? *Or*, What got the least votes? *Or*, How many people voted?)

Invite students to ask questions based on the information.

Provide students with graph/grid paper to recreate the bar graph.

Model for students how to draw the two axes: a vertical line near the left side and a horizontal line across the bottom.

Discuss aspects of the graph, such as the title and labels.

Differentiation

As a challenge for some students, have them turn the bar graph into a picture graph and then compare the two.

Differentiation

For students who have difficulty relating the bar to the numbered scale, use a yardstick and have the student trace his finger across to the corresponding number.

What would happen if you didn't title the graph and put on labels? (You wouldn't know what the graph was about.)

Model for students how to number along the side.

Instead of using sticky notes, let's draw and color in our bars.

Invite students to share their completed graphs.

> Emphasize the importance of drawing the bars accurately. Students could use a ruler or other straight edge (e.g., paper) to make sure the top of the bar aligns with the corresponding number.

Interpreting Bar Graphs

Students see parts of a bar graph and try to make sense of the graph until all parts are revealed. Students talk about how the essential components of the bar graph help to tell the data story.

Show students a portion of a bar graph.

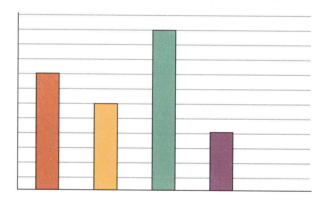

Have students describe the image.

What do you see?
How do the bars compare to one another?
What might the bars represent?

Show students the updated graph image.

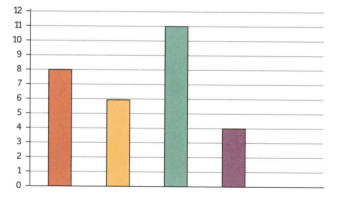

Ask students to describe what they see.

What new things do we know about the graph?
What is the value of the green bar?

Which bar has the least value?

What is the combined total for the orange and blue bars?

What is the difference between the orange and red bars?

How does the scale help us answer these questions?

Reveal the labels for the bar graph.

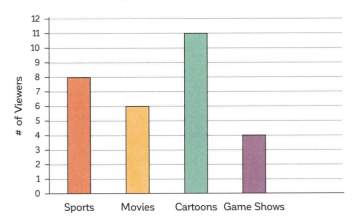

Ask students to explain how the labels help you to understand the data.

What do the bars represent?

What survey question might have been asked to collect the data?

What title might be added to describe the data?

Show students the complete bar graph with all components.

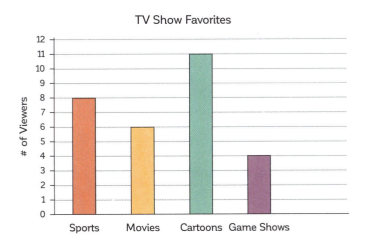

Have students consider how each component of the bar graph is crucial in understanding the data.

How do the labels help you to understand the graph?

How many people were included in the survey?

Five of the students watching sports watched soccer. How many of the students watching sports did not watch soccer?

How many more people watched cartoons than game shows? How do you know?

Distribute index cards and have partners write two questions that could be answered by looking at the graph.

Have pairs trade cards and answer each other's question.

The cards are then returned to the original pair to check the answers.

Creating and Using a Bar Graph to Analyze Data 😊|🖌️

Students use information to create a bar graph and develop questions to ask, based on the data.

Pose the following:

> Mrs. Cole's class is planning a school garden. She surveyed her class to find out which vegetables they like best.

Why would Mrs. Cole want this information?

> After the survey, Mrs. Cole shared the following information:
> 5 students chose peas
> 7 students chose tomatoes
> 7 students chose cucumbers
> 2 students chose green beans

How can we display the data so that it is easier to understand?

Provide students with grid paper.

> *Let's make a bar graph using the data that Mrs. Cole collected.*
> *What are some important characteristics of a bar graph?*
> *How can we organize the bar graph so that the information is clear?*

Allow students time to create their bar graphs.

> *Compare your bar graph with your partner's.*
> *What's the same? What is different?*
> *With your partner, write some questions that we can answer by looking at our graph.*

Have pairs take turns asking classmates their questions.

Creating Bar Graphs 😊|🖌️

Students create a design with pattern blocks and then make bar graphs to show the number of pieces of each type of block used in the design.

Distribute pattern blocks and allow students a few minutes of exploration time.

> *What is the name of the red block?*
> *How is the trapezoid different from the triangle?*
> *What do you notice about the hexagon and trapezoid?*

Distribute an 8.5 × 11-inch sheet of paper for each student to use as a work mat.

Have students create a design on their work mats using the pattern blocks.

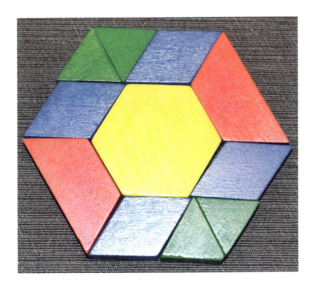

> Take a picture of each design, or have students trace their designs, to use in a center activity (described in Additional Ideas for Support and Practice).

Have students do a gallery walk around the room to see all of the designs created.

Create a bar graph to show the number of each type of block you used. Remember to include labels and a title.

Distribute graph paper.

As students work, circulate to monitor their progress on creating the bar graphs.

How are you keeping track of the pieces already graphed?
What labels will you need?
How high must your labels go to show the number of each block?
What title would describe your data?

Discuss the graphs with the students.

We have so many different designs in our class. I'm curious about which pattern blocks were used the most and which were used the least.
How can we figure this out?

Have students work in small groups of 3–4 students to tally the number of each type of block used and then show the totals on a group graph.

> The totals of the small group graphs can be combined using tally marks and skip counting to find class totals, but the quantity of blocks will probably be too great to actually graph the class data at a one-to-one scale.

Have students report their data and talk about which type of block was used most and least.

Distribute an index card to each student.

Ask students to record three observations about their bar graph or their small-group bar graph, using at least one of the following words in each observation: *more, fewer, equal, difference, total.*

FORMATIVE ASSESSMENT

Give students the following instructions:

> Create a bar graph to show the following data about second graders' favorite ice-cream toppings.
>
> hot fudge—9
>
> peanut butter—5
>
> chocolate chips—8
>
> nuts—4

Once students have completed their graphs, have them use the graphs to answer the following questions and explain how they got the answers.

> How many more students picked hot fudge than nuts? Show the equation you would use to solve it.
>
> How many second graders were surveyed for this graph? Show the equation you would use to solve it.

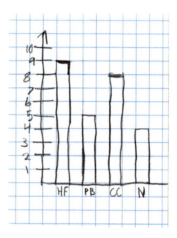

9−4=5 more students picked hot fudge than nuts.

9+5+8+4=26 students were surveyed for this graph.

This student shows a bar graph with the data accurately represented, but there is no title. Ask, "What does your bar graph show? How can you help people know what the graph is about?" The student shows a number sentence, correctly identifies how many more students picked hot fudge than nuts, and is able to add four numbers to find how many students were surveyed.

Graph and Compare

Decide on a class question and conduct a survey to find the answer.

Possibilities might include:

> In what season were you born: spring, summer, fall, winter?
> Which subject is your favorite: reading, math, science, social studies?
> What fruit do you prefer: bananas, strawberries, grapes, apples?

Split the class into two parts and have students in one part of the class work with partners to create bar graphs of the results, while students in the other part of the class work with partners to graph the results on a picture graph.

Have students talk with partners about what their graph shows.

Have a bar graph pair talk with a picture graph pair to discuss their observations and compare their graphs.

> *In what ways are the graphs alike?*
> *How are they different?*
> *Is one easier to use than the other?*

Have the new team of four design some addition and subtraction problems that could be solved using the graph data.

Have teams record equations that would solve their problems.

Have teams pose their problems to the class for others to solve.

Have the whole class summarize their observations:

> *What do bar graphs and picture graphs have in common?*
> *How are they different?*
> *Which graph do you prefer? Why?*

Additional Ideas for Support and Practice

The following ideas extend students' understanding of bar graphs and provide meaningful practice.

LEMONADE FOR SALE

Students see how a bar graph can be used in real life in *Lemonade for Sale* by Stuart J. Murphy.

Before Reading:

Briefly introduce the book.

> *This story is about a group of friends who sell lemonade. One girl uses a bar graph.*
> *Look at the cover. What do you think she might record on her graph?*

During Reading:

Read *Lemonade for Sale*.

Ask students to analyze features of the bar graph that the character Sheri makes, and how she completes it during the week.

> (p. 7) *Why would Sheri want to make a bar graph?*
> *What are some features you notice about Sheri's bar graph?*
> *How does she label the graph along the bottom?*
> *What do the numbers along the side mean?*
> *What counting pattern did she use?*
> (p. 10) *How does Sheri's graph show that they sold 30 cups on Monday?*
> (p. 14) *How many more cups of lemonade did they sell on Tuesday than they did on Monday? How do you know?*
> (p. 18) *They sold 56 cups on Wednesday. What did Sheri have to think about when she filled in her graph?*
> *Looking at the graph, what trend or pattern do you notice?*
> *Make a prediction. What do you think will happen on Thursday? Why do you think that?*
> (p. 22) *Did they sell more or less on Thursday than on Monday? How can you tell from looking at the graph?*
> (p. 30) *How many cups of lemonade were sold on Friday?*
> *How high does the graph go?*
> *Can you make a prediction of how many cups they sold?*

After Reading:

Display the graph shown on page 30.

> *Write three questions you could answer using the data that was collected.*

Have students take turns asking their partners questions. Listen for questions that might elicit meaningful conversation for the whole class.

To end the lesson, ask students to discuss the following with partners and then with the whole class:

> *The Elm Street Kids Club used a bar graph to keep track of how many cups of lemonade they sold. Can you think of other times people might want to use a bar graph?*

Matching Sets

Use the pictures of the pattern block designs, the student-created graphs, and the index cards of observations (see page 305) to create a matching exercise.

Choose the work of 5–6 students to place at the center at one time.

Have students match each design photo with the correct bar graph and index card of observations.

Differentiation

Second-grade students focus on a single-unit scale. The scale used on this graph is by tens, so it will extend their learning beyond the grade-level standard. Because students have been skip counting by ten, most should understand and be able to use this scale.

You may wish to recreate the graph on chart paper prior to the lesson, or display the graph on a projector.

Representing and Interpreting Data

MODULE 13

309

My Survey

Give students the following instructions:

> Decide on a question that has four possible answers.

Survey some classmates and graph the results on a bar graph.

Write a problem that can be solved with your graph.

Repeat the process at home with survey questions for your family and friends.

Possible survey questions:

> How many brothers do you have: 0, 1, 2, or more?
>
> Which after-school activity do you prefer: watching TV, reading a book, playing outside, or playing on the computer?
>
> Which sport is your favorite to watch: basketball, soccer, baseball, or football?
>
> Which sport is your favorite to play: basketball, soccer, baseball, or football?
>
> What instrument do you play: piano, violin, drums, or none?
>
> What is your favorite pizza topping: pepperoni, sausage, green pepper, or no topping?
>
> How do you prefer potatoes: french fries, baked, mashed, or chips?

> **Differentiation**
>
> Have a bank of possible survey questions to jump-start the activity. Limit the categories to three to simplify the task. For example: "Do you prefer cherry, grape, or lime popsicles?" "Do you come to school by car, bus, or do you walk?" "Would you prefer potatoes mashed, baked or french-fried?" "Would you rather read a book, go to the playground, or watch TV?"

Focus on the Question

Have students make a bar graph or picture graph to show the following data:

Coins	Number in My Bank
pennies	18
dimes	7
nickels	10
quarters	4

Pose the following problems for students to discuss using the data on their graphs. Use a different problem each day.

1. I used 7 nickels. How many did I have left? Tell how you would solve it.
2. How many more pennies than quarters did I have? Tell how you would solve it.
3. I bought a snack with all of my quarters and 4 dimes. How much did my snack cost? Tell how you would solve it.

> For more information on the Focus on the Question strategy, see Math in Practice: A Guide for Teachers, Chapter 2.

> This series of problems provides a review of money concepts. See Module 12 for more activities related to money.

Vocabulary

bar graph | picture graph
bars | pictures
data | tally marks
key | title
label

This activity revisits geometry concepts. For more on identifying and describing shapes, see Module 14.

ONLINE RESOURCES

General Resources
Additional Problems

Resources for Specific Activities
Data Charts:
- Favorite Lunch
- Recess Choice
- Transportation Home from School

Formative Assessment About Books Read

Ice-Cream Cone Cards

Picture Graphs:
- Favorite Books
- Favorite Colors
- Favorite Vegetables
- Musical Instruments

Roll and Picture It Cards

These resources are available at http://hein.pub/MathinPractice, keycode MIPG2.

4. I took the pennies and nickels out of my piggy bank and put them in my wallet. How many coins were in my wallet? Tell how you would solve it.

5. I took the pennies and nickels out of my piggy bank and put them in my wallet. How much money did I have in my wallet? Tell how you would solve it.

SHAPE SORT AND GRAPH

Prepare four different bags with various numbers of pattern blocks. Label the bags *Bag 1*, *Bag 2*, *Bag 3*, and *Bag 4*. Students choose a bag and create a bar graph based on the shapes inside. Students will need to identify each shape in order to label their graphs.

Extension: Students can share their graphs with each other and determine if they had the same bags, based upon their graphs.

IN THE NEWS

Search for bar graphs used in the news by browsing grade-appropriate children's newspapers, magazines, or almanacs.

Discuss what the graph shows and how the graph enhances the article.

MODULE 14

Describing Geometric Shapes

About the Math 2.G.A.1

At an early level, students recognize and name shapes based on their appearance. A triangle is a triangle because it looks like a triangle. In second grade, activities are designed to help students identify shapes that belong together because they have certain characteristics in common.

> The key ideas focused on in this module include:
> - **identifying and describing two-dimensional shapes based on attributes (e.g., circles, triangles, squares, rectangles, rhombuses, trapezoids, pentagons, hexagons, octagons, and other polygons)**
> - **identifying and describing three-dimensional shapes based on attributes (e.g., cubes, cones, cylinders, and spheres)**
> - **drawing shapes with specific attributes (e.g., four sides)**
> - **recognizing the category of shapes known as quadrilaterals.**

When students are looking for a square by appearance only, they may call a square a diamond because of its position (see Figure 14.1). Focusing students on why a square is a square helps them better understand shapes and allows them to identify shapes even when they are positioned, or oriented, in a different way. It also builds the language (related to attributes) and understanding that students need for experiences comparing and describing shapes in later grades.

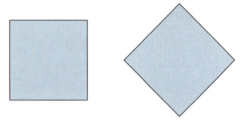

Figure 14.1 Although both shapes are squares, students may not identify the second shape as a square because of its orientation.

Students may not identify a triangle as a triangle unless it is an equilateral triangle, because that is what they are used to seeing. But, what makes a shape a triangle? Our goal in early geometry experiences is to help our students understand the attributes that define a shape (e.g., triangles are flat shapes with three sides and three corners or vertices). Triangles do not all look the same (as shown in Figure 14.2), but they do all have these attributes.

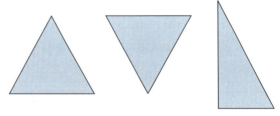

Figure 14.2 All of these shapes have the attributes of a triangle even though they differ in orientation, length of sides, and measure of angles.

Similarly, a square is defined by having four sides, four corners/vertices, a certain type of angles, and equal side lengths; its color, size, and position are irrelevant.

As early as kindergarten, we ask students to look at shapes based on sides and corners/vertices. We show triangles of different sizes and with different angle measurements to allow students to look past the way one triangle looks in order to generalize about what every triangle has (e.g., three sides and three corners/vertices). In first grade, students talked about characteristics, or attributes, of shapes that matter or do not matter. A square is a square no matter what color it is, but it cannot be a square if it doesn't have four sides. By second grade, our students recognize shapes based on their attributes and should be able to draw shapes with certain attributes. Although in the past they may have simply noted the number of sides or corners (angles/vertices) as attributes, they now begin to recognize the length of sides or the type of angle as important. As they point out a square, they are able to tell you why it is a square, including comments about the side lengths being equal and the angles being the

They compare side lengths and angles visually, not by measuring.

same, yet they understand that the square is also a rectangle because it has all of the attributes of a rectangle. And when asked to draw shapes with four sides, they might draw a rectangle, a trapezoid, or a square.

Students see connections between three-dimensional shapes as they explore their attributes, noticing that rectangular prisms can and cubes must have faces that are squares, while cylinders and cones have faces that are circles. Students discuss and reason about their observations as they refine their understanding.

At this grade, students are introduced to the term *quadrilateral* and start gaining insight into shapes having more than one name, understanding that a rectangle, rhombus, or trapezoid can also be a quadrilateral. Through hands-on activities and math discussions, we provide opportunities for students to visualize, sort, compare, discuss, and reflect on two-dimensional and three-dimensional shapes to help students gradually refine their understanding about shapes.

Exploring the Progression

PREVIOUS	NOW	NEXT
Grade 1	Grade 2	Grade 3
Exploring attributes that define shapes (e.g., number of sides) and those that do not define shapes (e.g., color); combining shapes to form new ones	Recognizing and naming shapes; drawing shapes based on a given set of attributes; being introduced to quadrilaterals	Naming the attributes of different shapes; comparing and contrasting shapes; identifying quadrilaterals

Learning Goals

I can describe flat and solid shapes by talking about their attributes.

I can draw shapes with certain attributes.

I can tell what a quadrilateral is.

Lessons in This Module

Exploring Shapes

Defining vs. Non-Defining Attributes of Shapes

Making Right Angle Finders

Exploring and Defining Shapes

Introducing Quadrilaterals

Quadrilaterals on the Geoboard

The Greedy Triangle

Describing Three-Dimensional Shapes

Ideas for Instruction and Assessment

EXPLORING SHAPES

Through the following interactive activities, students explore, sort, compare, and describe shapes to refine their understanding about their attributes.

Defining vs. Non-Defining Attributes of Shapes

Students observe and describe shapes to determine defining attributes.

> Give each pair a set of two-dimensional shapes, copied in several colors.
>
> *How would you describe these shapes?*
>
> *With your partner, pull aside all of the triangles.*
>
> *Turn and tell your partner what makes these shapes triangles.*
>
> *You just told me the attributes of a triangle. Those are the things that make it a triangle.*
>
> *If a shape has three sides and three corners, or vertices, it is a triangle.*

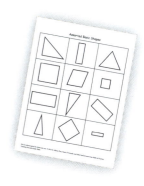

Students should be familiar with the term *vertices* from kindergarten and first grade, but a quick reminder by using the synonym, *corners*, and pointing to the vertices on several shapes may be helpful.

Write the word *attribute* on the word wall or Math Talk chart. Reiterate that these are the things about the shape that matter; they make it that kind of shape and not some other kind.

Add the words *sides*, *corners*, and *vertices* to the word wall or Math Talk chart, including illustrations to show their meanings.

Ask them to work with partners to pull aside all of the squares.

> *Turn and tell your partner what makes these shapes squares.*
> *You didn't mention the color of the squares. Why not?*
> *For shapes, which attributes matter and which do not matter?*

Continue, having students pull rectangles and talk about them.

> *What makes these shapes rectangles?*
> *How are these rectangles different from squares?*
> *Turn and tell your partner what is the same and what is different about these rectangles and a square.*
> *Do you think a square is also a rectangle? Why or why not?*

Listen to students as they share their thinking.

> *A square is a special kind of rectangle. It is a rectangle that has all the sides the same length.*

Common Error or Misconception

Students mistakenly believe that a rectangle must have two sides that are longer.

Following the discussion, have students write in their math journals: *What is a square? What is a triangle?* Remind them to use words, pictures, and examples to show what they know about the shapes.

Making Right Angle Finders **SHOW IT!**

Students fold a circle to form and visualize a right angle in order to develop the vocabulary to more easily compare and describe shapes.

Have students fold a small circle in half, and then in half again.

Students do not need to be able to measure to determine a right angle, but should be able to visually identify the angle. In most standards, knowing the term *right angle* is not an expectation at second grade, but students do need to be able to recognize the angles of squares and rectangles. Introducing them to the term makes it easier for them to talk about what they see.

Tell students that the corner of their folded paper is called a *right angle*. Add the term to the word wall or Math Talk chart.

Have students use their right angle finder to locate right angles around the classroom.

> *Where did you find right angles in our classroom?*
> *In what shapes would you see an angle like this?*

Give students a shape template and have them locate the shapes that have right angles.

Do all squares have right angles?

Do all rectangles have right angles?

Do all triangles have right angles?

Have students draw a triangle that has a right angle and one that does not.

Are both of them triangles?

Begin a class chart with labels: *Has a Right Angle/No Right Angles*

Turn and talk to your partner about which shapes go in which column on our chart. Be ready to share your ideas.

Have students help you add examples to each side of the chart.

After the chart has examples on both sides, have students fold a paper in half and make their own charts with shapes of their choice.

Thinking Through a Lesson

SMP3, SMP6, SMP7, SMP8

Exploring and Defining Shapes

Students explore sets of shapes to develop a definition for each shape.

Give students a page of assorted pentagons (some regular and some irregular).

With your partner, find ways these shapes are alike. (Each shape has five sides and five corners/vertices.)

What is the name of these shapes? (Pentagon.)

Do the sides of a pentagon have to be the same length? (No; some of these don't have the same length sides, but we call them all pentagons.)

We call a shape that has sides the same length a regular shape. Can you name a regular shape? (Square.)

Point to one of your pentagons that is regular.

Place a counter on any shapes on your page that are pentagons, but that are not regular. In other words, they do not have sides the same length.

> Students may not immediately see that all of the shapes have five sides and five angles, because some of the shapes look very different than a traditional (regular) pentagon. They may initially say they are all flat (which is true) or that they all have angles (which is true, but not specific). Continue to probe until someone counts the sides. The questioning in this lesson reinforces the definition of a pentagon as a flat shape with five sides and five angles/vertices. Equal side lengths is not a part of that definition.

> This allows you to walk through the room and quickly identify students who are able to distinguish between regular and irregular pentagons. The idea of pentagons looking irregular may be new to students. If they are having trouble with the concept, draw a few on the board, count the sides and angles, and reinforce that those are the defining attributes regardless of how long each side is.

> Having students write the word and draw an example helps them process the word and meaning, and helps them remember it.

> An important insight is that any flat shape with five sides and five angles is a pentagon, not just the regular pentagon they are used to seeing.

Add the word *pentagon* to the word wall or Math Talk chart.

Have students record the word *pentagon* on a sheet of paper and draw examples of three different pentagons.

Then have them write the attributes that make each shape a pentagon.

Are any of your pentagons regular pentagons?

Add the word *regular* to your word wall or Math Talk chart.

Have students draw a regular pentagon if they have not already drawn one. If they have, they can circle the regular pentagon on their paper.

Repeat the activity with hexagons and octagons.

Repeat the following day with rhombuses and trapezoids.

On day two, the idea of regular shapes can start an interesting discussion.

Are all rhombuses regular shapes? Can a trapezoid be a regular shape?

A rhombus is a regular shape because all sides are equal length. A trapezoid is not regular because the sides are not equal length.

> Spread this out over a couple days to allow students to digest the defining attributes for the various shapes, rather than introducing too many at one time. When students have created pages for all of the shapes you'd like them to explore, staple the pages together to make shape books.

FORMATIVE ASSESSMENT

Give students these instructions:

  Draw an example of a rectangle.
  Describe the shape using at least two attributes.
  Draw an example of a pentagon.
  Describe the shape using at least two attributes.

Students should be able to accurately draw the shape named and be able to tell the number of sides, whether sides need to be equal, the number of corners/vertices, and/or if they have right angles. Students might draw a square as a rectangle. This is correct, but *has equal sides* would not be a correct attribute for a rectangle.

Draw an example of a rectangle.
Describe the shape using at least two attributes.

Long
4 Sides

Draw an example of a pentagon.
Describe the shape using at least two attributes.

5 Sides
shapt like a houres

This student correctly draws both a rectangle and a pentagon, and can identify the number of sides they have. This student describes the rectangle as being long, but may have a misconception that a rectangle must be long. Conduct an interview and ask if the student can draw a rectangle that is not long. Likewise, this student describes the pentagon as the shape of a house. Provide examples of different pentagons and ask if the shape must be like a house.

Introducing Quadrilaterals

Students observe shapes to determine the definition of a quadrilateral.

> Put some photos or graphics on the board that are labeled *quadrilaterals* and some that are labeled *not quadrilaterals*.
>
> *Some of these shapes are quadrilaterals, and some are not quadrilaterals. Study them. What do you notice?*
>
> *Turn and tell your partner what you think a quadrilateral is. What do all of the quadrilaterals have in common?*

How are they different?

So, what does a shape need to have to be called a quadrilateral?

Write the word *quadrilateral* on the word wall or Math Talk chart. Have students write it in their vocabulary logs or math journals.

Draw three quadrilaterals and then write about what makes them quadrilaterals.

Have students share their examples with a partner.

What shapes do you already know that are quadrilaterals?

Is it okay that these shapes now have two names? Can a shape be a rectangle and a quadrilateral?

In your journal, add some names of shapes that are quadrilaterals.

Have students turn to a partner and share:

Is a trapezoid a quadrilateral? Why or why not?

Is a triangle a quadrilateral? Why or why not?

Quadrilaterals on the Geoboard

Students each need a geoboard, rubber band, and geoboard recording sheet.

Today we are going to make quadrilaterals.

Turn and tell your partner what your shape needs to have to be a quadrilateral.

Have students make a quadrilateral on their geoboards.

Have them look at their partners' quadrilaterals.

How are the shapes alike? How are they different?

Is a square a quadrilateral? Explain.

Is a trapezoid a quadrilateral? Explain.

Is a pentagon a quadrilateral? Explain.

Have them copy their quadrilateral on the geoboard recording sheet and then make a new and different quadrilateral.

Have them look at their partners' quadrilaterals and talk about how the shapes are alike and different.

Have students continue to make different quadrilaterals and record them on the recording sheet.

The Greedy Triangle

Students listen to *The Greedy Triangle* by Marilyn Burns to explore various shapes through the experiences of a greedy triangle who is not satisfied with his shape and yearns for more sides and more angles.

Before Reading:

Make a list of real-world items that are triangles, quadrilaterals, pentagons, and hexagons.

For more ideas on developing math vocabulary, see Math in Practice: A Guide for Teachers, Chapter 4.

Common Error or Misconception

If students have a hard time with this concept, have them think about other real-world items that have more than one name, one being more specific than the other (e.g., girls are children, apples are fruit, building blocks are toys). One name is a category name and the other name is more specific to help you know exactly what it is.

For more ideas on integrating children's literature into math lessons, see Math in Practice: A Guide for Teachers, Chapter 2.

We are going to read a book about shapes. Listen to see if you thought of any of the objects mentioned in the book.

During Reading:

Read *The Greedy Triangle*.

After Reading:

The book used the word quadrilateral.
What real world objects are quadrilaterals?
What is a quadrilateral?

Have students work in groups of 3–4 students with a large piece of string that is tied to form a circle. As you reread the story, have team members work together to create the shapes with the string. All team members must be holding a part of the string (except for when making the triangle if there are four members on the team) and can only touch the string with their fingers (no mouths or feet!).

Show me the triangle.
How do you know this is a triangle?
Do the sides have to be the same length?

As the shape changes, have students change their string shapes to show the newly formed shape.

Ask questions as they form their shapes.

How do you know it is a quadrilateral?
How is this quadrilateral different from a triangle?

> *How many sides should I see?*
> *Do the sides all have to be the same size?*

Continue with all of the shapes in the story.

Add the shape names to the math word wall or Math Talk chart, with an example for each one.

Have students use geoboards to practice making each shape on their own.

Describing Three-Dimensional Shapes

Students observe three-dimensional shapes to determine attributes of the shapes.

> Give each pair of students a bag of shapes (two- and three-dimensional) including a square, rectangle, triangle, circle, cube, rectangular prism, pyramid, cylinder, and cone.
>
> *With your partner, observe the shapes in your bag.*
> *How are they different?*
> *I noticed some of you calling them* shapes *and some of you saying* figures. *Can we say both?*
> *Turn to your partner and name some flat shapes.*
> *What do we call the other shapes?*
> *Turn to your partner and name some solid shapes.*

Ask students to select the cube and point to a face on the cube.

Observe to see that they understand the word *face*.

Write the word *face* on the word wall or Math Talk chart.

> *What do I mean when I say* face?
> *How many faces does a cube have?*

Count them together.

> *What do you notice about the faces of a cube?*
> *Show me the rectangular prism.*
> *How many faces does a rectangular prism have?*
> *What do you notice about the faces of a rectangular prism?*
> *Show me the sphere.*
> *How many faces does a sphere have?*

Have students work with partners to talk about the faces of the following shapes: cylinder and cone. Have them share their ideas about the number and shape of the faces.

Give each student a Faces of Solid Shapes recording sheet (see the online resources) and have them draw the faces for each shape and record the number of faces.

Different curricula use different terms to describe these shapes. Some say shapes, *others say* figures. *Some say two-dimensional, while others call them flat or plane. Although some terms may be used more frequently by different districts, states, or curricula, using synonyms and having students familiar with all of the terms makes sense because the different terms may appear on assessments or in subsequent grade levels. Whether talking about two- or three-dimensional shapes, frequently using synonyms helps students get comfortable with all of the terms.*

Students likely have used this term to describe three-dimensional shapes in first grade. If they seem unfamiliar with it, take a few minutes to have them point to and touch faces of various three-dimensional shapes.

If students have not heard the term rectangular prism *before, introduce them to it, write it on a word wall or Math Talk chart, and take a minute to explore how it is alike and different from a cube.*

After students have completed the task, have them talk about:

Why was a sphere not on your paper? Explain.

This activity can be repeated with a focus on vertices.

Additional Ideas for Support and Practice

The following ideas extend students' understanding of shapes and provide meaningful practice.

WHAT'S MY SHAPE?

Students practice describing shapes by writing clues for shape riddles.

Ask students to draw a triangle and think about the attributes of the shape.

Turn and share something you know about a triangle (e.g., flat, three sides, three corners).

Together, create a riddle with 2–3 clues to describe a triangle.

I am a flat shape.
I have three sides.
I have three corners.
What am I?

Have students work with partners to write a riddle for another shape.

Have them fold a paper in half and write the riddle on the front, and then write the shape name and draw a picture of it inside.

Have each pair pose their riddle to the class to see if they can guess and draw the shape (students might have individual whiteboards to draw the shape after hearing the riddle).

Option

The folded pages can be posted on the wall so pairs of students can read each one, talk about the solution, and then open the flap to see the answer.

DESCRIBING SHAPES

Students describe the attributes of shapes with the help of attribute cards. This small-group activity allows students to see the attributes and select the ones that match the shape.

For the two-dimensional shapes rectangle, square, triangle, pentagon, and hexagon, you would write the following attributes on small cards: 3 sides, 4 sides, 5 sides, 6 sides, equal sides, flat, solid, face, vertices, right angle. This can be modified for any group of shapes, including three-dimensional shapes. For three-dimensional shapes, you might include cards that describe faces like circle, square, rectangle, and triangle or 2 faces, 4 faces, 6 faces, etc.

> **Differentiation**
> Having word cards provides help for students who may be struggling to describe shapes and reinforces important geometry vocabulary.

Place a two-dimensional shape on the table so all students in the group can see it.

Have students take turns to pick an attribute word that describes the shape.

Have the student making the attribute selection explain why she picked that card as an attribute for that shape (e.g., counting the sides to show that 4 sides matched the shape).

Have everyone in the group show a thumb up or thumb down to indicate if they agree or not.

If a student disagrees, he must tell the group why (That triangle doesn't have a right angle, because the angles are all smaller than our right angle finder).

STREET SIGN SHAPES

Students identify attributes of street signs to determine their shapes.

Share pictures of street signs with the class.

Have students identify the shape of each road sign by describing the attributes of the shape.

SHAPE SORT

Students sort shapes in different ways to observe for attributes.

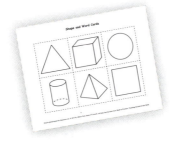

Use word cards or shape cards and have students group them:

| triangle | cube | circle |
| cylinder | square | pyramid |

How could you sort these shapes into two different groups?
Why did you choose to sort them that way? Explain.
Now sort them into three groups.
Why did you choose to sort them that way? Explain.

Describing Geometric Shapes

MODULE 14

TALK ABOUT IT/WRITE ABOUT IT

What makes a square a square? Which attributes matter? What attributes don't matter?

What is a triangle? Illustrate and give some examples to show that you understand.

What is a quadrilateral? Name some quadrilaterals.

A square is a rectangle because_____.

A cube and a rectangular prism are alike because_____.

How are a circle and cylinder alike? How are they different?

Name and describe this shape:

Bailey says that a cube has 8 faces. Do you agree or disagree? Explain.

Hasan says that the faces on a cube are rectangles. Do you agree or disagree? Explain.

Draw two different shapes that have 4 sides. What is each shape called? What are two objects in your classroom that have the same shape? Explain.

Which has more sides, 4 squares or 5 triangles? How do you know?

Describe what a cube would look like if it were unfolded.

FOLDED SHAPE BOOKS

Students create folded books to show what they know about various shapes.

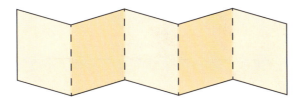

Have students fold paper in an accordion style.

Have them label the sections with shape names (e.g., trapezoid, hexagon, pentagon, square).

Have students show what they know about each shape with words (describe it), numbers (sides or corners/vertices), pictures (how does it look), and real-world examples.

SPIN AND DRAW

Students spin to determine how many sides are on their shape and then draw and label an appropriate shape.

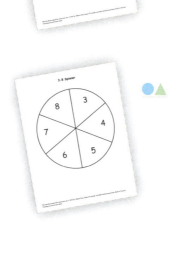

Students spin a spinner with numbers 3–6.

Students then draw a shape with the number of sides spun and write the name of the shape by their drawing.

Then, they spin again and draw and label the next shape.

If they get the same number of sides again, they must draw a different example than they did before.

Challenge: Use a 3–8 spinner and include heptagon (7 sides) and octagon (8 sides).

BUILDING TWO-DIMENSIONAL SHAPES

Students build shapes using plastic coffee stirrers and mini-marshmallows (or balls of clay) to practice creating shapes with specified attributes.

Provide a basket of stirrers, some cut to shorter lengths, and some mini-marshmallows or a small container of clay for students to make small clay balls to connect the stirrers.

Students pick a card with some attributes (e.g., 3 sides and 3 vertices, quadrilateral with 4 right angles) and then build the shape to show it.

Students record the clue and draw their shape on paper.

Then, students pick another clue, build the shape with the stirrers, and then record it on their paper.

BUILDING SHAPES

Students use soft modeling clay to show flat and solid shapes.

Give each student some clay and then describe a shape by using the following prompts:

Show me a shape that is flat and has three sides and three angles. (Triangle.)

Show me a shape that is flat and has five sides and five vertices. (Pentagon.)

Show me a solid shape that has no faces. (Sphere.)

Show me a flat shape that has four sides and four vertices. (Any quadrilateral.)

Show me a shape that is solid and has six faces. Each face is a square. (Cube.)

Then, have students each think of a solid shape and build it with clay.

When each student is done making her shape, have her turn to her partner and tell a clue about her shape so her partner can use the clue and look at the shape to guess its name.

> Having this recording component allows you to check student work to see that they are understanding the clues and accurately building the model.

QUADRILATERAL CRAYON RUBBINGS

Students cut out quadrilaterals and create art to show the different types of quadrilaterals.

Give students a piece of cardstock paper and scissors.

Students draw and then cut out as many different quadrilaterals as they can from the cardstock (e.g., square, rectangle, trapezoid, rhombus).

Students then place one quadrilateral under a sheet of white copy paper and rub over it with a crayon to allow the image to appear.

Quadrilaterals can be overlapped or creatively placed in any direction as students continue making their quadrilateral art.

> Integrating art and math is a great way to energize the classroom and reinforce math concepts.

DOT PAPER DRAWING

Students draw and compare shapes with various numbers of sides.

Students will need isometric dot paper.

Draw each shape on your dot paper:
Triangle
Quadrilateral

Vocabulary

angles	pyramid
attributes	quadrilateral
cone	rectangular prism
corners	
cube	regular
cylinder	rhombus
faces	right angle
hexagon	sphere
lines	trapezoid
octagon	triangle
pentagon	vertices

ONLINE RESOURCES

General Resources
- 3–6 Spinner
- 3–8 Spinner
- Additional Problems
- Assorted Basic Shapes
- Hexagons
- Isometric Dot Paper
- Pentagons
- Quadrilaterals

Resources for Specific Activities
- Clue Cards
- Faces of Solid Shapes Recording Sheet
- Geoboard Recording Sheet
- Shape and Word Cards
- Three-Dimensional Shapes Template
- Venn Diagram

These resources are available at http://hein.pub/MathinPractice, keycode MIPG2.

    Pentagon
    Hexagon
Compare your drawing with a partner's.
What's the same?
What's different?

Venn Diagram

Students compare shapes using a Venn diagram.

Give students a card for a flat shape and a solid shape (see the Shape and Word cards in the online resources).

Students receive one of the following pairs: triangle and pyramid, square and cube, or circle and cylinder.

Students label the two circles on the Venn diagram with the names of their two shapes.

Students then use the Venn diagram to record how they are alike (in the middle) and how they are different (the two sides).

Scavenger Hunt

Students identify three-dimensional shapes around the classroom.

Have students make a chart in their math journals with six columns. Using the left and right pages with three columns on each page works well.

    Label sphere, cylinder, cube, rectangular prism, cone, *and* pyramid *at the top of the columns.*
    Paste an image of each shape from the three-dimensional shapes template.
    Go on a classroom search for the three-dimensional shapes.
    List each real-world item in the correct column.

After students have completed their search, have them share the items they found for each shape.

Talk about the number of faces on each shape and the shape of the faces, being sure that each item is correctly identified.

Create a class list of real-world items for each shape.

For homework, have students look at home for more items to add to the list.

MODULE 15

Partitioning Shapes

About the Math 2.G.2; 2.G.3

Although the study of fractions does not formally begin until third grade, first- and second-grade students begin to develop foundational understandings about fractions as they engage in geometry investigations. As they partition circles and rectangles and discuss what they see, they begin to internalize some of the language of fractions (e.g., whole, parts, halves, thirds, fourths) and discover some big ideas about partitioning.

> The key ideas focused on in this module include:
> - partitioning circles and rectangles into two, three, and four equal shares and understanding the meaning of equal shares
> - understanding and correctly using terms such as *half of*, *third of*, *fourth of*, or *quarter of*
> - understanding that equal shares of a same-size whole do not have to look the same (have the same shape).

In first grade, students partitioned circles and rectangles into halves and fourths. They explored the concept of equal shares through hands-on explorations. During these investigations, they made discoveries like the following:

- Decomposing shapes into more parts means that the parts became smaller (e.g., fourths are smaller shares than halves of the same shape).
- Equal shares don't always look the same (don't have to be the same shape).
- Two halves make a whole and four fourths make a whole.

In second grade, students extend their investigations with geometric shapes to include partitioning circles and rectangles into thirds. They extend what they observed in first grade and discover that their insights about equal shares hold true for thirds, too.

At this level, our students use the words *halves*, *thirds*, and *fourths*, but do not use the fraction notation of $\frac{1}{2}$, $\frac{1}{3}$, or $\frac{1}{4}$. That notation is introduced in third grade. Students describe the whole as having two halves, three thirds, or four fourths and begin to recognize that when the whole is the same size, a half is more than a third because the whole is only split into two parts instead of three parts (see Figure 15.1).

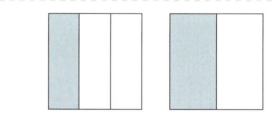

Figure 15.1 Students see that a third on the left is less than a half on the right.

Students begin to notice that the size of a half or a third changes if the size of the whole changes (see Figure 15.2).

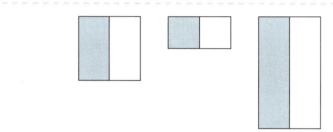

Figure 15.2 The size of half is different in each of these models. The size of half depends on the size of the whole.

Students also notice that equal shares do not have to look the same. A rectangle can be partitioned in different ways and as long as each section represents a third of the whole, the parts are equal (see Figure 15.3).

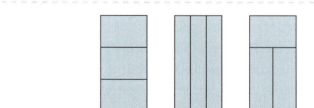

Figure 15.3 In each of these models, a section represents a third even though the shapes of the sections differ.

Second-grade explorations with partitioning shapes lay the foundation for a strong understanding of fractions. These opportunities introduce students to fraction concepts in very visual ways. Students' observations lead to insights about part-whole relationships and help them develop the language they need to delve into a formal study of fractions in third grade.

Exploring the Progression

PREVIOUS	NOW	NEXT
Grade 1	Grade 2	Grade 3
Introduction of partitioning circles and rectangles into halves and fourths	Partitioning circles and rectangles into halves, thirds, and fourths; understanding the meaning of equal shares	Introduction of fraction notation, fraction models (including sets and number lines), and equivalent fractions

Learning Goals

I can split a whole into halves, thirds, and fourths and describe the parts.

I can use the terms half of, third of, and fourth or quarter of to describe parts of shapes.

I can show that equal shares of a whole don't have to be the same shape or look the same.

Ideas for Instruction and Assessment

PARTITIONING SHAPES INTO HALVES, THIRDS, AND FOURTHS

Through a variety of investigations, students revisit partitioning circles and rectangles into halves and fourths and are introduced to partitioning into thirds. They discuss their models to develop insights about partitioning into equal groups and to build related vocabulary.

Brownies and Cupcakes: *Introducing Thirds*

Students draw models of a brownie (square or rectangle) and a cupcake (circle) and are introduced to the concept of thirds.

Lessons in This Module

Partitioning Shapes into Halves, Thirds, and Fourths

Brownies and Cupcakes: Introducing Thirds

Sharing Granola Bars

Creating Fourths

Size Matters

Pose the following problem:

3 friends want to share a brownie so each person gets the same amount.

What shape might a brownie be?
Draw a brownie and show how you would split it.
Show your brownie to a partner. Do they look the same?

Have a student who made a square brownie show his model and ask if anyone else split a square brownie in a different way.

Show both ways on the board.

Turn and talk: Are these both showing a brownie split in thirds?
Did everyone make a square brownie?

Have a student who made a rectangular brownie show her model and ask if anyone else split a rectangular brownie in a different way.

Show another possibility (e.g., one student splitting it vertically and another student splitting it horizontally).

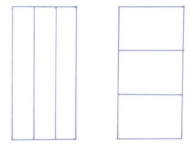

Which is right?
Do they both show thirds?
How many thirds are in the whole brownie?

> 3 friends want to share a cupcake so that each person gets the same amount.

What shape would a cupcake be?
Show how you would split the cupcake.

Have some students share their models. Discuss whether each friend would get the same amount of cupcake.

Common Error or Misconception

It is difficult to split a circle into thirds and exact partitioning is not expected. Some students, however, may simply draw vertical lines to split the circle into three sections as in the example to the far right. Discussing this example will generate good discussions about the meaning of equal parts.

When you split something into 3 equal parts, you call each of them a third.

Write the word *third* on the word wall or Math Talk chart. Draw an example similar to what students have drawn.

How many thirds are in the whole cupcake?
Will each student get the same amount of cupcake?

Add a square and/or rectangle model of thirds to the word wall or Math Talk chart.

What do we know about thirds?

FORMATIVE ASSESSMENT

Give students the following prompts.

Show how you would cut this cookie into thirds.

How do you know it is cut in thirds? Explain.

Show two different ways to cut these crackers into thirds.

Are you sure they are cut in thirds? Explain.

> For additional formative assessment techniques, see Math in Practice: A Guide for Teachers, Chapter 5.

Show how you would cut this cookie into thirds.

How do you know it is cut in thirds? Explain.

There are 3 peces

Show two different ways to cut these crackers into thirds.

 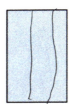

Are you sure each one is cut into thirds? Explain.

There are 3 peces

This student's understanding seems to be limited to drawing horizontal and vertical lines to decompose a shape. When cutting the cookie into thirds, the student is missing the importance of each share being equal in size. Prompt the student to try partitioning from the center of the circle to make it easier to cut the cookie into thirds.

Show how you would cut this cookie into thirds.

How do you know it is cut in thirds? Explain.

Because they are even.

Show two different ways to cut these crackers into thirds.

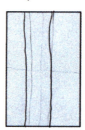 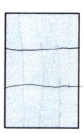

Are you sure each one is cut into thirds? Explain.

Yes becuse they are both even.

This student has an understanding of equal shares. The student's explanation would improve by identifying that there are three equal parts. Ask the student if the number of pieces is important information to explain.

Sharing Granola Bars

Students partition wholes into halves, thirds, and fourths.

> Give each student a recording sheet with four granola bar templates.

>> You have 4 granola bars on your recording sheet.
>> Imagine that you were sharing the bars with your friends.
>> Write 2 by the first granola bar because 2 people will be sharing it.
>> Write 3 by the next granola bar because 3 people will be sharing it.
>> Write 4 by the last two granola bars because 4 people will be sharing each one.

Work with a partner to show how you would split each granola bar so it is fair and each person sharing it gets the same amount.

Have students partition each bar using a pencil or crayon to trace around the part of the granola bar (halves or thirds or fourths) that each person gets.

Observe as students partition the rectangles, looking for different ways that they might have shown each type of partitioning.

Call on students to share how they partitioned the granola bar for 2 people to share.

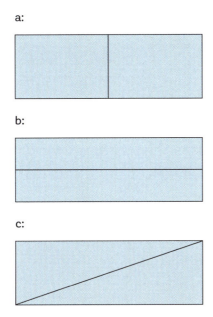

Initially, have a student who partitioned it as in the first image share her work. As she shares her model, ask questions like:

What is the name for one part?
How many halves are in your whole granola bar?
Are both halves the same size?
Are both halves the same shape?
Did anyone split their granola bar in a different way?

Select a student who partitioned the bar in a different way. Use similar questions as this student shares. If students used other ways, share those as well.

Call on students to share how they partitioned the granola bar for 3 people to share. Use similar questioning for thirds as you did for halves.

If all students partitioned the shape the same way, ask, "Can you think of a different way to split the granola bar?" "What if I did it like this (model partitioning like the second or third picture)? Can we do that? Does each part have the same size and shape?"

a:

b:

c:

d:

Select a student who partitioned it so the parts are not congruent (or share an example if no students did).

Is each part the same shape?

How do we know they are the same size if they don't have the same shape?

Ask students to talk with partners to find a way to prove that all of the parts are thirds.

How do you know the parts are equal?

How do you know that each person got the same amount?

Is it okay if they don't look the same?

> You may wish to have students explore this further by cutting apart and recomposing the pieces.

Repeat with students' partitioning the rectangle into 4 equal shares, challenging them to partition the last granola bar into 4 equal shares in a different way.

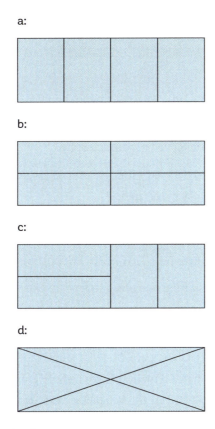

Share with your partner.

Would you rather have a third or a fourth of the granola bar? Why?

Use questions such as these for a final discussion:

What is more important when we partition a whole: size or shape?

How can you prove shapes have the same size even if the shapes are different?

What happens to the size of the pieces when we have more parts?

Common Error or Misconception

Students may think that a fourth is more than a third because of their understanding of whole numbers (4 is more than 3). Activities in which they can visualize thirds and fourths helps them see that the size of the parts gets smaller as the whole is shared by more people. This is the beginning of an important fraction concept that will be developed further in third grade: thirds are a larger portion of the whole than fourths, because the whole is partitioned into fewer equal shares.

Thinking Through a Lesson

SMP2, SMP4, SMP6, SMP7

Creating Fourths SHOW IT!

Students further explore decomposing shapes into fourths.

Show two rectangles split into fourths.

Rectangle A   Rectangle B

Turn and talk: In which rectangle are the pieces larger?

Allow students to talk with partners and then share their ideas with the class.

> This question is intentionally ambiguous to assess students' thinking about what it means to be large. Some may be thinking of larger as longer, while others may think of it as wider. Allow them to struggle with this a bit and debate with partners before you begin a class discussion.

Which one has larger pieces? (A because they are longer. *Or,* B because they are fatter. *Or,* Neither; they are the same.)

How can we decide?

Allow students to share some ways they might be able to prove their answers.

Let's do an investigation to see which rectangle has larger sections.

Give each pair of students two paper rectangles.

Have one partner fold it to show fourths as in rectangle A and the other fold it to show fourths as in rectangle B.

Have them trace the fold lines on their rectangles.

How could we compare the sections? (We could put them next to each other. *Or,* We could cut one out and put it on the other.)

If no students suggest cutting out a section from one rectangle, you might suggest it with a think-aloud.

Will a section from one rectangle fit on a section from the other?

Observe as students try to compare. Look for students who think about cutting one section to make it fit on the other one (e.g., cut the section from rectangle A in half and lay the two pieces next to each other to cover a section of rectangle B).

What do you notice? (They do cover exactly. *Or,* They didn't look the same, but they are the same size. The shape was just different.)

Draw a rectangle on the board.

Split the rectangle in half horizontally as in the rectangle below-left.

Then, split each half in half again by drawing a horizontal line on one half and a vertical line on the other half.

> **Common Error or Misconception**
> Students may think that fourths must be congruent (same size and shape), when they can be different shapes as long as each of the four parts is the same portion of the whole. Investigations in which students explore this idea with hands-on materials help them better understand this concept.

> Asking students to prove their answers gets them thinking more deeply about their ideas. Students might think about how a model could prove their thinking or some reasoning about what they know about fourths.

> Have students share some ideas about how they might compare the size of the sections with the whole class to jump-start students who may not have ideas about how to begin.

> If some students simply place one section over another and still look at length or width, ask questions as you watch them work, such as the following: "But is it bigger just because it is longer?" "Is there anything else you could do to compare them?"

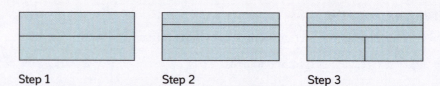

Step 1   Step 2   Step 3

Turn and talk: What do we call each part in our rectangle? (A fourth.)

Are all of the sections the same size? (Yes; they are all fourths.)

Are all of the sections the same shape? (No, but they are still the same size because they are half of the same size piece.)

To close the lesson, have students draw two examples of a square cut into fourths and write about how they know the parts are fourths.

FORMATIVE ASSESSMENT

Have students show two different ways to decompose a rectangle into fourths.

Then have them show another way to decompose a rectangle into fourths that are different shapes.

If there are not four shares, ask:

How many shares are in fourths?

Count your shares. How many do you have?

If partitions are not equal sizes, ask students if any of the parts are larger than others.

Show two different ways to decompose rectangles into fourths.

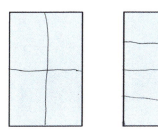

Show a third way to decompose a rectangle into fourths that have different shapes.

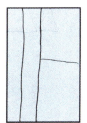

This student shows the first two rectangles partitioned into four equal pieces. The third rectangle is also partitioned into fourths. This student shows an understanding that fourths do not have to be the same shape in order to be the same size.

Size Matters

Students explore partitioning shapes when wholes are different sizes.

Pose this situation:

Molly had a cupcake, and Angel had a large cake.

Model drawing one small circle for a cupcake and one large circle for a cake. Have students draw models for each on their papers.

Show one half of each.

Have students talk with partners and then share their ideas about the following with the class.

Are the halves the same? Why or why not?
What do you notice about half of a cupcake compared to half of a cake?
Name two halves that would not be the same.

Pose another example:

Mallory had a brownie, and Harrison had a tray of brownies.

Model drawing one small rectangle for a brownie and one large rectangle for a tray of brownies. Have students draw models for each on their paper.

Show one quarter of each.

Have students talk with partners and then share their ideas about the following with the class.

Are the quarters the same? Why or why not?
What do you notice about a quarter of a brownie compared to a quarter of a tray of brownies?
Name two quarters that would not be the same size.

Have students turn to partners and share:

What would you tell someone who said that half of one thing is always the same size as half of something else?

To close the lesson, have students answer the following question in their journals, supporting their answer with drawings:

Why is the size of the whole important?

Additional Ideas for Support and Practice

The following ideas extend students' understanding of partitioning shapes and provide meaningful practice.

Which Is More?

Give three paper rectangles to each team of three students.

Fold one of your rectangles into fourths.
Label each section fourth.

Cut the four sections apart.

Have them do the same for thirds, labeling each section *third*.

Have them do the same for halves, labeling each section *half*.

Turn and talk: Which is biggest—the half, third, or fourth? Why? Does that make sense?

If students are confused by this, have them put the rectangles back together.

How many halves make the whole? Thirds? Fourths?
Which had the most pieces? Which had the largest pieces?
Does it make sense that halves are bigger than fourths? Explain.

CIRCLES OF CLAY

Prepare several circle shapes made from soft dough or modeling clay. This can be done by rolling clay and using a circle cookie cutter or an upside-down drinking glass to cut the shapes.

Give each pair two clay circles and a plastic knife.

Have them cut one circle to form two halves.

Have them cut the other circle to form quarters.

Have students draw the models in their math journals, labeling them *halves* and *quarters*.

4 FOURTHS FLAGS

Split a rectangle into fourths and create a 4-color flag.
Make four different flags.

Variations:

Split a rectangle into thirds and create a 3-color flag.
Make three different flags.

Split a rectangle into halves and create a 2-color flag.
Make two different flags.

TALK ABOUT IT/WRITE ABOUT IT

What is a third? Draw two examples.

What is a quarter? Draw two examples.

Do fourths have to be the same shape? Explain.

Colin has a brownie. Will I get more of it if he gives me a third or a fourth? Explain.

Do these both show fourths? Explain.

THE PIZZA PARTY

Students draw and write to show their understanding of halves, thirds, and fourths.

Pose the following problem:

> Mrs. King ordered 3 pizzas.
> She cut one into 2 equal pieces.
> She cut another into 3 equal pieces.
> She cut the last one into 4 equal pieces.

Draw a diagram to show how Mrs. King cut the pizzas.
Label each pizza with words to tell how Mrs. King cut it (e.g., 2 halves, 3 thirds, 4 fourths).

Observe as students draw and write about their shapes.

Have them continue to draw to show their understanding of partitioning with prompts like the following:

Show one half of the pizza with pepperoni. Explain.
Show one fourth of the pizza with green peppers. Explain.
Show one third of the pizza with pineapple. Explain.

> **Differentiation**
> Allow students to work with partners to complete this task.

VOCABULARY SORT

Students work with a team to sort the following words and representations based on their math meanings. Once they have placed the words into groups, they decide on a title for each group that describes why those words belong together. Teams then share their groupings with the class or another team and justify their decisions.

> There is not one way to sort the words, but the groupings must make sense based on the math meanings of the words and representations.

circle
column
equal
fourth
half
partition
rectangle
row
shares
third
whole

Partitioning Shapes **341**

MODULE 15

Folded Books

Have students create a folded book about partitioning shapes.

Have each student fold a paper in half and then cut three flaps.

Have students label the flaps *half*, *third*, and *fourth*.

Ask them to show what they know about each with words, pictures, numbers, or examples.

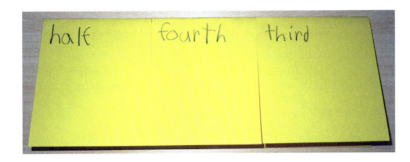

Split the Shape

Have students draw a circle (or square) and then spin a spinner with sections labeled *2*, *3*, and *4*.

Students then split the shape into that number of parts.

Students say, "I split the whole shape into ____ parts. There are ____ halves/thirds/fourths in a whole."

Then, students spin again.

For more ideas on developing math talk and writing, see Math in Practice: A Guide for Teachers, *Chapter 4.*

Vocabulary

fourth	parts
half	quarter
halves	third
partition	whole

General Resources
Additional Problems

Specific Resources
2, 3, 4 Spinner

Formative Assessment—Partitioning into Fourths

Formative Assessment—Partitioning into Thirds

Granola Bars

These resources are available at http://hein.pub/MathinPractice, keycode MIPG2.

ONLINE RESOURCES

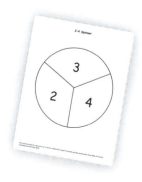

Recommended Children's Literature

Burns, Marilyn. 2008. *The Greedy Triangle*. New York: Scholastic.

Fisher, Doris, and Dani Sneed. 2007. *My Even Day*. Mount Pleasant, SC: Sylvan Dell Publishing.

———. 2007. *One Odd Day*. Mount Pleasant, SC: Sylvan Dell Publishing.

Hall, Pamela. 2003. *The Odds Get Even: The Day the Odd Numbers Went on Strike*. Franklin, TN: Piggy Toes Press.

Lionni, Leo. 1995. *Inch by Inch*. New York: HarperCollins.

Murphy, Stuart J. 1997. *A Fair Bear Share*. New York: HarperCollins.

———. 1997. *Lemonade for Sale*. New York: HarperCollins.

———. 1998. *The Penny Pot*. New York: HarperCollins.

———. 2000. *Missing Mittens*. New York: HarperCollins.

———. 2006. *Rodeo Time*. New York: HarperCollins.